SECOND SUNRISE

Nuclear War: The Untold Story

SECOND SUNRISE

Nuclear War: The Untold Story

Michael Pogodzinski

Thorndike Press • Thorndike, Maine

Library of Congress in Publication Data:

Pogodzinski, Michael.
    Second sunrise.

    Bibliography
    1. Atomic warfare.   I. Title.
U263.P63   1983   355'.0217   83-9317
ISBN 0-89621-072-3 (hard)

This book was typeset in 10 point Garth Graphic
by The Comp Shop, Augusta, ME.

Book and cover design by Abby Trudeau.

*To the memory of the late Dr. Edward
Nehls, who, two decades ago, taught me
about Graham Greene, George Bernard
Shaw, and ways to get at the truths in
history.*

TABLE OF CONTENTS

PART I

A Modern Primer

PART I

A Modern Primer

1 Nuclear War: The Untold Story

*And when he broke the second seal, I heard the second
figure say, Come and look; and a second horse came
out, fiery-red, whose rider was empowered to take away
all peace from the world, bidding men slay one another;
and a great sword was given to him.*

The *Apocalypse* of the Apostle John

What you have been told, if you are an average American
citizen, is that a nuclear exchange between the United States and the
Soviet Union is unthinkable, that it would lead to the destruction of
the core institutions of both nations, and that it could kill a large percentage of the population of the northern hemisphere. All of this is
true, as far as it goes.

From the beginning of the nuclear age in 1945, you have also been
told that America must maintain the growth of its nuclear capabilities,
in terms of technology and numbers of weapons, as this is presumed
to be the best way to ensure that an attack upon the nation will never
occur, because the effect of our retaliation would be too great to
justify any such attack. To most Americans, this makes some sense,
though a growing awareness of the danger has recently set off a public
desire to search for a better way.

The result of this sincere desire for a ''better way'' to peace has been
the renewed and daily attention paid to the subject by the mass media.
Today the average American citizen is again being told things about
nuclear war: that it is unwinnable; that it cannot be survived by anyone; that it inevitably means the extinction of the human race. These
are very dramatic assertions, and the major staging for the protest
movement. Yet such arguments stand as a gross over-simplification,
an exercise in sheer rhetoric in which only the very worst case — that
of a planetary holocaust — is taken into consideration. In this spate of

11

new-found media attention it often seems that everyone everywhere is automatically a target for direct nuclear assault. This is a problematic and a limited view, at best.

One result of the new American nuclear debate has been a questioning of the accuracy and reliability of available public information. On one hand, those who insist that the nation must always have a demonstrable nuclear superiority, or who have some defense technology to sell, argue for ever-increasing efforts to perfect the deadly art of nuclear weaponry. Proponents of a strong defense cite the Red Menace and do their best to scare folks.

On the other hand, critics of the endlessly burgeoning nuclear arms race argue, sometimes with more emotion than knowledge, for hugely over-simplified arrangements that are probably unworkable as well as unachievable. To many anti-nuclear activists, even giving thought to the possible limitations of nuclear warfare serves to increase the likelihood of the weapon's use, as if human intelligence — the stuff that got our species to its dominant position on the planet — must not investigate the circumstances of the nuclear age. Like their pro-military counterparts, critics of the atomic age cite the sheer horror available in modern military arsenals, and they too try their best to scare folks.

The result is a huge gulf between two opposing philosophical extremes, that leaves the majority of the American population somewhere in an unexplored middle ground. Neither side does much to provide adequate information about the effects of nuclear weapons, about who is an early target and why, about the practical steps that might be taken if worst ever came to worst. The loudest voices from both the pro-nuclear and anti-nuclear schools of thought have plenty of advice on what the public should *think*, but neither side offers much useful information about what the public can or should *do*.

This lack of genuine, useful information stems in part from a conscious American policy decision made several decades ago to downplay civil defense, because this was in keeping with the American doctrine that stability could only come when both sides feared "mutual assured destruction." This same policy, however, also required giant increases in the number of nuclear warheads, making nuclear war far more dangerous for everyone.

This book will attempt to establish a more "centrist" view of nuclear war. It will tell you, frankly, about nuclear effects still largely unexplained, and it will try to give you a basis for determining your own odds for the future. All of us today live in some degree of hazard under the nuclear sword of Damocles. For some, the odds are much worse than for others, depending upon a host of factors such as area and type of residence, lifestyle, and general awareness of emergency procedures. The working assumption of this book is that knowledge is a very good thing, and common sense is incredibly valuable. To begin, let us look at a brief history of the nuclear age, for this retrospective points out some of the flaws in most conventional nuclear points of view. Things are not always as they seem in the nuclear age and, on occasion, history has turned because one side intentionally misled the other, with the view of gaining some essential advantage.

It is important to approach the subject of nuclear war in this substantive way, starting with history and what can be known of the "facts." The contemporary debate in America about nuclear war is too often couched in seeming certainties based on abstractions. Little attention is paid in the press, for instance, to the disparities between the U.S. and the U.S.S.R. — what the experts call "asymmetries" — caused by geography and basic cultural differences. Still less attention is paid to the human foibles that have so often influenced events in the past. Both sides of the current debate seem to assume that all the advanced technology would work precisely as designed, although it has, thankfully, never been tested in full, and cannot be. Would human fingers flinch on the nuclear trigger? Might a nation's leader be bluffed into surrender rather than chance the decimation of his people? How sure of success must an attacker be — the notorious "first strike" case — before he dares commit his nuclear forces? The answers to some of these questions lie rooted in what little history has transpired in the nearly 40 years since the nuclear genie was released from its eternal bottle.

PAX AMERICANA

Since the invention and first use of the atom bomb in 1945, the world has never again come truly close to actual employment of nuclear weaponry. The human stricture against the use of nuclear weapons has, in fact, proved stronger than the similar agreement not to use chemical warfare. We probably came closest to a nuclear shooting war during the Cuban Missile Crisis of 1962. Yet even that time was marked by intense negotiations, behind the scenes, to prevent the possibility of a nuclear exchange. In the two decades since those events, maintenance of the tender peace has been marked by a constancy of private communication between the U.S. and the U.S.S.R. Thus, while there is no evidence that these two governments are necessarily any wiser than their predecessors, they clearly *know* the implications of the horrid power they both possess. Both have thus acted appropriately at moments when, in earlier human history, the chips might have been allowed to fall where they may.

Despite the best efforts of the brightest minds, there is still no known way by which man might destroy all life on the planet with complete certainty. While this mild note of comfort might irritate those few scientists who fear Dr. Strangelove's "mineshaft gap," the truth remains that there are still not enough weapons to allow one or more to be targeted upon every place on earth. People who live, for instance, within 25 miles of a high-priority military target today are confronted with an entirely different problem than those who live 100 miles away, assuming only that the latter group has some knowledge and facility to handle fallout. (Please see the subsequent chapter on fallout for more detailed information.) It is theoretically possible to build a doomsday weapon, a bomb so big and ferocious that, while it could not be delivered by ordinary means, might still poison much of the earth's atmosphere with some form of radiation. In this way, according to the science-fiction presumption, a dying nation might arrange to take everyone else with it. But, according to such leading weapons designers as Los Alamos' Ted Taylor, such a device would be too big to hide — perhaps as much as a mile long or wide and five hundred feet high — and its detonation might simply blow a large hole in the earth's atmosphere and rather than spreading its contamination, blow it into space. Proclaiming your own suicidal intentions has never proved to be an effective way to motivate other human beings.

The seemingly endless arms race between the U.S. and U.S.S.R. has usually involved economic factors amidst military decisions. American policy, for instance, has always been to confront the Soviet Union with a whole series of independently launched threats. For example, the United States has long insisted on maintaining an aging force of manned bombers and, more recently, announced its decision to introduce a new model to its bomber fleet. This is not because U.S.

Air Force generals necessarily want to fight the next war with the techniques of the last — though such is a constant theme in most military thinking — or because our national policy makers secretly believe that manned aircraft dropping gravity bombs are necessarily the strongest threat of our famous weapons "triad" (aircraft, land-based rockets, and sea-launched missiles). Instead, this maintenance of a manned bomber force, in the face of evidence that much of it would be intercepted and shot down in flight, is based largely on the fact that it compels the Soviets to maintain a large and very expensive force of interceptor aircraft. Thus, the American commitment to manned bombers puts more heat on the already-tight Soviet economy. Ironically, this American doctrine produces several other results. For one, it substantially heightens the danger facing those Americans who live fairly close to domestic bomber bases. For another, it gives rise to the near-wishful thinking that, one day, the world might revert to manned aircraft as the principal technique of nuclear deterrence. Such retreat from the instantaneous and irrevocable quality of the missile age might, ironically, give leaders a bit more time to think during a crisis. Once launched, a modern ICBM is but minutes from its target, and it can not be recalled. Manned bombers, much slower (if less certain), take hours and therefore provide time to think. They may also be recalled at the last moment, since they remain under human control all along the way.

Technology itself is a double-edged sword. To a regrettable degree, the argument put forth by those of the anti-nuclear persuasion usually conveys some form of disdain for technology. Technology gave us the bomb, the argument goes, and so technology should not again be called upon to do the human race any favors. Technology is non-human, it is said, and the answers it can provide are too narrow to solve the nuclear quandary we find ourselves in. The problem with this argument is that it overlooks the contributions technology has made, including those that have helped make the world safer for us all in the hair-triggered nuclear age.

RECONAISSANCE SATELLITES

Today the Pax Americana that has so influenced the world since the end of World War II is watched over from on high by an elaborate network of early-warning and reconnaissance satellites that is remarkable in its performance. Every American President since John Kennedy has had access to precise knowledge of the military alert status of the Soviet Union from moment to moment, knowledge that contributes to rational decision-making. In the late 1960s, President Johnson said that military spy satellites over the Soviet Union had allowed him to save billions of dollars, because he knew very precisely the strength of the opponent. Every President since Johnson has had such valuable information on a real-time basis.

American satellites such as the Discoverer, MIDAS, and SAMOS series, and the new Big Bird photographic series, gather huge amounts of electronic information. Some are stationed so far in space that, to date, they lie beyond the reach of Soviet anti-satellite weaponry. Others can be sent up quickly, in a matter of hours or days, and may then have their orbits changed while in space. Some measure infrared frequencies and can determine that a rocket, or a whole flock of rockets, has been launched; the sensors pick up heat from the rocket exhausts. Other American satellites, such as the Vela series, watch automatically and visually; a sure and certain sign of a nuclear detonation on earth is the brilliant flash of white light emitted. Nothing else known to man produces such a light, and the Vela satellites look for this. Most American spy satellites today have the ability to communicate with men on the surface of the earth, or beneath it, on a real-time basis. The systems, taken together, are reliable and accurate, and they are redundant. Such space devices are apt to be among the very first targets of an attack on either the United States or the Soviet Union, and there is precious little hope on the part of any would-be aggressor that his assault might go undetected. Attacks on any part of this highly sensitive space network are today generally considered to be tantamount to an act of war, and the agreement appears to be bilateral, if largely unspoken. Because of its geographic position and its lead in solid-state electronics, U.S. satellites today can be stationed in deep space, away from harm but connected to human authority by an invisible circuit of microwave channels that girdles the earth. For their part, the Soviets still bunch relatively shorter-lived spy satellites, keeping them in orbit for a week or two, stationing them in groups near trouble spots, and recovering the data the devices gather by means of landing capsules dropped by parachute from the satellites. Examples of such Soviet procedure can be seen in the gathering of

Russian satellites over the Middle East during the Yom Kippur War of 1973 and, more recently, the series of satellites the Soviets launched over the Falkland Islands in the South Atlantic early in 1982.

EFFECTS OF TECHNOLOGY

If advanced technology has sometimes been able to stabilize an otherwise frightening international situation, advances in technology may also serve to further global tension. Sudden breakthroughs in laser or proton-beam weapons and especially in antisubmarine warfare techniques may de-stabilize the situation, and not necessarily in the way that would seem most likely. The nation that knows it is falling behind might, for example, elect to pre-empt a worsening situation. In the odd logic of the nuclear age, it is the impending loser who may be more tempted to start a war, rather than the winner, who knows that time is on his side.

President Reagan's 1983 proposal that the United States concentrate its efforts toward *defense* against nuclear attack highlights the uncertainties of our age. On the surface, Reagan's new policy appeals to many people, based as it is not on mass destruction but on an emphasis on defense against holocaust. Yet, though there are few scientists who believe that such a system will become operational within the next human generation, (in the early 1980s, it is still all too easy for the aggressor to flood any conceivable defense with offensive weapons), the immediate Soviet response to Reagan's proposal was negative in the extreme. The problem the Soviets perceive is that the United States, with its larger technological base, *might* indeed one day deploy a reasonably effective defense against nuclear attack. To Soviet strategists, the very notion that America might invent ways to disable their nuclear arsenal implies that the U.S. might then be able to conduct nuclear blackmail. For all its novelty in proposing sweeping changes in the way mankind thinks about security in the nuclear age, the Reagan proposal still falls on stony ground.

The effect of present technology is largely that it greatly inhibits the possibility of a sudden, Pearl-Harbor-like nuclear attack. It is virtually impossible for either of the superpowers to bring its forces to readiness without the victim's space sensors detecting the preparations. Any modern, nuclear war is far more apt to start with attempts to impair the opponent's early warning and electronic communications, rather than to eradicate its entire population with the first blow.

Americans, probably because of the cultural inheritance of the Japanese attack on Pearl Harbor, tend to think about nuclear attack in terms of a sneak assault. But, even given a true "first-strike" capability, the issue of "first-strike" must be placed in perspective. What level of assurance would the attacker require that his assault would disable the victim's retaliatory forces and minimize the harm to himself? After all, such huge systems have never been used in war, and war has a habit of changing things, bringing up surprises. Would 90% certainty of success be enough to tempt the attacker? Not if the remaining force was certain to wound the attacker deeply in return. And, even if he had a known first-strike ability, what targets would the attacker choose first, if his choice helped determine how much damage he himself would receive? Even the Japanese attacked the U.S. Naval facilities at Pearl Harbor, not the population of San Francisco.

HOW THE WAR MIGHT START

Despite popular conception, the best current thought on how a nuclear war might start holds that thermonuclear hostilities are likely only after a prolonged period of visibly increasing international tensions. Experts at the Rand Corporation and other major American think-tanks sometimes suggest that World War III might one day start more like World War I than World War II. The dangerous period of the future may arrive after a prolonged, tortuous, diplomatic dispute, after "mobilization" in its modern form of arming rockets, and readying aircraft, when a slight miscalculation anywhere could begin the irrevocable slide toward war. "Things fall apart," as Yeats put it, "The centre does not hold." The central assumption of this thesis is that modern reconnaissance is certain to give clear warning of enemy intentions, either way, and even the absence of such information implies great danger.

In theory, then, an aware person will presumably know if and when nuclear war clouds gather by listening to the news. Reliable information received about any mass movements of people is a sign that serious things are afoot.

In contemporary America, mad for electronic gadgets, the sudden absence of communications, or of electricity, would be an ominous sign. In the words of one government scientist, ''If you suddenly lose one station on your beachfront transistor radio, could be anything's happened. If more than one station has gone off the air simultaneously, and especially if you get no signal whatever, it's come time to check the same signals on another instrument in the vicinity. If you still have no-go, try receivers with different power sources. One form of nuclear attack possible today — use of the electro-magnetic force emitted by a nuclear explosion at high altitudes — can severely damage electronic communications and related equipment. This kind of attack can be thought of as resembling a major power outage. It isn't supposed to affect things with antennas as small as those in transistor radios, but the more we learn, the more the evidence indicates that this 'pulse' is a powerful phenomenon, strong enough to disrupt normal communications in this country entirely. Some phone circuits will be best protected because they are underground, but even that system will likely overload. If the lights go out in your house, it's probably a thunderstorm. If you can't get anything at all on a transistor radio at the same time, then there's bigger trouble. If the phones are dead out at the same moment, then we are probably already at war. Don't panic, because there's nothing you can do about it just then on any grand scale. Get your people together in one place as best you can, see if the car will start, count your resources of that moment.''

Sources

Although the judgments expressed in this chapter, as throughout much of this book, are largely those of the author, considerable information is available to the reader who seeks to pursue specific aspects of nuclear war, the weaponry designed for it, and the general plans of the United States and the Soviet Union.

At present, the daily newspapers and the broadcast news reports frequently carry stories about nuclear war and its implications. Many of these, however, provide little background information upon which the general audience might reach its own, independent conclusions. Some of the present-day coverage of nuclear subjects is, in fact, simply wrong or lacks the contextual perspective required for clear thought. Among daily news-papers, for instance, the *New York Times* stands alone in providing adequate coverage of the myriad aspects of nuclear war, a status this newspaper achieved at the very outset of the nuclear age and one it still proudly upholds. If you wish to know more about what is truly what in the nuclear field, reading the *Times* is a minimum requirement.

Other publications, most of them more technical in nature, can provide a reasonable amount of unclassified but up-to-date material. Notable among these is *Aviation Week & Space Technology* (McGraw-Hill, publishers), a weekly magazine that provides excellent coverage of current developments in both American and Soviet technological advances. This is a sophisticated publication, often breaking stories just beyond the pale of government classification.

Among the military journals, the most useful for the average reader today is the *Proceedings* of the U.S. Naval Institute, an independent, non-profit professional society headquartered at Annapolis, Maryland, 21402. Especially worth a close check each spring is the ''Naval Review Issues'' of *Proceedings,* which provides an annual checklist of world developments of strategic significance. Subscriptions to this publication are relatively expensive, but it can usually be found in a good local library or in the libraries of colleges and universities.

The same can be said for the entire series of the world-famous *Jane's Yearbooks,* published in London but distributed in the United States by Franklin Watts, Inc., New York. Three of the yearbooks, *Fighting Ships, All the World's Aircraft,* and *Weapons Systems,* provide the best single compendium of the weaponry threatening the world today, and the back issues of these annuals can provide considerable historical perspective about developments during the course of our age.

The Bulletin of the Atomic Scientists, hard to obtain except through the good offices of a competent librarian, is also extremely useful and comes highly recommended for its objective coverage of scientific doubts and developments. This publication has already played an historic role in the United States by bringing to light scientific issues in nuclear technology that might otherwise go unpublicized by the government.

Readers interested in learning more details of the amazing developments in satellite reconnaissance of the past two decades should seek out an excellent book, *Secret Sentries in Space* by Philip J. Klass (Random House, New York, 1971). Many of the judgments expressed in Chapter One about the utility of spy satellites in helping to keep the peace between the two great superpowers are derived in part from this very strong book, which also happens to provide an excellent review of Soviet and American developments, actions, and pronouncements of the past quarter century, all in the context of what each side knew of the other from its silent spies in space. Mr. Klass, long a knowledgeable debunker of everything from UFOs to myths of Soviet military prowess, has been a senior editor of *Aviation Week & Space Technology* and writes with great authority.

The best general introduction to the theory of nuclear weapons themselves is, ironically, contained not in a weapons textbook, but, instead, in John McPhee's marvelously entitled *The Curve of Binding Energy* (in hardcover from Farrar, Strauss and Giroux, New York, 1974, and in paperback by Ballantine, 1975). This book first appeared as a series of exceptionally well written articles in *The New Yorker* magazine in the early 1970s. Its principle focus is on the threat posed by the spread of nuclear weapons, including the frightening possibility that nuclear materials might be fashioned into a crude weapon by a small terrorist band with a modicum of technical knowledge. Mr. McPhee tells his powerful story in the form of a series of interviews with nuclear weapons designers and, in the course of making his selective point, provides excellent information about the design and effects of various forms of nuclear weapons. Information on this subject is extremely useful to anyone who wishes to understand the nuclear hazards inherent in modern life, and *The Curve of Binding Energy* provides the requisite tutorial material in very palatable form.

Less well known but also useful for its summary of the current state of weapons technology is *Overkill — The Weapons of the Nuclear Age* by John Cox (Thomas Y. Crowell publishers, New York, 1977). This book also includes an excellent summary of the nearly 600 nuclear devices that have been fired in the course of testing since 1945, a subject that may be of special interest to many general readers.

2 A Short History

Here lie the people of Leningrad
Here are the citizens — men, women and children —
And beside them the soldiers of the Red Army
Who gave their lives
Defending you, Leningrad,
Cradle of Revolution.
We cannot number the noble
Ones who lie beneath the eternal granite,
But of those honored by this stone
Let no one forget, let nothing be forgotten.

Inscription on the wall at the eternal flame,
the Soviet war monument at Leningrad.

One day, the nuclear spore set down in the New Mexico desert with the first atom test in 1945 may yet bloom in an ugly mushroom at Hartford, say, or Portland, or Boston. To the children of the second generation of the nuclear age, it may seem that humankind has always lived with our dreadful lot, has always existed on the brink of annihilation. But this is not so.

The truth is that the number of nuclear weapons that threatens the future has grown like a cancer in a single lifetime. From just a few atomic weapons in the mid-1940s to more than enough to eradicate civilization in the early 1980s, the world's nuclear armory has grown in clots of new weapons and ever-higher technology.

To reach a true understanding of the means of survival in the 1980s and '90s, it helps to know how it came to pass that there are so many weapons at hand today, for that gives a clue to where and why those weapons might be used. The history of the nuclear age tends to divide (perhaps too neatly) into convenient five-year periods, each of them marked by some great but basically unpublicized advance in atomic technology. Given the progress of science since World War II, the mistakes — the international deceptions, the "disinformation" planted by both sides — serve as a tidy but ironic counterpoint to show that human wisdom is not necessarily on a par with human knowledge.

1945-1950

It began with the "Trinity" test of the first plutonium bomb in the southwestern U.S. desert in July, 1945. Within a month, the United States had dropped two atom bombs, the uranium-235 "Little Boy" on Hiroshima and the plutonium-239 "Fat Man" over Nagasaki. Those two cities remain the only ones in history to have endured atomic attack, and on-going postwar health studies on them are still the only reliable guide available to the long-term effects of nuclear weaponry.

The atomic bombings of Japan brought the war to a sudden close in a dramatic way. Overnight, most of the world came to believe that America alone had mastered modern physics in a way that would leave it perpetually the strongest nation on earth. But the truth, made available to the public only in recent years, was that the bombings themselves were a gigantic deception. In September of 1945, for instance, the United States possessed so little nuclear material that only one more bomb could conceivably have been used, anywhere, before the spring of the following year. The every-three-day schedule established had been a psychological ploy, a trick designed to induce rapid surrender from Japan. The problem, it turned out, was that you could certainly make bombs, if you had the right materials. But the materials themselves were very rare, hard to make, and dripped from the nuclear supply spigots only in tiny drops.

Nothing that happened in the first year after the war served to mitigate the misunderstandings. While the Soviets secretly rushed their own atomic project to conclusion — the reactor to produce the enriched uranium was put on-line in Russia in 1946 — America did what it still could to foster the conviction that no power on earth could withstand the might of the American air force, its bomb bays loaded with atomic weapons. In fact, U.S. plutonium-producing reactors at Hanford, Washington, were then undergoing a perfectly predictable swelling of their cores, with the result that one had to be shut down entirely and the other two operated at greatly reduced power to prolong their safe lives. In the early summer of 1946, America detonated two more A-bombs — one of them was to have been dropped on Tokyo the previous September, had not the Japanese surrendered in time to forestall the use of "Big Boy" — at Bikini atoll in the Pacific. The idea was to test what might happen when a nuclear weapon was fired at or under the sea, since nobody had the foggiest idea about such things yet. In the process, the U.S. used up the majority of its available supply of nuclear combustibles.

With the outbreak of the Cold War, America maintained the public deception, fostering the loud debate about a proposed "75-wing air force" composed of then-heavy B-29 bombers that could threaten Russia with atomic destruction if necessary. In fact, when the first chairman of the U.S. Atomic Energy Commission went to check how many bombs we had in early 1947, he was amazed to learn that there were essentially none at all in the American arsenal. The material for a couple of the beasts existed at an airbase in New Mexico — it was shortly moved to much tighter security at Fort Knox — but the civilians who knew how to put an A-bomb together had long since scattered after the end of the war. Besides a total of ready bombs that came to zero, the U.S. had no B-29s in Europe, which meant that no American plane could easily have reached any important Russian target until long after the Red Army had conquered western Europe. Ways to rectify the weak American position became a secret, high-priority, national program.

The surprise came in September, 1949. An American plane in Alaska picked up irrefutable evidence that the Soviets had exploded an A-bomb: the radioactive trace elements in the air were a sure and certain sign. Within weeks, President Harry Truman announced that America's nuclear monopoly was over. American scientists had expected it — improvements in U.S. production facilities for nuclear material had given the nation perhaps 200 atomic bombs by then. But no one had expected the Soviets to catch up so soon.

1950-1955

In 1950, the United States began the first formal target study of military and civilian objectives for atomic bombing in the Soviet Union. The photographs used, taken mostly by the Germans in World

War II, enabled the physicists to calculate what type and amount of nuclear force would be necessary to destroy a suitable percentage of each area. The decision was also made by the United States to proceed with the Super-Bomb, the thermonuclear weapon.

Such devices had been known to be theoretically possible as far back as the Manhattan Project during World War II. But nobody yet knew quite how to put together the immense pressures and star-like temperatures required to ignite elemental hydrogen, and thus make a weapon whose force was greater over that of the atomic bomb as the A-bomb was over conventional chemical weapons. After a fit of semi-public debate, the United States detonated the first thermonuclear device in November, 1952, eradicating an entire Pacific island. Two new manmade elements were discovered in the radioactive detritus from Project Mike-Ivy, and wags sought to name them frenetium and pandemonium. But the explosion itself had been caused not by a bomb but a warehouse-sized device 100 feet square and 50 feet high to house the refrigeration equipment then thought necessary to create the thermonuclear event. That first beast would never fly, of course. No bomber could ever be big enough to carry it.

The following spring, the Soviets achieved their own first atomic milestone in history: they detonated a true hydrogen bomb in Siberia. By the end of that same year, 1953, the U.S. too was prepared and had its own version of an actual H-bomb. America began to build its air defenses against presumed Russian bombers, to teach its school children how to duck beneath window level if they saw a terribly bright light, and to build huge offensive bombers.

Understanding of the sheer power of the modern, thermonuclear weapon came slowly to all but the most far-sighted of the scientists. The technology of H-weaponry was still such that huge bombers with large bomb bays were thought necessary to lug the forces of nuclear justice. But the explosive force and long-lived radioactivity — a U.S. weapons test of the time had salted a Japanese fishing boat a hundred miles away from the explosion and harmed the crew — began to make it seem that even a few H-bombs, if successfully delivered upon a nation the size and character of the United States, might be enough to bring down the institutions of the country.

There was more disquiet during that time. Not only had the Soviets caught up, but it now seemed that the manned bomber might not be the best way to launch an attack. The German rocketry of World War II had neither the power to lift the heavy warheads, nor the accuracy to bring them close enough to destroy their presumed targets. But might the H-bomb not change all that? An intercontinental rocket, even one armed with an A-bomb, which it might be able to lift, was still not very good because it was not apt to drop its warhead within 50 miles of its target. But, if H-bombs could be made smaller and lighter while just as powerful, might rockets then be used instead of the much slower airplanes?

1955-1960

The dread began to come true at this point in history. Late in 1954, scientists had worked out ways to make smaller H-bombs. One could be made, in fact, that weighed less than a ton, and this meant such a bomb might fit into the small payload atop a rocket. Assuming that the Russians caught onto this idea as swiftly as they had to everything else nuclear to that date, there was fear that Soviet missiles might now endanger the continental U.S. in a wholly new way.

In October, 1957, the Russians provided the first great cultural shock to America — they launched a 180-pound-plus Sputnik into space. We had been unsuccessful in numerous earlier tries. Our own first satellite was to be but an eight-pound sphere, about the size of a grapefruit. The Russians obviously had rockets big enough, or surely would have soon, to launch H-bombs right through American defenses. Word began to leak from the high councils at Washington that the Soviets might have skipped an entire generation of military hardware, by-passing the manned bomber for the next higher step, the intercontinental rocket armed with a thermonuclear bomb.

America went on a nationwide crash program, half in secret. Atomic submarines, half-completed and designed to be ship-chasers, were modified in mid-construction, lengthened, broadened, and fitted out to carry the newly-developed small H-bombs of the U.S. arsenal. The U.S. spent great sums to build its own land-based rockets, the intermediate-ranged Thor and Jupiter and the intercontinental Atlas and Titan. Giant new warning radars, intended to give as much alert as possible against incoming missiles over the North Pole, were hastened to completion at Thule, Greenland; Clear, Alaska; and Flyingdale

Moors, England. The British and then the French, no longer believing that an American President might be willing to risk New York to halt a Soviet land attack on Paris or London, began to build their own nuclear arsenals. The nuclear genie had not only successfully escaped from his physics bottle, he had reproduced, as well.

By the late 1950s, the United States, still principally reliant on its nuclear bombers, had at least dispersed them as widely as possible and improved its internal communications with them at all times. With the possibility growing that the Russians might attack the country with as little as an half-hour's warning, it seemed sensible to keep as many planes on station in the air as possible.

In the 1960 presidential election, John Kennedy made points with the public by highlighting the so-called "missile gap," a circumstance that presumably left the nation vulnerable to Soviet nuclear blackmail or attack. On his way out of office, but with knowledge that Kennedy would only acquire in his first months as President, Dwight Eisenhower warned of the power of nuclear weapons and the growing influence of what he called the military/industrial complex.

1960-1965

The Soviets, as the first spy satellites revealed, had never built whole fleets of nuclear-armed rockets. The Russians had simply acted as if they had, rattling their sabres and shouting angrily about American destruction. It had been a Soviet bluff, and it worked all too well.

Sure that the nation had the necessary military strength, John Kennedy chose to back the Soviets down in public over the presence of their missiles in Cuba. To assuage the Russians, Kennedy agreed to remove our own similar missiles in Italy and Turkey. With the third-generation rockets in the late 1950s, the United States would soon no longer need land-based missiles stationed overseas. Instead, there was a fleet of impossible-to-find subs with nuclear-tipped missiles. Soon there were going to be more solid-fueled Minuteman missiles alone than the number of missiles the Russians had in total. The satellites told all.

There were further breakthroughs in the miniaturization of thermonuclear weapons design, but none favored the defense. Nuclear warheads now provided so much bang for the relative buck that it was far cheaper to build more attack-oriented launchers than to try to invent expensive defense systems. American policy makers abandoned the idea of building defenses against non-existent Russian bombers, eliminated Nike anti-aircraft sites — these still sit unused upon many a New England hilltop — and cut back on the civil defense programs of just a few years before. Now the operative policy was "mutual assured destruction," or MAD. The suggestion intended for Soviet ears was simple: there is no defense against modern nuclear weaponry because we can develop offensive systems more quickly and far more cheaply than you can build defenses against them. The offense, much cheaper — not much more than one million dollars per megaton — can clearly swamp any conceivable defense. So, if you attack us, you will still inevitably die in the course of our reaction.

There were several technical tries at new forms of defense during the Kennedy years. Could small, local, anti-aircraft rockets, such as the once-deployed Nike, carry small defensive nuclear warheads? Yes they could, but the cure — two nuclear explosions close above an American city — seemed worse than the disease. Could some new nuclear effect somehow cook incoming warheads or disable their electronics by bathing them in a kind of nuclear broth in space? This was a new idea in the early 1960s, but the answer did not bode well for the defense; high altitude weapons set off an electromagnetic pulse (EMP — please see Chapter Four for more details) that short-circuited conventional electrical lines on earth. The effect was proved during one of the last American atmospheric tests, when an H-bomb lifted by rocket and fired 20 miles above Johnston Island in the Pacific knocked out half the electricity and communications in the Hawaiian Islands.

By the mid-1960s, the Soviets had clearly begun their long build-up. Both the satellites and surveillance of the Pacific proved it. In the autumn of 1964, to everyone's great surprise, the Chinese fired their own first nuclear weapon, making five members in a once-exclusive world club.

1965-1970

In this period, the U.S. decided aginst building another manned bomber, fitted out and sent to sea the last of its missile-firing submarines, and deployed the last of its Minuteman I missiles. The first

Atlas rockets, by contrast, had stood tall and obviously exposed at their above-ground gantries. The second-generation Atlas and Titans, though buried underground and thus less sensitive to nearby nuclear attack, still took hours to load with dangerous liquid fuels. But Minuteman was small, hard, reliable, stable, and apt to last as a potential attack launcher for years to come. Only the warheads had to be made smaller to be configured properly for the smaller missiles. The U.S. began its policy of small warheads delivered in waves upon waves with great accuracy. The age of the silent silo had begun.

The agony of Vietnam occupying its public mind, the nation overlooked the obvious increase in Soviet nuclear capabilities. The Russians were building missile subs, deploying huge missiles capable of lifting enormous warheads to America. There was some debate, but the scientists who knew the most understood that there was still no effective defense against saturation nuclear attack. The U.S. could either invest in another whole round of offensive rockets, newfangled bombers, or some form of defense as yet undiscovered. The best bet was to improve the accuracy and internal electronic intelligence of the present warheads. This might help to preserve some semblance of an American lead in nuclear firepower, even while the Russians continued to build up their own forces.

1970-1975

Under Richard Nixon the decision was made to forego all attempts to install expensive defensive systems and, instead, to multiply the number of hydrogen warheads that might be carried atop each individual missile. The idea was formally known as "multiple-independently-targeted-reentry-vehicles," or MIRV. If you could drop a thermonuclear warhead right in the proverbial bushel-basket from half a world away, you could certainly plunk them down close enough to the Russian missile silos to destroy them. The era of fear of "first strike" was born, for now both sides might have the capacity to wipe out the other's land-based missiles simply by attacking first.

Technological advances were again at the root of the changes. Science had known for some time how to pack a cluster of several warheads atop each rocket, then cast them in the general direction of their targets without guidance, like so many unstabilized shotgun pellets fired at a passing waterfowl. But MIRV technology was substantially more sophisticated; it provided that the warheads be carried aboard a kind of robotic space ''bus,'' smaller than the later U.S. space shuttle and obviously not under direct human control in flight. As the bus descended toward earth, it would be capable, thanks to its miniature computers, of dispensing warheads over a vast area. In addition, researchers discovered, a small rocket motor could be added to the rear of each warhead to provide mid-course corrections and to add velocity as it returned to the earth's atmosphere. The last factor, in particular, helped to improve accuracy considerably.

Taken together, these advanced technologies allowed America to confront the Soviet Union with a multiplicity of nuclear weapons, each of which could be guided to its target with remarkable accuracy. (Please see the next chapter for examples and definitions.) If there could be many warheads atop each rocket, and if each warhead was accurate enough to land close to its target it was obvious that one super-power might theoretically target the offensive missiles of the other, since the positions of the launching silos had long since been precisely mapped by satellite.

In the early 1970s, in response to the continuing Soviet build-up, America's strategic forces went MIRV, on the assumption that it was the least expensive way to ensure the continued safety of the U.S. The nation upgraded its Minuteman land-based missiles to design-stage III, which meant rapid re-targeting capability (an assumption is that the entire target plan of these missiles may be changed in as little as seven hours), more secure communications, methods to launch the missiles from aircraft if the ground control centers should be destroyed, still harder and more stable silos, and MIRVed warheads, with three to ten weapons atop each rocket. The technology of the time required that such multiple warheads be considerably smaller in their yield, but the effective firepower increased nevertheless, because three warheads, say, exploding in a well-designed pattern in the area of a target actually could do considerably more damage than a single warhead of much more power. United States policy was now based on the theory that it is better to shoot many small warheads, each of high precision and accuracy, and use volley-fire techniques and mass numbers, rather than trying to obliterate the same targets with single, large, high-yield weapons.

1975-1980

During this period the Soviet Union caught up in true measure, even though it had taken nearly 20 years since its embarrassment in Cuba. Avoiding the need to make smaller warheads, which was not their special technical competence anyway, the Soviets opted instead to maintain much larger H-weapons atop their own rockets, but to surpass American capabilities in total number of launchers and in the total weight of the attack, all the while adding MIRV-type nosecones that could begin to match the heralded American accuracy.

Monitoring Soviet missile tests from giant radar stations in Turkey and Iran, and watching the warheads land in the central Pacific from specially equipped research ships, the United States took due note of the ever-increasing range, firepower, and accuracy of the Soviet weapons. Midway through his term, President Jimmy Carter, among the least warlike of all American leaders of the 20th century, announced, for the first time, a re-targeting of the entire American missile system. Left unsaid was the fact that the missiles had previously been aimed largely at the Soviet population and the infrastructure of the Soviet nation. Loudly announced was the fact that American missiles would henceforth be targetted first upon Russian military facilities, missile silos, communication chokepoints, and the leadership of the Soviet Union itself. More than one observer suggested at the time that the Carter re-targeting announcement was apt to be interpreted by the Soviet leadership as a direct and personal threat. The Soviet resonse was simply to deploy still newer missiles and larger numbers of them, as if its build-up was inexorable. For the early 1980s, the working assumption became that the U.S.S.R. could conceivably destroy most if not all of the American land-based Minuteman missile system, leaving the U.S. only its aging bomber fleet and nuclear submarines as a last deterrent.

In this same period, India became the latest nation to explode an atomic weapon to prove to itself that it could make one. The technology had by then become so commonplace, so widely known by so many people throughout the world, that no one who wanted to build the bomb really had to test it.

Sources

With the passage of time since World War II, much of the earliest American thinking about nuclear war has come to public light with the declassification of official documents, such as the minutes of policy meetings of the U.S. Joint Chiefs of Staff during the late 1940s. Many such documents have only recently become available to professional historians and the public alike, and the disclosures have set off a spate of newly published books on the early history of the atomic age. Much of the material in Chapter Two is drawn from such sources, as well as private interviews with retired officers and scientists who once played an active role in American decision-making.

By far the best and most objectively striking of the new histories is *The Winning Weapon — The Atomic Bomb in the Cold War, 1945-1950,* by Gregg Herken (Alfred A. Knopf publishers, New York, 1980). Mr. Herken's study is based on exhaustive and comprehensive reviews of recently declassified records of the American Joint Chiefs of Staff from the early Cold War period. Some of the records are available to the interested reader through the Department of Defense and other official government publishers. Of special interest in Mr. Herken's book is the enumeration of the gradual increase in the numbers of atomic weapons deliverable by the U.S. in the late 1940s. This theme is played out against a contrast of the almost-bizarre U.S. Air Force planning for a huge manned bomber fleet at a time when the weaponry to be placed in the proposed bomb bays was almost invariably lacking.

There are a plethora of books available about the earliest days of the atomic age, the U.S. Manhattan Project, which secretly built the atom bombs used in World War II. The best general book on the subject is *Manhattan Project* by Stephane Groueff, (Little Brown & Company, Inc., Boston, 1967). Many of the scientists who participated in the original nuclear work have contributed valuable memoirs, and the transcripts of the security hearings involving J. Robert Oppenheimer, the father of the bomb, (M.I.T. Press, Boston, 1980) are also useful as a demonstration of the growing U.S. policy of that time to proceed with the development of the H-bomb by way of response to the first Soviet test of an atom bomb in 1949. Also useful because it provides insight into both the Manhattan Project days and the earliest tests of thermonuclear devices in the early 1950s is *The Uranium People,* by Leona Libby, a scientist who survived irradiation herself during World War II and went on to participate in the development of the H-bomb (Little Brown & Company, Inc., Boston, 1979).

Numerous other works on this period are also worth citing, including official government reviews of the development of the Thor and Atlas rockets in the 1950s (available with the help of your local librarian) and three books by Richard G. Hewlett, who served as the offical historian of the U.S. Atomic Energy Commission. The first of these, *The New World, 1939-1946,* by Hewlett and Oscar E. Anderson, (Pennsylvania State University Press, 1962) covers the titled period of history. The second in the series, *Atomic Shield, 1947-1952,* (Pennsylvania State University Press, 1969) is co-authored by Hewlett and Francis Duncan, the assistant A.E.C. historian. The third of the series, *Nuclear Navy,* by Hewlett and Duncan again, (University of Chicago Press, 1974) provides detailed information about the U.S. policy decisions to develop a submarine-based nuclear strike force and valuable insight into the degree of influence wielded over American policy by former Admiral Hyman G. Rickover, widely considered the father of the nuclear navy. The entire series is replete with excellent official information then available only to historians occupying the unique positions held by Hewlett and Duncan. The writing is, however, concerned largely with government decision-making itself rather than the larger social and policy issues at hand.

Another book, *The U.S. Nuclear Navy* by retired admiral Herbert J. Gimpel (Franklin Watts, Inc., New York), gives superb detail of the first U.S. atomic weapons tests in the Pacific, but is otherwise lacking in useful perspective for the average lay person.

Material concerning ABM and MIRV developments covered in Chapter Two is largely drawn from private interviews by the author with retired military personnel and with various senior officials of private companies engaged in defense projects involving the appropriate technologies. Unlike the Soviet Union, the United States is clearly an open society, in the sense that much can be gleaned about current technological developments simply by reading the employment ads of the major newspapers around Boston, New York, and in California. The author's personal file of such want ads, appearing in such newspapers as *The Boston Globe* in the early 1970s at the height of public debate over MIRV and ABM, provide a perfect backdrop against which the twists and turns of each policy decision can be measured. The author is also indebted to numerous scientists at M.I.T. and Harvard for the valuable insights provided into these subjects during interviews at that time, with special thanks to Dr. George Wald of Harvard and Dr. Jerome Weisner, former Provost of M.I.T., who also served as Science Advisor to President Kennedy.

3 Modern Strategic Balance

Rise up, mighty land,
Rise up for the deadly battle. . . .
Let noble anger
Boil like a wave.
We march to the People's War,
The Holy War . . . .

Lyrics of a popular song of the Red Army
in World War II

No question in American politics can raise more hackles than the question of whether the Soviets might have grown militarily stronger than the United States. The issue has raised its head, in one form or another, in most American national elections since World War II, and it has been a major factor in the elections of Presidents Eisenhower, Kennedy, Johnson, Nixon, and Reagan. On the whole, the American body politic has been conservative, usually voting for larger defense expenditures. There is not an abundance of evidence to indicate that the general public, however, ever quite understands the real state of affairs. In the late 1950s, for instance, Soviet successes in space gave rise to the concern that a potential enemy had skipped an entire generation of military technology, the manned bomber, for a newer and potentially more powerful one, the intercontinental rocket. Hastily, we threw up giant radar stations in impossible places like Greenland and Alaska, so that we could get maximum warning of any impending attack. In public there arose the question of a "missile gap" — the notion that the Soviets were, in fact, presenting a genuine threat to our existence.

MISSILE GAP

In response to the restiveness, the United States embarked on an emergency program. We cut up half-built submarines and installed new missiles in them. The missiles themselves were rushed into production at high cost. We designed and began to build the entire first generation of American strategic rockets, the Atlas and the medium-ranged Thor and Jupiter. The American race to get something, anything, in place was so great no one noticed that these early rockets were clumsy and vulnerable. They stood exposed on tarmac plains like single cornstalks scattered on a field. Their liquid fuels were volatile, and they took hours to load into war-launch condition, during which time they were vulnerable even to a near-miss by any nuclear weapon. In fear of the "missile gap," we built several different early generations of such rockets and put them in place in New York and Kansas and Arkansas, sometimes in areas fairly close to population centers. The medium rockets went to Turkey and Italy and Britain, and their presence in those places likely gave rise to the Soviets' attempt to arm Cuba with nuclear missiles.

In 1960 and 1961, American spy satellites began to indicate that the Russians had never truly launched a crash rocket-building program. They were clearly capable of doing so, but they had chosen not to do it, for they had fewer than 100 rockets deployed and had little operational capability. The Soviet missile-rattling of the late 1950s, the bluster of Khruschev, had been something of a bluff. Talk of the "missile gap" disappeared.

In the early 1980s, the United States has again regarded apparent developments on the Soviet side of the world and come to the conclusion that certain Russian advances in technology and its deployment represent an attitude so aggressive as to border on the hostile. As a result, the nation has embarked upon a military and nuclear build-up unparalleled since World War II. The costs of this program have been so high, but the political support for it so great, that there was bipartisan agreement upon one of the largest tax increases in American history, at a point less than two months before the next national election.

Satellite and other electronic intelligence provide hard proof that there could be reason for concern. In the past 15 years, the Soviet strategic nuclear capability has clearly grown to match that of the United States, if not exceed it in certain technical respects. The notion of strategic parity between the two superpowers is a new one in American life, and one that may frighten the electorate.

EAST AND WEST ASYMMETRIES

Any real comparison between the nuclear strength of the Soviet Union and that of the United States is no easy task. It is not necessarily adequate merely to consider sheer numbers of launchers, or even of warheads, for the two nations have different perceived needs, and they have conducted themselves accordingly. What is "safe" for one may not be for the other, for a host of reasons the roots of which lie at the very core of differences between the two nations. Before we look at the likely numbers involved in a modern nuclear war, let us look first at some of the huge differences that set the two nations apart and make their needs hard to reconcile.

Geography

The United States is the smaller nation, a major factor in considerations of nuclear war, where distance can mean safety. Worse still, almost three quarters of the American population lives and works in about 400 population centers, most of which are within 75 miles of the two long coasts. Industry and property are highly centralized in these same areas with almost one half the population concentrated in 75 cities. The general picture is one of massed clusters of targets, if an enemy chooses to target civilian populations.

By contrast, the Soviet Union is a vast nation that subtends 11 time zones. Most of the population resides in a long crescent-like belt starting in the northwest of Baltic Russia and running southeast past Moscow toward the northwest border of China. Although the population is larger than that of the United States, there are only 150 Soviet metropolitan areas of more than 100,000 population. Much of the population is scattered in villages and towns along the same huge arc, bypassing the emptiness of Siberia, where the Soviets deploy some of their intercontinental missiles.

Moreover, much of the Soviet population lives in the west, where the prevailing winds would tend to take fallout away from clusters of human population. For the United States, the majority of the population lives to the east of the major missile fields, which would be high-priority targets.

Latitude favors the United States, as does ready access to the earth's major oceans. The Soviet Union is much farther north than the continental United States, a factor with considerable technical influence. For one, because American missile-test and launch sites in California and Florida are much closer to the equator, it is, technically speaking, much easier to put early-warning satellites into a geosynchronous orbit (one in which they maintain the same relative position above a particular point on the surface of the planet). American satellites, therefore, tend to be much longer-lived, and perhaps more sensitive, than their Soviet counterparts. The northerly position of the Soviet Union also severly limits the number of daylight hours in winter, a factor that can complicate the problem of how to intercept manned aircraft.

To offset its geographic disadvantage, the Soviet Union, for the past decade, has done much of its development from the major site at Tyuratam, east of the Aral Sea, in the Central Asian Military District with headquarters at the southern city of Alma Alta, about as far as it is possible to get from the Arctic Circle. Stations specifically monitoring Tyuratam were lost by the United States in the course of the Iranian revolution.

From Tyuratam and other such southerly bases as Kapustin Yar, 150 miles northwest of the Caspian Sea, military reconnaissance, communication, and weather satellites are launched in a northeast direction. Tests of early models of rockets intended for field deployment are accomplished now mostly from Tyuratam, with the target/impact area thousands of miles away in the central Pacific, east of Japan. The same target area was first used in 1974 for test launches of long-ranged rockets from Soviet *Delta*-class nuclear submarines firing from the Barents Sea north of Norway. The range of such tests established that the Soviets had accomplished two strategic goals. They could now target virtually any area in the United States for attack by submarine, without ever having to send the submarine much beyond sight of its own base. The principal Soviet submarine base is at Severomorsk, near Murmansk, and when a *Delta* submarine fired a missile into the Pacific Ocean near the Kamchatka Peninsula in February, 1974, the opinion of Western military analysts was that the Soviets had attained a major new operational capability: they no longer had to trust their submarine captains for long undersea voyages; they could avoid the narrow passages leading from Russia and carefully guarded by U.S. surveillance vessels and sensors, and yet they could mount a new attack threat aimed at any point in the United States, literally while the submarines were sitting aside their dock stations.

Operational Soviet missile fields have been reported at several points, including north of Moscow, in the northwestern U.S.S.R.; in the Ural Mountains; and in various spots around Siberia. Some tests of operational Soviet nuclear rockets are staged with an impact area on the barren island of Novaya Zemlya, far above the Arctic Circle, east of the Barents Sea.

By contrast, American satellites are generally launched from favorable "window" positions in Florida and California, and operational tests of deployed U.S. Minuteman missiles are conducted from California facilities, with the target far out in the Pacific, southwest of Hawaii. Both nations closely monitor each other's rocket-firing tests, for much can be gleaned from this electronic intelligence.

To keep the major targets as far away from population centers as possible, American policy has been to place its major land-based missile forces in fairly empty areas in Wyoming, Montana, New Mexico, North Dakota, South Dakota, Kansas, Missouri, and Arkansas. The older facilities tend to be closer to population centers, such as the bases near Little Rock, Arkansas. Heavy bomber wings are scattered in three dozen airbases. Some late model versions of America's aging B-52 bombers are stationed in an arc starting in Maine and running through upstate New York and northern Michigan in a band along the northern tier of states.

All areas in the general vicinity of any of these bases in either nation are high risk areas in the event of a nuclear war, for they are apt to be among the primary targets of the opponent.

Culture

The United States is a highly mobile, ultra-modern society. Its internal communications are excellent, its resources and capacity to organize its industrial strength are very high. It is an open society, whose citizens are unaccustomed to the government's giving them direct orders for prolonged periods of time.

The Soviet Union is much younger, apt to be more divisive among its internal factions, and much less rich in consumer goods. The Soviet citizenry is more accustomed to regimentation than the American populace, and the general mood of life is far different in the two nations.

Electronic communication, gadgetry, motor vehicles, and readily available food are common in America, much less so for the average Soviet citizen. The sheer size of the Soviet Union argues against any system of roads such as the American interstate highway system. Long-range transportation in the U.S.S.R. is a matter of rail, air, and water, not roadway. Soviet design engineering, however, tends to favor intense concentration and vast spread in factories devoted to a single, large, industrial product, such as a tractor or truck.

These asymmetries suggest that each society has somewhat different chokepoints, areas most vulnerable to attack. The American reliance on imported oil, for instance, leaves the nation vulnerable, and offers a concentration of soft-skinned domestic oil facilities for Soviet targeting specialists. Yet very little of the nation's oil supply is devoted to food production and so the assumption is that the U.S. could better afford constriction of oil availability than could the Soviet Union, where so much of the available oil is used for agricultural production that a relatively small shortfall might still lead to starvation.

History

Since the American Civil War, which caused by far the greatest casualties in U.S. history, it has been national policy, always honored if largely unspoken, to avoid military circumstances that could bleed the nation's generations white. We went late into World War I and managed our affairs in World War II so as to lose "just" 400,000 people. We feel, as a nation, that we were forced into both wars. Yet, of all the participants only America emerged a stronger nation.

By comparison, the U.S.S.R. lost more than 20 million people during World War II, a conflict which they regard intensely as strictly a defense of their homeland. The Soviet motherland suffered invasion through a third of its breadth, endured the very largest land battles in the history of warfare, and repelled the German invaders only with massed artillery fire that exceeded in power everything but the atom bomb. Memory of both the carnage and the winning-strength still lives vividly in the mind of the average Russian. It is impossible to believe that any Soviet leader, mindful of the suffering of his people in the recent past, could ever again allow another attack upon the motherland.

The Soviet Union survived the war, but the ordeal impoverished the nation and gave it a national sense of inferiority, an abiding awareness that outsiders could again pose a grave threat. Accustomed to privation, harsh winters, and the hard rule of centralized authority, the Russian people today have a far more organized and practiced civil defense system and share vivid memories of times in which shelter was a prerequisite to survival.

In contrast, Americans laughed at fallout shelters in the early 1960s, as part of a national policy to concentrate on offense rather than defense in the nuclear age. American policy came to mean that there was no conceivable defense that would work well against all-out nuclear war, short of arming ourselves so strongly that no one would dare attempt an attack. Even today, rational debate about some form of civil defense for the United States is nearly impossible, overwhelmed by a backdrop of howling laughter at clearly unworkable Federal evacuation plans for large cities. The debate about civil defense in the United States has been oversimplified to a preposterous degree, and the subject should once again undergo serious analysis.

Military Doctrines

The two superpowers approach the subject of nuclear war from vastly different standpoints. The United States, with a long seafaring tradition, maintains its strongest nuclear threat aboard its nuclear submarines, whose captains have relative freedom to roam the seas. The Soviets, having beaten the German Wehrmacht with massed guns and armor, put three quarters of their nuclear force into land-based strategic rockets and tend to think of the missiles as a form of giant artillery.

In the United States, two of the three major military arms, the U.S. Air Force and the U.S. Navy, are given joint assignments to carry out American strategic nuclear deterrence. In the Soviet Union, far more of this role is given exclusively to the Strategic Rocket Forces. The official Russian name for this organization, now nearly half a million strong, is *Raketnye Voiska Strategicheskogo Naznachemiya,* or "Rocket Troops of Strategic Designation." The roots of this organization date back to the Stalinist era, when such a force was viewed, in the Soviet perception, as properly belonging to the artillery corps of the Red Army. Born artillerymen, with a history of success, the Soviets have traditionally given heavy emphasis to the "weight-of-metal" they can bring down upon the head of their adversary.

In May, 1960, just prior to Khrushchev's ignominious facedown in the Cuban Missile Crisis, and at a time when the Soviet Union had perhaps only 35 intercontinental rockets deployed, the Strategic Rocket Forces were elevated to the higher status of a full, separate service. No such corresponding organization exists in the United States. The growth of the Soviet Strategic Rocket Forces since they were removed from the Red Army has been unprecedented.

Today, high rank in the Strategic Rocket Forces is considered to be a ticket to the fast-track for those who hope to rise from the military to power in the Soviet Politburo. The commander-in-chief of the Strategic Rocket Forces, though he sits on a panel of senior officers governing the military in roughly the same way that the American Joint Chiefs of Staff conduct their business, always takes precedence over the other military chiefs, regardless of rank. By contrast, general commanders of the ballistic missile forces in the U.S. Air Force and Navy are not directly represented in high military councils.

The Soviet preference for centralization of authority is clear in this tight-fisted wielding of nuclear power. Although both nations are very cautious in their deployment and control of warheads, the American system is far more flexible and allows local field commanders considerably greater leeway of action than is Soviet practice. During the 1960s, for instance, United States nuclear technology had produced miniaturized tactical nuclear warheads so small they could be fitted onto a bazooka-like rocket that could be fired by a private. This weapon system, known as the Davy Crockett, was initially deployed in Europe, then removed because of the objections of field commanders, who worried about the security of so widespread a system. By comparison, there is some evidence that physical control of Soviet nuclear weapons is vested in the KGB, until such time as central authority may release the rockets for use by specialists. In America, the weaponry is "owned" by the President of the United States, but maintained and managed in the field by the responsible local military force.

Substantial differences also exist in the philosophy-of-use of such weaponry. The Soviets have generally opted for very large missiles carrying huge thermonuclear warheads. Until the last five years, the accuracy of these missiles, when compared to their American counterparts, was considered lacking.

American warheads mounted atop both Minuteman land-based missiles and Polaris/Poseidon/Trident rockets aboard nuclear submarines are generally much smaller in their destructive force — below a megaton, or million-tons-of-TNT-equivalence — though there are usually more of them and they have set the standard for accuracy.

"Accuracy" itself, among missilemen, is a relative term that essentially helps to measure the confidence the user has in his product. The technical measure of "accuracy" is a standard entitled "CEP," for circular-error-of-probability — a way of measuring what percentage of rockets are apt to fall within a certain distance of their targets.

Until the early 1970s, the CEP of most deployed Soviet missiles was on the order of a mile or two, accurate enough to destory such soft, sprawling targets as cities, but too wide a range of error to allow for precise targeting on specific, hardened "point" targets, such as missile silos. By comparison, the accuracy of the U.S. Minuteman III rockets, the design of which was frozen in 1963, has been considered to have a CEP of 100 feet or less, sufficient to bring even a small warhead down precisely enough to eradicate a hardened target.

American policy has concentrated on "hardening" of silos in an effort to protect the nation's offensive power. "Hardening" is generally measured in terms of how much air overpressure the facility can withstand in pounds per square inch. A typical wooden frame house, for instance, is apt to be destroyed by an overpressure (see Chapter Four for more details) of as little as five pounds per square inch. Since the early Atlas series of intercontinental rockets, virtually all U.S. missiles have been placed in buried concrete silos of increasing hardness. The earliest American silos were concrete-hardened to withstand forces of several hundreds of pounds per square inch (the equivalent of many hundreds of tons of pressure on each surface). Some contemporary Minuteman installations in the western U.S.

may, in fact, be hardened to many thousands of pounds of over-pressure to the square inch. The best public information is that recent Soviet missile silos may now be hardened to sustain overpressure forces of up to 3,000 pounds per square inch. All such hardening compels any potential adversary to think through the precise likelihood of his offensive warheads eradicating the enemy's retaliatory force. In general, a huge thermonuclear weapon hitting a mile or two away from a missile silo will not disable the rocket within the silo, but a much smaller warhead landing precisely on the silo housing the rocket may do so because it focuses its force on that particular area.

Several technical milestones can serve as measures of the degree of sophistication of nuclear weaponry. One such yardstick is the capacity for "cold launch" and not just "hot launch" of missiles. In hot-launch procedures, the earliest generation of rocketry techniques, the missile's main motors are fired while it is still in its silo, and the energy thus generated is used to lift the rocket out of its concrete hole. The missile must be considerably smaller in diameter than the silo, to allow release of exhaust gases from the main rocket motors. One main disadvantage is that the silo is virtually ruined and not readily re-loaded with another rocket. In addition, the necessary space left between the sides of the missile and the interior walls of the silo serves to weaken the whole assembly, making it more vulnerable to nuclear destruction.

In the newer cold launch technique, the entire missile is first forced into the air by compressed gas or similar force, and sometimes the missile is protected by a kind of "sabot" or cover. The main rocket motors of such weapons as the Minuteman are thus not fired until the missile has been expelled from its silo. The advantages to the technique are numerous. For one, the user gets a missile of larger diameter for the same size silo, which translates to greater range for the rocket. More important, making missile and silo wall virtually flush with one another serves to strengthen the entire installation and make it more resistant to shock and blast damage. Finally, the silo is far more read-ily re-loaded, since the exhaust gas effluents do little damage.

The entire generation of new rockets introduced by the Soviet Union in the 1970s evidently has a cold launch capability.

Another standard of measurement, one that applies to "accuracy," is the extent to which the warheads can be guided or boosted in space after launch. Fine-tuned accuracy can be achieved only by means of adding post-boost guidance systems, usually in miniaturized computer form, to the re-entry nosecone. In the most advanced American system now made public, the warheads are contained within a kind of space "bus" that releases them at appropriate points along its run toward its own target on the other side of the world. Thus a large intercontinental rocket with eight or even ten thermonuclear warheads aboard can be targeted on a general area, with each of its weapons assigned to a particular point in a large elliptical "footprint" on the surface. The more advanced the system, the finer the accuracy of any given warhead.

American Defense Department officials have been quoted as saying that the U.S. Minuteman missile system, the nation's chief source of land-based deterrence, becomes vulnerable to destruction when large warheads can be targeted to a CEP of roughly 370 meters. Soviet test flights of the new SS-18 giant missile in 1977 and 1978 averaged a CEP accuracy, determined by American spy ships, of 180 meters. Large rockets capable of delivering heavy warheads with such accuracy essentially eliminate any theoretical possibility of hardening a silo sufficiently for it to survive a blast. It is this Soviet accuracy — especially in the giant SS-18 rocket — that has given rise to speculation in the American press about the theoretical new "window of vulnerability" of the American land-based missile force. The Soviet advances thus have raised once again the fear of a "first strike" that might disable a substantial part of the American retaliatory force.

The issue of "first-strike" capability is one of the least understood of modern strategic ideas. It relates to the ability to fire rockets first, with the other side's land-based missile forces as primary targets. To be capable of a degrading "first strike," the aggressor must have large. numbers of big rockets, each carrying several warheads sufficiently accurate to hit small targets with enough yield to assure destruction of the hardened silos.

Critics of the arms race diminish the notion that the U.S.S.R. perhaps already has the ability to eradicate the U.S. land-based Minuteman missile forces. "So what," they say, in effect. "The U.S. has enough bombers and submarine missiles to assure the total destruction of Russia even if the Minutemen were wiped out." While on paper this is true the fact remains that the land-based missiles of both sides represent by far the largest retaliatory force either has on instant-alert status. For the U.S., the land-based strategic missiles represent roughly 60 percent of the retaliatory power that could be fired in the first half hour of war. The rest of the force, bombers and submarines, could be used only hours or days after the initial attack and mostly consists of weapons not accurate enough to be targeted upon hardened silos. Hence there is a disquieting scenario sometimes discussed in Washington in which, with their first-strike capability, the Soviets eliminate our Minuteman missiles while avoiding attacks on populations centers. Having done so, the Soviets then announce that they have intentionally avoided nuclear holocaust by not hitting American cities, but any subsequent American retaliation on Soviet cities, by means of bombers or submarine attacks, would mean a second Soviet wave of assaults upon the American population. In this way, pressure might be placed on an American President to surrender rather than risk the inevitable destruction of the fabric of American life.

Strategic Forces

According to a study done by the Congressional Budget Office in 1978, the Soviets are projected to support a fully deployed force of as many as 2,688 strategic launchers for nuclear warheads by mid-1985. The study assumes that the pattern of updating and future deployment, just within the guidelines established in the 1972 SALT I agreement, will be similar to the pattern exhibited by the U.S.S.R. since the signing of the original agreement. In some respects, the Soviets have clearly not deployed as many new rockets as they potentially could have. (An example is the new SS-17 rocket for which total operational numbers reached roughly 100 in the very early 1980s, much more slowly than the Soviets could have proceeded.) Total Soviet warheads of that time are projected to be 8,794.

The same sources estimate that the American strategic nuclear forces of 1985 will number precisely 2,179 launchers. But most of these will have been MIRVed. Accordingly, America will field almost exactly 13,900 strategic nuclear warheads in 1985, providing some continuing lead in total numbers over Soviet forces. Both estimates, incidentally, are far below the commonplace ''50,000 warhead'' total usually cited by American anti-nuclear critics. (Please see Table 1 for

TABLE 1 Strategic Nuclear Forces

(Estimated 1985 Totals)	USSR	USA
Land based ICBMs	1,398	1,053
Total number of warheads (ICBMs)	6,654	2,154
Total delivery capability (in megatons)	7,131	1,508.5
Submarines	73*	41
Total warheads	1,560	6,650
Total delivery capability (in megatons)	840	454
Manned aircraft	390**	390
Total warheads/bombs	640**	5,190***
Total delivery capability (in megatons)	2,300**	1,662
Total nuclear force (in megatons)	10,271	3,624.5

Sources: U.S. Congressional Budget Office, U.S. Air Force Strategic Air Command (SAC), and private sources

  * Includes deployment of 20 older *Gold* and *Hotel* class submarines.

  ** Includes 250 "Backfire" bombers.

*** Includes deployment of 3,300 cruise missles on B-52s by 1985.

a summary of strategic nuclear forces.)

From the American point of view, the world appears as a rivalry between the Giant Russian Elephant, the Red Army, and the Great American Whale, the United States Navy. Much of the strategic nuclear firepower of the United States is vested in its nuclear missile-launching submarines. Our nation maintains a fleet of 41 such nuclear missile submarines, the bulk of the boats dating back to classes commissioned in the early 1960s. Though this fleet is aging, and its replacement is limited by SALT I, the equipment aboard, including the rockets and nuclear reactors, have been updated to modern standards periodically, and the basic designs were sound in the first place. So the boats still sail freely, ranging throughout the oceans on long missions undersea, and they do so with an efficiency still higher than that of the Soviet Navy for keeping-on-station. A baker's dozen plus another or two are at their general station at sea at any given time. This alone is sufficient nuclear firepower to assure the destruction of every city and town in the Soviet Union with more than 100,000 population.

Another 13 American subs are in transit to or from their appointed grounds at sea. Should a crisis intervene, virtually all these craft may be alerted instantly, essentially doubling U.S. nuclear sub firepower. The remaining third of U.S. boats are at their home ports and would require varying amounts of time to go onto a full war-footing.

In the mid-1980s, these American nuclear submarine forces are assumed to be equipped with three basic models of missile:

Poseidon   Equipped with a relatively small warhead of 40 kilotons, 10 warheads to each missile, each warhead having a bit more than twice the destructive power of the Hiroshima A-bomb. 21 of the older nuclear submarines will continue to carry this particular weaponry into 1985. Like all submarine missiles — it is impossible to fit a 200-foot high rocket into a 40-foot tall submarine — Poseidon is quite small, less than 30 feet high, and its ability to deliver a powerful nuclear punch is attributable to American breakthroughs in nuclear weapons miniaturization in the mid-1950s. Because Poseidon has a limited range, the 21 older U.S. nuclear submarines must approach Soviet waters more closely. The United States often stations two Poseidon boats in the Baltic Sea, where their proximity minimizes any potential warning time for the Soviet Union. It is no accident that the presence of such craft near western Europe also serves as a kind of heavy-artillery back-up against any potential Soviet land attack through Germany. The concentrated firepower of 32 such missiles, 320 multi-kiloton warheads detonated in an area of a few thousand square miles, is clearly sufficient to obliterate the mightiest tank attack yet envisioned.

Poseidon C-4   Essentially the same model of missile, but fitted with a newly-designed thermonuclear warhead of roughly 100 kilotons, or two and a half times more powerful than the original Poseidon. Ten American submarines are to be outfitted with C-4s by 1985, with each sub carrying 16 missiles and each missile eight separately targetable warheads.

Trident I   The newest American undersea-launched missile, to be deployed aboard 10 new and far-ranging *Trident* type submarines by 1985. In the case of Trident, the warhead is the same version used in the Poseidon C-4, a 100-kiloton model, with eight warheads to each missile, but the missile itself is entirely new and much longer-ranged than anything previously sent to sea. In combination with its firing platform, the advanced nuclear submarine, the Trident makes a ferocious weapons system. Accuracy has been improved substantially over earlier sea-launched ballistic missiles; estimated CEP for Trident is on the order of one third a mile or so from target, for one half the missiles fired.

In contrast to American policy, the U.S.S.R. puts much of its nuclear power in the control of the land-based missilemen. Slightly more than half the Soviet strategic launch vehicles projected for 1985 will be land-based missiles, and more than three-fourths of all the warheads will be atop those particular rockets. The emphasis on land-based missiles of immense size and power is in stark contrast to the American preference for the sea.

Different sources give varying estimates of the precise power of the Soviet Union today, and for the immediate future. But most analysts agree that, while the U.S.S.R. has embarked on an extended and massive build-up of its power, it has also *not* added to its forces quite as fast as it could have. Whether this implies that the Soviet Union is quietly willing to talk about true limitation of nuclear weapons, or whether the fact is that the Soviets have encountered unexpected technical trouble with their rockets, so far it is impossible for anyone to tell. (Please see Table 2.)

While Soviet motives may forever be held in suspicion, the massive extent of their build-up and modernization is quite clear. The process has been going on since the early 1960s, and the U.S.S.R. actually overtook the U.S. in sheer numbers of land-based missiles in 1970. The chief surprise since then has been the rapid improvement in Soviet technology. The missiles of the U.S.S.R. have become very accurate in recent years, while actually increasing their range and payload.

Because most Soviet missiles are land-based, they can be quite large, and their ''throwweight,'' or how many tons they can carry, can also be huge by American standards. The average warhead on an American strategic missile will have the power of two to five times the

TABLE 2   Estimated 1985 land-based missile strengths

	SS-11	SS-16	SS-17	SS-18	SS-19	Minute-man	Titan
			SOVIET UNION			UNITED STATES	
height in ft.	62	66	80	121	89	56	90
weight in tons	53	40	72	243	86	40	110
diameter in ft.	8	6	8+	10.5	8+	5	10
total number* deployed/1985	330	66	200	308	500	1000	53
date first deployed	1966	1975	1974	1974	1974	1963	1961
number of warheads	1-3	1+	4	1-8	6	1-3	1
warhead type	MIRV	MIRV?	MIRV	MIRV	MIRV	MIRV	single
yield per warhead, in megatons	1=1.5 3=.33	2.0	.6	1=25** 8=1.0	.8	1=1.0 3=.17	9
max. range in miles	6550	5585	6225	7475	6219	6650	6330
accuracy, in C.E.P. (miles)	1	.6	.5+	.1	.6+	.1	1.5

* Source: U.S. Congressional Budget Office, "Counterforce Issues for the U.S. Strategic Nuclear Forces," 1978

** By the provisions of the SALT I Treaty, all Soviet SS-18s are counted as having eight MIRVed warheads. However, Western intelligence sources believe that approximately 50 of these giant rockets carry a single very-high yield 25 megaton or larger, warhead.

power of the Hiroshima A-bomb. The very smallest nuclear warhead in the Soviet missile inventory in 1985 — when Soviet warheads will have grown smaller — is projected by U.S. Congressional sources as 600 kilotons, or thirty times the size of the Hiroshima bomb. Most Soviet missile warheads are, in fact, expected to be in the megaton range, or higher.

The Soviet interest in large weapons has existed for some time, but what surprised most Western analysts during the 1970s was the rapid progress of Soviet missile and space technology. As far back as the mid-1960s, for instance, the U.S.S.R. had startled U.S. test-watchers by firing a giant intercontinental rocket over record ranges with then-high accuracy. By 1966, this missile, the SS-9, was being deployed with its companion, the SS-11 (a less accurate missile intended to destroy sprawling areas like cities), at the rate of one every two days. Production and deployment of these two weapons was then increased by the U.S.S.R., while the technology was further improved.

In 1973, the Soviets again startled American analysts by conducting three tests of the SS-9 in the Pacific, each time with three independent warheads atop the rocket. The three warheads were still just MRV (multiple re-entry vehicles), independent of each other but not capable of being precisely aimed by computer. The tests were something like the firing of a shotgun, the pattern containing several pellets, none of which is precisely aimed. These tests were most interesting, for they consistently formed the geometry of the typical U.S. Minuteman missile complex. The following year, the Soviet Union tested still newer missile systems that incorporated all the latest design technology, from cold-launch to MIRV to super-accurate warheads. By 1985, virtually none of the original SS-9s in the Soviet nuclear inventory are expected to be in continued deployment.

Here is the projected land based missile force of the Soviet Union for 1985:

SS-11 Estimates of Soviet deployment of this rocket vary. American authorities, who tend to believe that the Soviets will continue to target virtually all American population centers of 50,000 or more, project that the U.S.S.R. will maintain a force of 330 of these missiles, each with a single 1.5 megaton warhead and accuracy of slightly more than one mile from target for half the missiles fired. European and NATO sources believe that the U.S.S.R. will have retired virtually all SS-11s by 1985, replacing them with the newer missiles described below.

SS-16 This missile was specifically banned in the SALT II treaty, although that treaty was never ratified under President Carter and was shelved by President Reagan. It remains to be seen whether the Soviets will fully deploy this particular missile. Most defense analysts believe that at least 60 such missiles will be deployed by the U.S.S.R. by 1985. Quite likely, this missile is mobile despite its large size (nearly 70 feet high). When only the top two of the three stages are used, the resulting launcher is known as the SS-20, an intermediate-range rocket whose deployment has caused a recent furor in Europe.

The SS-16 is the Soviet Union's first successful solid-fuel missile, and it incorporates a kind of space "bus" in its warheads capable of targeting warheads precisely over a wide area, and it contains advanced devices to help it plow through modern electronic defenses.

There is concern about the missile's status. No tests of it have been seen since 1975, when it had completed a successful string of launches to demonstrate its capabilities. The evidence since then, however, is that this particular missile has rarely been deployed. Whether this strange absence is intentional or the result of bugs in the system is almost impossible to determine. Both British and some American analysts at the Department of Defense believe it possible that the U.S.S.R. has produced this particular missile in considerable numbers, but because of mobile deployment possibilities, the rockets are being stored for use in the event of war. The SS-16 carries a warhead rated between one and 1.5 megatons.

SS-17 One of two basic designs evidently competing within the U.S.S.R. for the role of replacement launcher for the aging SS-11s, the SS-17 is 80 feet high, a bit more than eight feet wide, and weighs roughly 72 tons at launch. It is a "cold-launch" vehicle, incorporating advanced space bus and terminal-boost technologies, and some reports state it as solid-fueled. Best estimates of its intended role is as a city-killer. One version, arrayed with a single, high-yield thermonuclear weapon, is assumed to be accurate enough to give the SS-17 some capability to back up other Soviet missiles aimed at American silos. The SS-17's main models are reported to carry four warheads, with yields in the 600-800 kiloton range per warhead. Deployment of the SS-17 began in the Soviet Union in 1975, but has proceeded somewhat more slowly than the Soviets might have done. The implications of this Soviet decision — it might have been influenced by a decision to switch to the competing SS-19 model — are unclear.

SS-19 Presently competing in the Soviet Union for the job of replacing the SS-11, the SS-19 can deliver a warhead/payload four times greater than the SS-11. Some debate exists about whether it is cold-launched, but tests of this missile have indicated an accuracy on a par with Soviet missiles intended for American hard targets, such as missile silos. The SS-19 appears to be the victor in the competition with the SS-17.

SS-18 This missile, intentionally listed out of numerical sequence here, is the chief cause of American concern over a Soviet "first-strike" capability. First tested early in 1974, the SS-18 was deployed that same year. It is a gigantic rocket 121 feet high, ten and a half feet thick, and capable of targeting almost any point on the planet. The SS-18 can carry up to 10 tons of thermonuclear warhead machinery (as much as a heavy manned bomber), and the missile itself weighs more than 240 tons at launch.

One clear purpose of the SS-18, in American eyes, is to be a terror weapon. Reports persist that some SS-18s have been deployed with extremely high-yield thermonuclear warheads of up to 50 megatons. (The largest hydrogen weapon ever exploded on earth was a 58-megaton blast by the Soviet Union in the late 1950s.) A weapon of such size, most analysts agree, has no military purpose.

Most Western analysts today rate the high-yield version of the SS-18's warhead at 18 to 25 megatons, still the largest presently deployed on the planet. The alternative version of the SS-18 is a MIRVed model, with most observers estimating from eight to ten warheads per missile, each warhead rated somewhere between 600 kilotons and 1.5 megatons. Because a provision of SALT II (intending to limit the total numbers of warheads, not launchers) called for a formula by which, if a single MIRVed version of any missile should be deployed, all missiles of that model would be considered as MIRVed toward a ceiling limit, American defense officials traditionally count the SS-18 as carrying eight separate warheads and estimate that 2,464 large warheads will be deployed on this Soviet missile in 1985. British sources, however, give figures that allow the Soviets roughly 50 of the giant SS-18s with the huge, terror warhead, with the remaining several hundred already deployed carrying 10 MIRVed warheads of 600 kilotons each. Both British and American defense analysts agree on a top figure of precisely 308 Soviet SS-18s deployed by 1985, probably because this figure was established as the limit for this missile under SALT I.

If the size of the SS-18 is awesome, its accuracy is sufficient to raise qualms throughout the American defense establishment. During 1977 and 1978, numerous SS-18 warheads reached their impact area in the Soviet test zone in mid-Pacific. These test shots demonstrated an average accuracy for the warhead that brought it to earth within 200 yards of its intended target, from half a world away. Such accuracy, combined with the sheer power of the SS-18 warheads, is enough to provide the Soviet Union with a presumed first-strike capability that could decimate American land-based missile forces. For all practical purposes, it is virtually impossible to harden any spot on earth targeted by one of these missiles enough to avoid absolutely assured destruction. The capabilities of this missile, fully realized by Western defense analysts, gave rise in the early 1980s to entirely new thinking of how American land missiles might be based. Early in 1983, Congress rejected the ''dense-pack'' arrangement of a number of new American missiles — the MX in particular — in silos packed quite closely together and extensively hardened. The theory is that the first incoming warhead would obviously destroy an American missile or two, but the rest might survive as later-arriving Soviet rockets might destroy their own internal mechanisms from the ''fratricide'' effect of the first warhead.

Assuming that the Soviets deploy 308 SS-18s during the early 1980s, and each such missile carries 10 of the MIRVed warheads that have proved so accurate in tests, the Soviets would then have the theoretical capability to aim three warheads at each and every American Minuteman or Titan silo, with a few left over for other targets. A single SS-18, if targeted toward a region rather than a specific point, is able to cover 10 targets in an area as large as New England and portions of New York and Canada.

Missiles such as the Soviet SS-18 and the American MX are at the heart of modern concern about a first strike, because each missile carries enough very accurate warheads to represent a threat to the other side's land-based missile force in a preemptive attack. Perhaps a wiser and more realistic course for proponents of a nuclear freeze would be to restrict the freeze to this type of weapon in particular. For those concerned about diminished U.S. retaliatory capabilities in the 1980s and 1990s, a wise course might be to propose a series of much smaller, mobile missiles armed with but one warhead apiece. Compared to the vast cost and the potentially destabilizing influence of such giant rockets as the MX, the smaller one-warhead missiles would be considerably cheaper, probably less vulnerable because of their mobility and scattered basing, and represent something of a reduced threat to Soviet leaders because such new weapons would not add to America's first-strike capabilities.

The weapons postures of the two super-powers diverge widely in the 1980s. The second large American nuclear striking force is housed in its far-flung missile silos, precisely 1,053 of them. This is the force presumed to be in danger of pre-emption by the Soviet SS-18. Officially speaking, the U.S. Air Force's Strategic Air Command (SAC) is responsible for the 1,000 Minuteman missile silos and the 53 aging, second-generation Titan missiles. All these rocket complexes are scattered west of the Mississippi River. A brief description of the American land-based missile facilities follows:

Minuteman II   An updated Minuteman first deployed in the mid-1960s to carry an extremely accurate single warhead with a one megaton yield. The basic Minuteman design calls for a fairly small, solid-fueled rocket with intense hardening of its protective silo, communications and control facilities, extreme accuracy, and silo-storage stability. It is still considered reliable, and the entire system is evidently retargetable in as little as seven hours, thanks to advanced communications. There have been 450 Minuteman II missiles deployed in the U.S. since the 1960s, and there will likely still be 450 such missiles deployed in 1985.

Minuteman III   Still more advanced, the Minuteman III carries three MIRVed warheads of about 170 kilotons each. These weapons hold the world standard for accuracy, with half the missiles having a CEP of as little as 100 feet from target. There are 550 Minuteman III missiles in the American arsenal today, and that many are projected as still deployed in 1985. As with the Navy's Poseidon missile program, there is a plan built into the American defense build-up of the 80s to double the yield of each Minuteman III warhead to roughly 350 kilotons.

Titan II   Early versions of this second-generation missile, designed in the late 1950s, served well as vehicles in the American space program, and 53 are still deployed with the operational U.S. missile forces. Each missile carries a single, large, nine megaton warhead, the largest currently in the U.S. missile inventory, but accuracy is not nearly as good as that of Minuteman. In recent years, as the Titans have aged in Arkansas and New Mexico, they have acquired the reputation of being dangerous to handle; the liquid fuel is both toxic and very volatile, and leaks are commonplace. Accuracy of Titan II leads several observers to believe these missiles are aimed at the huge populations of China, rather than at targets in the U.S.S.R. In 1980, a

Titan missile exploded in its silo in Arkansas after a workman dropped a wrench that ruptured a fuel valve, bringing America's aging inventory of Titans to 53. Current projections are that these missiles will still be on-line in the U.S. in 1985.

Separately from its large land-based missile force, the U.S.S.R. maintains a fleet of ballistic missile launching submarines of considerable range and firepower. About 900 missiles are projected for the Soviet submarine missile force in 1985, and these are clearly thought of as a second-strike weaponry aimed at cities and population centers if a nuclear holocaust should transpire.

In 1985, the Soviet Union is projected to maintain a missile submarine fleet of about 75 ships. Only about 10 percent of the Soviet submarine force is on station at any given time, and deployments in such critical areas as the North Atlantic have periodically seemed to fall short of Soviet desires. The long range of the newer Soviet sea-launched missiles, however, allows some Soviet subs to fire at American targets without going far from port.

In 1985, two thirds of the 900 submarine missiles of the U.S.S.R. will take the form of two older models that date back to the 1960s and two much newer models accounting for the rest. The four basic models are outlined below:

SS-N-6 46 feet long, with 16 aboard each 34 *Yankee*-class Soviet submarines of the 1960s, the missiles carry a one-to-two megaton warhead, with another version providing three smaller warheads of lower yield. Accuracy is not sharp enough to allow targeting on hardened, point targets, and so the vehicle is assumed to be targeted on American cities. The missile was introduced to service by the Soviets in 1967, and later improvements in range allowed it, in official U.S. Defense Department estimates, to reach any part of the continental United States from any point along the 100-fathom contour along our shores.

SS-N-8 When this submarine missile first appeared in Soviet tests in 1971, the then-Chairman of the U.S. Joint Chiefs of Staff announced that its range was greater than 2,000 miles more than any other sea-launched missile in the world. By October, 1974, further Soviet tests, fired from a new Soviet *Delta*-class submarine — there are roughly 18 such ships, and they are giant-sized to carry the N-8 conveniently — in the Barents Sea north of Norway to an impact area in the central

Pacific, indicated a maximum range of nearly 6,000 miles, about enough to let the submarine fire its missiles at an American target without having left its moorings.

SS-N-17 and SS-N-18 Both of these are still considered experimental by the American defense community, but they appear to be sufficiently successful and advanced as to be considered certain for operational deployment by 1985. The N-17 variant may be the first successful solid-fuel Soviet missile designed to be fired from a submarine. The N-18 appears to be a large vehicle of very long range and very high accuracy, equipped with significant advances in the state of the art of firing submerged ballistic missiles. Some of the items noted during Soviet test flights of the N-18 in 1977 and 1978 indicate levels of operational technology not planned for introduction in the advanced Trident of the U.S. Navy for another decade.

Oddly, the dimensions given by early Western intelligence reports correspond to no known Soviet submarine's missile chambers. They may, however, relate to a still-newer class of Soviet nuclear submarine named the *Typhoon.*

On paper, advances in electronics, radar, and rocketry should have all but eliminated the manned bomber from strategic consideration. Yet both super-powers maintain something more than just a negligible capability in manned bomber-type aircraft. (Please see Table 3.)

On its part, the United States evidently intends to keep 330 of its aged B-52 bomber fleet on active duty well into 1985, or at least until that aircraft can be replaced by a much newer bomber. The airplane itself, originally designed in the early 1950s as a high-altitude penetration bomber, has now been in service for more than two decades and has seen more changes in its mission than any other operationl aircraft in U.S. history. Current U.S. planning is that B-52 bombers could fight their way through massed Soviet fighter interceptors and sophisticated surface-to-air (SAM) missiles, presumably by approaching their targets at breath-taking treetop level, or by using some form of stand-off missile that lets them fire their weapons before having to penetrate the stiffest defenses. The American cruise missile falls into this latter category. The first such B-52 wing to be so armed became operational at Griffis AFB, near Rome, New York, in mid-1982.

Early in 1983, the U.S. Air Force announced a reduction in the total number of air-launched cruise missiles once proposed for the aging

TABLE 3   Comparison of Manned Bomber Strengths, 1985 estimates

aircraft type	SOVIET UNION			UNITED STATES	
	Bear (Tu-20)	Bison (M-4)	Backfire (Tu-26)	B-52G/H	FB-111A
wingspan/ft	159	166	113	185	70
length/ft	155	155	132	157	74
no. engines	4 (prop)	4	2	8	2
combat weight (in tons)	170	186	135	189	47
crew	5(?)	4(?)	4	up to 9	2
max. speed (mph)	540	560	1,320	590	1,580
range without refueling (in miles)	7,800	6,825	2,110	6,785	3,165
year first deployed	1956	1955	1974	1953	1969
gravity bombs/ missile warheads	1	1	2	20-22 missiles 4 bombs	2 missiles 2 bombs
weapons yield (megatons)	20	5	.2	bombs = 1.0 missiles = 0.2	bombs = 1.0 missiles = 0.2
aircraft deployed	100	40	250	330	60

Sources: U.S. Strategic Air Command, U.S. Congressional Budget Office, private sources, Jane's *All The World's Aircraft* (London, several editions).

B-52 fleet, from more than 3,000 to less than 1,500. Whether the reduced number is the result of continuing technological difficulties or is an acknowledgement of the increased efficiency of the Soviet air-interception forces (cruise missiles might be shot down by fighter aircraft with "look-down/shoot-down" radars that highlight the small target against the ground below) is currently impossible to determine.

B-52s carry four bombs of a one-megaton yield for their gravity-powered weapons, and normally carry six short-range attack missiles with warheads of 200 kilotons each. Some of these latter missiles, and other defensive weaponry, may be configured to fly down the pipe of an encroaching radar beam and eliminate the air defense. The United

States believes that the aging airplane is still capable of penetrating the Soviet air defenses of the 1980s. The bomber's comparatively heavy nuclear firepower also counts as a plus as the mere existence of the B-52 compels the U.S.S.R. to maintain an extremely expensive air defense system against manned aircraft.

The only other present-day U.S. aircraft capable of reaching the Soviet Union on a strategic mission is the FB-111 bomber. This aircraft, originally the famous TFX fighter plane of the McNamara era of the 1960s, has now found itself a place as a reliable supersonic medium-bomber. About 60 of these aircraft are officially counted in U.S. projections of force levels for 1985, and each plane can carry two single-megaton gravity bombs, plus two of the short-range attack missiles.

On the Soviet side, the most formidable air threat is probably the Tupolev Tu-22 swingwing supersonic bomber, better known by its Western codename of "Backfire." About 250 such aircraft might be capable of reaching selected points in the United States at twice the speed of sound, provided they were on one-way missions or had adequate air refueling along the way. Different authorities give varying estimates of the Backfire's capabilities, but official U.S. estimates for 1985 suggest that each Backfire could carry two bombs of 200 kilotons each on such missions.

The U.S.S.R. also maintains a fleet of 40 Myasishchev M-4 "Bison" bombers. The Bison is a four-jet aircraft originally designed in the 1950s as a heavy, intercontinental bomber, but since reduced to roles in mid-air refueling, maritime reconnaissance, and electronic warfare. Nevertheless, U.S. defense officials estimate that Bison bombers could each carry a single five-megaton H-bomb to points in the domestic U.S. in 1985.

The Soviets also maintain a long-range, four-engined turboprop intercontinental airplane, the Tu-20 "Bear" bomber. This type of aircraft is used by the U.S.S.R. for electronic surveillance of the United States on long-range flights, often involving a stop in Cuba. About 100 of these aircraft are expected to be on active duty in 1985. Each could presumably carry a single 20-megaton gravity bomb, which earns this ancient bomber — it has been in Soviet service for a quarter century — the dubious honor of carrying the world's most deadly airplane payload.

Flights of Soviet Bear bombers, going ostensibly to and from Cuba on the Great Circle route from Moscow, are a frequent occurrence close to the New England coast, where the planes are often intercepted by U.S. fighters from Cape Cod.

FUTURE TRENDS

In the ever-tense 1980s, when neither side is certain of the intentions of the other, both the U.S. and U.S.S.R. have shown signs of further development of their nuclear war-fighting capabilities. Major questions still to be answered include Soviet intentions at this moment of comparative parity between the two nations. Will the U.S.S.R. slow its long build-up or be persuaded to halt its development entirely? Will the United States persist in its expensive new nuclear armament program? Will both sides continue to behave in circumspect fashion?

On its side, America has announced a major new program to introduce the cruise missile, in forms that may be launched from the ground, from the sea, and from the air. The technology involved is a major extension of the newly-discovered prowess of long-range, remotely piloted vehicles, first used extensively in the Vietnam war. With the cruise missile, the basic concept is to produce so many of these relatively inexpensive electronic marvels — they are to find their way precisely to their targets, over distances of thousands of miles, according to programmed terrain files in their computer memories — that they could potentially flood any conceivable Soviet air defense. The idea is to use ultra-modern computer and sensor technology to hearken back to manned bomber days, only to do so without taking a pilot aboard.

The technology to do all this is currently American technology, but there remains doubt about its effectiveness. Constant rumors abound about the misfires and inaccuracies of the early cruise missiles, and it could be that the idea will need more years to fully prove itself in the field.

On its side, the Soviet Union is presumed to continue its own constant build-up, at least through the deployment of the SS-17, 18, and 19 land-based missiles. There are indications that the Soviets have still newer missiles on the drawing boards, but, to date, both sides have been careful to live close to the provisions of the SALT treaties, even if they are not fully enforced.

Areas not well defined in the SALT/START process are arenas of hot technical competition between the two super-powers. The U.S. continues advanced work in anti-submarine warfare technology, though no break-through seems imminent on this front by either side. The U.S. also probably holds the current lead in hardening its electronic communications, and research into aircraft whose shape, size, and composition would render them nearly invisible to radar. The latter project is the so-called "Stealth" bomber prematurely announced by President Carter's administration during the course of the 1980 election campaign.

"Stealth," like many such advanced research projects, is not really a singular aircraft, but rather a compilation of different theories about radar reflection. The Stealth principles incorporate such ideas as non-metallic skin surfaces for the airframe, radar-beam absorbent materials, all surfaces curved, and other laboratory notions. The difficult thing may be to produce a single airframe that can fly incorporating all the anti-radar ideas.

The area of most intense interest is probably that of laser and charged-particle defensive beams that might destroy or incapacitate enemy warheads as they rose to the attack. For once in the history of the nuclear age, this idea supports the defense rather than the offense, for the U.S. officially considers such advanced weaponry "benign" — meaning that it can disable satellites or warheads but poses little threat to people. This technology is at the heart of President Reagan's proposed "defensive" strategy.

The public information and related technical literature are so sparse as to make it virtually impossible to determine which nation might be in the "lead." The Soviets are said to maintain a laser and charged-particle experiment at Semipalatinsk in the Central Asian military district, not far from Mongolia. The U.S. program of research into the same fields is said to have the codename "Sipapu," an American Indian term for the concept of "sacred fire." A few Western observers feel that operational laser/particle beam weaponry is feasible by the late 1980s but most analyists agree that this capability is much farther away.

Sources

Considerable variation appears in published projections of the military strength of the U.S. and U.S.S.R. In particular, sources in the United States and military analysts in Western Europe often seem to disagree strongly with regard to their estimates of the deployment of various kinds of Soviet weapons systems. The figures given in this chapter are the author's personal composite of two basic sources, NATO estimates combined with the publication, "Counterforce Issues for the U.S. Strategic Forces," published by the U.S. Congressional Budget Office and released in July, 1978 (available on occasion through local Senators and Representatives or from the Superintendent of Documents, Government Printing Office, Washington D.C. 20402). Material provided by the U.S. Strategic Air Command was also considered in the compilation of total 1985 strength of the U.S. and U.S.S.R.

The asymmetries visible in the comparative vulnerabilities of the United States and the Soviet Union are strongly highlighted in a most useful government report, *The Effects of Nuclear War*, published by the Congressional Office of Technology Assessment in 1980, available at Federal bookstores in the larger cities or through the Government Printing Office whose address is given above. Also helpful is the official handbook on the U.S.S.R. given to diplomats and produced by the U.S. Department of State. This is often available at good local libraries.

An excellent new book on Soviet power and Soviet thinking is *Russian Military Power* (originally published in London by Salamander Books in 1980 and now distributed in the U.S. by Bonanza Books Division of Crown Publishers, One Park Avenue, New York, New York 10016). This is a superb compendium highly recommended to anyone interested in understanding the Soviet perception of the contemporary world. A series of essays contributed by highly qualified consultants, from Western Europe and NATO for the most part, is combined with remarkable graphics illustrating Soviet advances in military technology. Of particular interest is the section on the Soviet Strategic Rocket Forces, written by the late Dr. James E. Dornan, Jr. of the Catholic University of America. This section is by far the best and most comprehensive such report available to the general public.

Material on the abortive deployment of the U.S. Davy Crockett is drawn from the author's interviews with former and present U.S. Army officers who questioned the security of this idea from the outset. Because some of the now-retired officers may have had their careers shortened by their outspoken questioning of official U.S. policy, no mention will be made here of their contributions by name. They were simply proven right, as subsequent American policy clearly revealed.

The interested reader may get a further introduction to the mathematics of "circular-error-probable," or C.E.P., in Herman Kahn's now-classic *On Thermonuclear War* (first edition, Princeton University Press, 1960). This is a seminal work in American theory about nuclear war, and its author is today widely viewed as the leading American theoretician on the subject, given his experience at the RAND Corporation and other government-sponsored think tanks. An abridged, though no more simple, version of this book exists under the title *Thinking About the Unthinkable,* which is no easier to follow than the original, and the reader is referred instead to the first, classic work. Material in Chapter Three about the recent accuracy of Soviet warheads is drawn mostly from the author's private sources in American industry, all of whom are engaged in the arcane business of monitoring Soviet missile tests.

The same sources must be cited for the author's comments about post-boost guidance systems of recent development. Statistics about the Soviet SS-17, SS-18, SS-19, and the experimental, new Soviet submarine-launched test vehicles were largely supplied by European sources connected to NATO, who must remain nameless here by agreement. Little is yet known about the latest Soviet submarine-launched missiles and still less has appeared in print in this country.

The accident involving the Titan missile silo in Arkansas was widely covered in the U.S. press when it occurred. By contrast, the comments at the close of Chapter Three about new advances in anti-radar vehicles, laser and charged-particle weapons, and the earlier comments about Soviet advances in extremely accurate naval missiles must inherently be limited for reasons of classification and genuine national security matters. Little is known as yet of many such developments. The author's private estimate, for instance, is that, with the completion of the Navy's "Navstar" satellite series in the mid-1980s, new U.S. Trident missiles may begin to achieve accuracies closely approaching those of the land-based Minuteman missiles, a conjectural development that will allow the U.S. additional flexibility in assignment of its strategic nuclear forces to Soviet military targets.

4 Prompt Effects

There was once a fifth horseman in the roster of the prompt killers incorporated in any nuclear explosion: the immediate radiation let loose in the course of the explosion itself. To fire a nuclear weapon, a chain reaction must occur. Neutrons must, in some way, be agitated to fly about and penetrate other atomic nuclei. The addition of a neutron to an atomic nucleus will render it unstable, or radioactive. When it decays, or splits, more neutrons are released, along with other forms of radiation, continuing and increasing the chain reaction. In the process, some of the original matter is converted to pure energy according to Einstein's famous equation, $E = mc^2$. If the explosion itself is a "small" one, something like an atomic laboratory accident, or the crude, first-generation A-bombs that fell on Hiroshima and Nagasaki, or is a contemporary "neutron" bomb, then a person standing quite close to the explosion might conceivably survive the blast, but still be killed by the neutron flux — the "immediate radiation" — emitted by the reaction. In Japan in 1945, because the bombs were fairly small, there were some casualties attributed to "immediate radiation." But neutrons that must travel through the dense atmosphere of the earth are quickly absorbed. The lethal range of such free neutrons released in a thermonuclear blast is much less than the lethal range of the blast and heat.

NEUTRON RADIATION

Neutron irradiation, of course, is clearly one of the worst local effects of any nuclear reaction. Other types of radiation do clearcut damage, but neutrons kill by causing the elements of the organism to become radioactive in their own right. Yet, at a range of two miles from the point-of-reaction, virtually all of the free neutrons have been absorbed by the earth's sea of air. And, since a modern thermonuclear weapon's initial fireball can extend far beyond the range of immediate radiation, scientists expect very few human casualties from *immediate* radiation in the event of nuclear war. In this odd way, modernity has removed the fifth horseman — immediate radiation — from the panopoly of things that can kill promptly during a nuclear weapon's explosion.

This non-quaint "oddity" of recent history implies a number of other things about contemporary nuclear times. The variables in any study of the effects of nuclear war are extremely great. For example, the U.S. government has, over the years, commissioned any number of privately contracted studies of the effects of nuclear war. Virtually all of these must inevitably make certain statistical assumptions: that there are so many people per square kilometer in Leningrad at noon on any given day; that there are so many people crowded into downtown Boston on a Wednesday afternoon in Christmas-shopping season. Now, assuming that data, if a nuclear weapon of known characteristics were fired above such a population at the studied moment, what might be the results in terms of casualties? Quite clearly, the only constant in all such calculations is man's precise knowledge of the physical effects of nuclear weapons, for the simple reason that physics is much easier to quantify than the vagaries of human life.

What we know today of the effects of nuclear weapons is quite precise; most nuclear matters can be determined down to a precise quantity. One of the most evident variables in the equation is the wide disparity of effect according to the weapon itself and how it is fired. Circumstances, in short, have great influence on the effect of nuclear weapons.

DETONATION VARIABLES

Among the most significant variables that determine the precise effect of any given nuclear explosion are the height at which the weapon is fired above the surface of the earth, the yield and design of the weapon, the general weather and wind direction at detonation, the time of day, and the season of the year. These variables are listed in order of significance below.

Altitude

A modern nuclear weapon may be exploded deep beneath the earth or sea, on the surface, at various altitudes above the earth, or high in space. Its effects differ radically according to its height above the planet, in this order:

Subsurface Blasts   Used to create ground-transmitted shock waves that might cause highly reinforced structures of various kinds to topple. The effect is roughly that of an earthquake, and it can be monitored over most of the earth by seismographs. If the explosion is fairly close beneath the surface of the earth, half a mile or less, it may vent radioactive gases into the atmosphere, causing a kind of local fallout. But, if the explosion is well contained, blast, heat, and shock are penned in, except for the ground wave, and fallout may be contained at a minimum.

Surface Bursts   These are the type apt to be used to vaporize missile silos. Because the fireball of the explosion physically touches the ground, a high intensity of fallout can be predicted for areas far downwind. The fireball in effect sucks up the highly irradiated motes of dust, concrete, and flesh, then carries the radioactive material high into the sky, where it will be scattered by the prevailing wind. For many people along the U.S. east coast, fallout carried from Soviet surface bursts upon U.S. Minuteman missile silos west of the Mississippi may be the greatest danger in the event of nuclear war.

Airbursts   Used to destroy fairly "soft" targets, such as cities. To modern targeters, the airburst is the method-of-choice when the target consists of a population center not likely to be reinforced against blast. An airburst kills and destroys by extending the area of air overpressure. By contrast, a groundburst destroys a specific, or "point" target by maximizing the overpressure at that particular spot. The excess pressure is measured, quantitatively, in terms of a number of pounds per square inch of exposed surface. An overpressure of five pounds per square inch, which amounts to hundreds of tons of pressure on any given wall, is likely to destroy most modern wood-frame housing. The use of airbursts reduces the maximum over-pressure at a point directly beneath the detonation, but extends the area of five pounds-per-square-inch (PSI) overpressure to its greatest range in a concentric circle around the explosion. Airbursts also tend to have extended visual and thermal effects. The use of airbursts is often recommended for catching early-launched bombers in mid-air, not far from their takeoff points, around the time their home bases have been obliterated. Almost all areas in a fan-shaped arc extending for 100 miles north of U.S. bomber bases are today assumed to be targets for Soviet attempts to eradicate those few aircraft that might have gotten off the ground in the event of sudden war.

High-altitude Explosions   There is no atmosphere in space and very little in the high reaches above the earth's air envelope. Hence nuclear explosions occurring in these regions high above the surface of the earth — particularly in the area 19-25 miles above the earth's surface — do not dissipate much of their released energy in the form of blast or shock. Instead, thanks to the enormous difference in electrical potential from one side of the detonation to the other, such bursts emit a tremendous pulse of electromagnetic energy. The phenomenon, known as ''EMP,'' or electromagnetic pulse, causes no harm to living organisms, but is extremely disruptive to all electrical circuits not protected against it. The surge of energy measured in antennas/receivers more than one meter in length — EMP most likely can affect much smaller receiving circuits, such as transistor radios and computers — strikingly resembles the profile of a lightning pulse, except that the energies recorded are vastly higher and come upon the electrical circuit much more quickly, swiftly enough in fact to defeat conventional ''lightning rods.''

Weapon Variables

The notion that the yield of the weapon has a great influence on the damage caused is readily grasped. A 25-megaton bomb is, most simply stated, 1,250 times more powerful than the 20-kiloton bombs dropped on Japan at the end of World War II. Increase the yield of the weapon, and its sheer beastliness is similarly augmented.

The idea that the design of the warhead and its carrying vehicle also serve to influence the likely damage done is dependent upon two nuclear factors that are somewhat harder to comprehend.

The first factor is the ratio of fission versus fusion built into the weapon to achieve its theoretical yield. To create the physical circumstance that produce a thermonuclear reaction — enormous pressure and stellar heat are required — the designer must use an atom bomb for a trigger. Unlike the thermonuclear or "fusion" reaction, in which atoms of hydrogen fuse together to produce tremendous energy, the A-bomb works on the principle of nuclear "fission" — the nucleus of an atom of plutonium-239 or uranium-235 is broken into fragments to release energy. Each of these fragments is a new element, but usually in non-stable or radioactive form. Hence fission reactions produce as a by-product "fission products," nearly 300 separate kinds of them in fact, and virtually all of them are highly radioactive. Some, like the man-made elements californium and berkelium, are so unstable that they emit high radioactivity for short periods before decaying and losing their potential for radiation-damage. Others, such as cobalt-60 and strontium-90, decay far more slowly and present a potential hazard for some time after their creation. Therefore virtually all fission reactions are much "dirtier" than fusion reactions, in terms of radioactivity, and the proportion of any given weapon's yield that is accounted for by fission, rather than fusion, affects the hazard from subsequent radiation.

Man has had the capacity to decide, in advance, how much fission and how much fusion he will build into his bombs since the late 1950s. Originally, fission weapons were considered lower-powered, generally in the sub-megaton range. Thermonuclear fusion weapons, by contrast, were giants, with yields generally measured in megatons, or millions of tons of TNT equivalency. Moreover, by the 1950s, the weapons theoreticians already knew that there is, in effect, no design limit to the size of a thermonuclear weapon. This was because, in stages, the trigger A-bomb first fused the hydrogen to create a thermonuclear reaction, which itself released swarms of extremely energetic neutrons so intense that they were capable of setting off still another nearly-simultaneous fission reaction in a blanket of ordinarily non-fissionable material, such as uranium-238. Thus giant bombs could be designed on this fission-fusion-then-fission again process. But the huge bombs were also apt to be "dirty" because of the proportion of yield stemming from fission rather than fusion. In the 1980s, the biggest and the smallest bombs are apt to be dirtiest in terms of their potential for radiation damage, while those in the middle yields — a megaton or two — are somewhat less likely to maximize danger from radiation after the explosion.

For the lay person who wishes to know more about the nuclear threat to his own survival in the 1980s and 1990s, a good working assumption is that the modern arsenals of the two superpowers contain weapons of a variety of designs. Indeed, some warheads might be designed with high fission ratios as "kamikaze" weapons.

There is a final eerie factor in the variation of effects in nuclear weapons. While, on paper, a 25-megaton weapon should be considerably more powerful than, say, the combination of ten 40-kiloton weapons that typically ride atop an American Poseidon or Trident missile, the actual damage produced by the two dissimilar warheads may be very much alike. In fact, under some circumstances, and depending mostly upon how the cluster of smaller warheads is aimed, the damage produced by the string of smaller yields may be somewhat greater than that produced by the single, much larger weapon. This is because a 25-megaton warhead dissipates its energies comparatively quickly according to the distance from ground zero. The ring of five pounds-per-square inch overpressures from such a blast, though it extends over many miles, may not be presumed to demolish as many wood-frame dwellings in a given area as a series of similar overpressures produced by ten smaller weapons aimed to have each explosion occur in precisely the right place. In terms of damage potential, the cluster of smaller warheads can be designed to obliterate very specific targets in an area — a particular factory complex, dockyards, clusters of tightly packed apartment dwellings — and the resulting human harm may therefore be much greater. In grisly fashion, comparatively small American submarine warheads are the rough targeting equivalent of much larger Soviet land-based missiles, when it comes to area targets containing high human populations.

Weather

The weather and wind direction that prevail at the moment of a nuclear explosion have a major influence on the extent and type of destruction caused. Dry, clear weather generally serves to extend the effects of the blast, especially in terms of the thermal, or heat, effects produced. A misty, rainy, muggy, cloudy day, by contrast, cuts down considerably on the effects of flash and heat alike.

Wind, of course, is an obvious factor. The surface winds in the local area will determine where the most severe fallout, if any, will occur. The steering currents, at much higher altitudes, will carry radioactive particles downwind for much greater distances, assuming that the explosion was of sufficient force and yield to insert its nuclear detritus high into the sky.

Rain, snow, and other precipitation prevailing in the immediate vicinity at the time of a nuclear explosion would also affect the precise effects very strongly. Local thunderstorms and rain showers may create unexpected "hot spots" of radiation danger in very specific places, depending largely upon luck. Snow may be dangerous in some places because it can retain the radiation in drifts and piles along the ground, making some places much hotter than others. Like a summer sun-shower that leaves one side of a residential street soaked but the other bone-dry, rain showers in the hours after a nuclear blast can swamp specific areas with high radioactivity while washing out much of the accumulated detritus and greatly lowering the intensity of radiation in other places just a bit further away. Assuming that you are the same distance from a nuclear explosion on two consecutive days, one rainy and the other clear and dry, you will be much safer from the heat effects of the weapon on the rainy day than on the dry one, but the rain itself may be a hazard if there is any fallout.

Time of Day

The time of day when any nuclear explosion occurs is a major factor in the amount of human harm apt to be caused. During the business hours of the work week, for instance, people are concentrated in clusters around their factories and places of work, with most families widely separated from each other and many people congregated in the downtown areas of the larger cities. Time of day is a primary consideration for the establishment of any rational plan for survival of the individual and those he cares about.

Moreover, the time of day can be a major factor in the kinds of dangers the victims immediately face. At night, the effects of temporary flash-blindness caused by the intense light of the explosion will be far more widespread, up to 75 miles or so for the potential danger zone on a clear, winter's night. On the other hand, at precisely that time, the majority of people are more apt to be inside their dwellings, where they will be somewhat protected from the immediate effects of the intense heat and light in the first few seconds and minutes of the explosion. Despite the number of executive studies commissioned by the U.S. over the years, virtually none of the government-recommended civil defense programs have considered the time-of-day factor in their plans.

Season of the Year

Like the weather and time of day, the season of the year can have some influence on the likely damage produced by any nuclear weapon. The flash-blindness and thermal effects of a large weapon, for instance, are maximized when the terrain around the blast is covered by shiny, crusted snow. In such circumstances, the ground itself may serve to reflect the light and heat energy emitted and carry them over longer distances.

The season of the year also may have major effects on the prospects for long-term survival of populations. A nuclear exchange taking place in the winter months, for instance, would maximize human travail from cold-weather and disease, but might allow sufficient time — fallout decreases in intensity in a matter of hours, day, and weeks, not years — for farmers to get in their spring planting, if any. A fallout-producing war in late spring or early summer, when young plants are most vulnerable to radiation, would likely reduce the yield of the crops, but might allow some harvesting. A war at harvest time would make fields temporarily unsafe for crop-gathering, which would lead to an increased chance of starvation the following winter.

Now that we have seen how variable the effects of nuclear weapons may be, let us look at the specific and most-immediate effects of the weaponry itself.

Electromagnetic Pulse (EMP)

Though this particular effect of nuclear weapons was somewhat anticipated, neither its results nor its widespread nature were, and so the extent of electrical disruptions caused by certain American atmospheric weapons tests in the Pacific in the late 1950s and early 1960s came as something of a surprise. In recent years, the effects of EMP on a modern society have come to be recognized and a small industry specializing in protection against this effect has developed commercially in the United States.

Any nuclear weapon releases its enormous energy in a variety of ways, through blast and heat and light, via radiation, and also by the propagation of an intense electromagnetic pulse. For weapons exploded at surface level or in the lower regions of the atmosphere below 50,000 feet, this intense electrical pulse has a relatively short range, affecting only those receivers likely to be greatly damaged by other principal effects of the weapon. This is because a substantial portion of the yield of a nuclear weapon close to the surface of the earth is used up in the generation of the great blast and the intense thermal effects at the bottom of the sea of air in which we all live.

When the same weapon is detonated at much higher altitudes — about 100,000 feet is optimum, or 19 miles above the earth — more of the total energy emitted takes the form of this electrical pulse in the almost airless regions of near-space. The precise effect is evidently caused by the lack of perfectly spherical release of energy in all directions evenly and simultaneously, which provides a massive electrical potential expressed as the EMP. The range of this effect is quite phenomenal, the theoretical possibility existing that a single large-yield Soviet weapon, designed specifically for this purpose and detonated 19 miles above the U.S. Strategic Air Command headquarter at Offut AFB near Omaha, Nebraska, could knock out the entire power and communications grid of the United States.

Though this effect of modern nuclear weapons poses no threat to humans directly, its potential for major economic damage is quite clear. EMP resembles super-fast and super-powerful lightning in its effects upon wiring, unprotected cables, transmission towers, and virtually any thing much more than a yard long that can serve as an antenna to absorb the incoming signal. Ordinary lightning rods and similar protective devices do not work against EMP because the pulse itself typically reaches its maximum voltage a hundred times faster than lightning. In terms of power to generate higher strengths of electrical field, EMP produces thousands of volts in a receiving antenna while a conventional radio signal could be measured in a thousandth of one volt, or less. EMP can burn out electrical, electronic, and communications circuits wherever they are connected to an antenna, or where power lines themselves can serve as an antenna. The range of EMP caused by a nuclear explosion at 100,000 feet is estimated to be in hundreds or even thousands of miles.

Precisely how much damage might be done by EMP and how small the "antennas" that would be affected remains controversial among nuclear specialists. An apocryphal story that makes the rounds of the U.S. defense establishment is that the EMP effect was first noticed, but not yet recognized for what it was, by observers at American weapons tests in the Nevada desert in the 1950s, whose cars would sometimes no longer start after a test. Officially speaking, EMP became a nuclear phenomenon to be considered after U.S. tests in the Pacific left the electrical grids of the Hawaiian islands in shambles. Since that time, the U.S. has taken steps to protect its essential national security communications and military-emergency power against EMP, though most U.S. radio and television stations are not required to be so protected, which leads to the conclusion that public information in any nuclear emergency might be quite hard to disseminate adequately.

In addition, some experts now opine — public release of technical studies in the field has been quite sparse — that EMP could serve to damage much smaller antennas, such as those found in transistor radios and small computer systems. If these scientists are correct in their speculation, and the EMP effect is found to extend to automotive circuits and consumer electronic circuitry, the EMP effect of any attack would be that much greater, though no direct human harm would result.

According to a U.S. government document of limited distribution, the "Checklist Guide for Nuclear Emergency Operations Plannings" issued in the late 1970s by the U.S. Defense Civil Preparedness Agency, a step to be taken by local authorities ensconced in their shelters thanks to advance official warning of attack is to:

> Protect against EMP by (1) disconnecting...all radio base stations from commercial power by opening master switch at electrical service entrance and transferring load to emergency generators; (2) disconnecting all electrical and electronic equip-

ment not essential to immediate operations by unplugging line cord or opening switch in power lead; (3) disconnecting antennas over five feet in length or employing multi-story antenna leads from transmitters and receivers, and employing mobile equipment as alternate base stations where required to maintain operational control of mobile fleets; and (4) continuing essential communications by telephone, teletypewriter, and other wire-line systems.

This somewhat rosy view of EMP's potential effects is intended for local officials apprised in advance to establish themselves in government shelter facilities and intended to keep a minimum of U.S. Federal, state, and local systems operating in the event of nuclear war. The entire system is connected to the U.S. "Nudets," or nuclear detonation evaluation grid, a series of sensors placed in the ground throughout the United States and designed to communicate confirmed seismic evidence that nuclear explosions have taken place on U.S. soil. This evidence is necessary to Presidential decision-taking, and the entire grid communicates to a hardened central point in Maryland often dubbed the "What's Left Department" by wags aware of its function in assessing the exact damage done to the nation by a nuclear attack.

Outspoken critics of U.S. defense posture insist, however, that EMP is apt to prove far more disruptive than the government believes. These analysts insist that the only protection for many devices handy in an emergency, such as transistor and CB radios, may advance storage in a modified "Farraday Cage," a device familiar to most students of high school physics. The emergency radios and communications equipment, these scientists suggest, must be kept insulated and placed inside a metal cabinet that is itself very well grounded. Nothing short of being kept "off-line" and protected in such a cabinet will shield them from EMP.

The entire subject of EMP is still shielded by the U.S. government from full public view, though most nuclear strategists today assume that one nation might raise the level of its threat against another in a period of tension by intentionally detonating a thermonuclear device or two high over the territory of its antagonist as a show of strength and an indication of its willingness to go the ultimate course. Such saber-rattling would clearly be a strong indication of the attacker's willingness to dispense with the long-established precedent that nuclear weapons not be used again in anger on the earth. It would be, even if no subsequent attack occurred, a spectacular demonstration that issues central to the attacker's sense of his own survival were at hand, and hence that the attacker was willing to do a kind of nuclear "property damage," while still refraining from hurting people directly. Some analysts also believe that an EMP attack on communications would be a sure early sign of an outbreak of full nuclear war, a precursor for the more awful events shortly to follow.

In the context of this mixed opinion concerning the hazards and significance of the EMP, it is perhaps most prudent to note here that the same limited distribution Federal booklet quoted above, a codified battle plan for the management of what might be left of the United States after a nuclear attack, assumes that its reader has had private forewarning of trouble, on a limited-information-only basis. The reader is cautioned, "Actions shown on this page are unlikely to result in more than a minimum public concern, even if they are reported by the news media." The specific "event" milestone that governs the actions to be taken, in the guidelines, is defined as "Decision to commence internal government actions." The prudent reader is here cautioned, then, that a useful assumption is that some people will hear the news of any impending war long before others do.

LIGHT AND HEAT

In the moment of a nuclear explosion, more than a third of the energy emitted takes the form of visible light and thermal energy, or heat. The light comes from the air itself, fired to incandescence at temperature levels equalled only in the hearts of stars. According to one government study, witnessing a nuclear explosion is "roughly analogous to the effect of a 2-second flash from an enormous sunlamp." Says another source, a defense scientist who must remain unidentified here, "We might all be better off if, every 20 years, all our world leaders were compelled to witness such a blast from 50 miles, because if you have ever seen such a thing, you will never forget it. We should let every world leader feel the heat of the explosion on his face at that enormous distance. We'd probably do a bit of future damage with long-term fallout by resuming such atmospheric tests. But they might well serve as a reminder, and that could make things safer for everyone."

The visual and thermal effects of modern themonuclear weapons are the longest-ranged, potentially most damaging, and clearly most awful of all the prompt effects that cause human harm. Heat from a one-megaton hydrogen bomb — travelling at just a little less than the speed of light — can cause first degree burns, roughly equivalent to a bad sunburn, at distances of about seven miles from ground zero. Under ideal weather conditions, such heat might conceivably extend as far as 11 miles from the center of the explosion, at which distance the intense light and heat may set dry leaves afire and burn the inked letters out of a dry newspaper neatly. A 10-megaton warhead, ten times more powerful, increases the range of harmful thermal effects by a "factor of two," as the nuclear physicists tend to put it.

For a 25-megaton nuclear weapon, the largest currently deployed by the Soviet Union, people living in a 30-mile radius of ground zero on a clear day will have a problem with the thermal effects of the weapon, depending upon such factors as weather and local geography. Within 20 to 25 miles of the target, the effects will rapidly increase in their lethality, to the point where any survivor of the blast is apt to be badly burned as well. A current working assumption of U.S. defense analysts is that American cities, even at the greatest building density, are sufficiently spaced out to make any "firestorm," such as occurred during the conventional bombings of Hamburg and Tokyo in World War II, quite unlikely. The problem would be burn injuries to, potentially, millions of people at the same time. The impossibility of arranging for proper assistance in such a situation has not been helped by American unwillingness to face hard facts in allocating resources. For instance, recent medical advances in the specialized treatment of burn victims have indicated that such patients can be treated successfully far more often than in the past, but such care and supportive treatment is expensive and very intensive. One 1980 estimate reported fewer than 2,000 such specialized burn-care beds in all of the United States, and virtually all of those were located at hospitals in downtown areas. In the same year, the U.S.S.R. was assumed to have only 200 such beds available.

Hence the thermal effects of any nuclear war are apt to be among the most horrifying, leaving behind many helpless victims, badly burned, for whom help cannot be made available. The range of burn injuries around each weapon detonation is very large, the largest of all immediate effects, and the potential for each bomb to leave thousands or hundreds of thousands of such victims is clear.

Only one of the prompt effects of nuclear weapons exceeds thermal radiation in range, and that is the visible light emitted at the instant of the explosion. It is possible that the visible light may cause permanent eye injury in the form of retinal burns. For this to happen, however, the victim must be literally willing to stare at the precise spot of the explosion long enough to let the light focus on the retina. At Hiroshima and Nagasaki, there were many authenticated cases of flash blindness, but only one case of permanent retinal burn.

The dangers of flash blindness, atop those of long-range burns, are apt to contribute to panic and, quite clearly, would be exceedingly dangerous for those caught while, say, driving in modern traffic. Again, the local conditions may have a pronounced influence on the exact effects of any nuclear explosion. Heat from the blast has been demonstrated to occasionally bounce off low-hanging decks of clouds and reflect down in one area far away, but not in others. A deck of white clouds over comparatively clear air can produce increased range of danger from flash blindness and thermal burns. Ice or crusted snow can also increase the range of these effects in unpredictable ways.

Ironically, one factor in modern weaponry adds a very slight touch of comfort for those in the immediate vicinity (25 to 30 miles) of a nuclear explosion. Thermonuclear weapons give off their heat over a longer pulse than did the first-generation fission weapons of Hiroshima and Nagasaki. A modern H-bomb may emit heat in a pulse lasting as long as 20 seconds. Persumably, this duration allows the knowledgeable person caught in the vicinity of such a blast a few seconds to seek emergency cover. Lighter-toned clothing and fabrics, white-painted houses, and other light objects tend to reflect some heat rather than absorb it as readily as darker-hued tones. Anyone in the proximity of a nuclear detonation will know it instantly, and without doubt, because of the stupendous light and heat, and should seek instantaneous shelter until it is time to worry about the next effect of nuclear weapons, probably less than a minute away.

BLAST

This effect of nuclear weapons is the same concussion and crushing effect witnessed in conventional explosions, but on a scale thousands and millions of times greater. The largest "blockbuster" of the World War II era contained ten tons of high explosive, and the Hiroshima bomb produced a blast equivalent to seventeen thousand tons of TNT. A 25-megaton hydrogen warhead, the largest currently known to exist on the planet, is substantially more than *two million times* more powerful than the most powerful weapon of a generation ago.

Scientists have determined that what is loosely called "blast" is composed of two separate and identifiable forces: air overpressure, measured in pounds per square inch (PSI), which has the sudden, crushing effect of a mailed fist slammed down upon an empty paper cup, and dynamic overpressure, which is a fierce wind blowing outward from the explosion at hurricane velocities.

These two wavefronts travel outward from the explosion faster than the speed of sound. The static, or air, overpressure is experienced, evidently, as a sudden and enormous concussive force, as if the atmosphere itself had suddenly grown much heavier than normal. Overpressures of as little as one PSI are enough to shatter glass and send the shards flying. A standard yardstick used by target planners is a ring of five PSI around a blast, because within that circle one half of the population can be assumed to be killed instantly and 80 percent of the survivors badly injured.

The larger the yield of the weapon, of course, the bigger the ring that defines the areas exposed to five PSI and more. Such overpressures seem small when measured in square inches, but simple math shows they translate to forces of many tons placed suddenly upon walls and supporting structures of buildings. The net effect, demonstrated during American A-bomb tests in Nevada in the 1950s, is to flatten ordinary houses instantly. For a one-megaton thermonuclear warhead fired at optimum altitude above a city, the area of five PSI and greater overpressures is a circle with its center at ground zero and a radius of roughly five miles. A ten-megaton weapon, ten times more powerful, extends the range "only" to ten miles. (This ratio of twice the effect for ten times the strength is roughly true for most nuclear weapons effects.)

Dynamic overpressure, the companion of static overpressure, appears as a sudden ferocious wind of hurricane force or greater. This wind is the air being pushed outward with great velocity from the blast, and the winds are obviously stronger the closer one is to the epicenter of the event. At a point, say, five miles or so from ground zero, the nuclear wind will reach velocities of 160 miles per hour or more. Winds of 100 miles per hour, sufficiently strong to lift people caught in the open and slam them into obstructions or drive loose objects dangerously around, can extend outwards from the blast to ranges from 12 to 15 miles from a one-megaton blast; everything within 30 miles or so of a 25-megaton blast will feel a wind of at least 35 miles per hour, or higher. This blast effect of nuclear weapons tends to push houses and buildings over, scattering the debris in circles outward from the site of the explosion.

In their calculations of the blast effects of nuclear weapons, U.S. defense statisticians traditionally assume that one half the people in the five PSI ring will be killed instantly. The damage is done not by direct nuclear effect on the human body, but by mechanical injuries produced when people are caught in their demolished buildings and homes. Virtually any location within 25 miles of a modern nuclear weapons explosion is apt to feel some of the effects of blast, though the lethality of the effect grows rapidly as one comes closer to ground zero. At areas within the 12 PSI ring around a blast, the assumption is that 98 percent of the population will be killed instantly and the few survivors will be badly injured and probably impossible to reach. This area can be defined as any point within three miles of ground zero for a one-megaton weapon and about seven miles from a 25-megaton blast.

Homes of ordinary frame construction are generally assumed to be vulnerable at about five PSI. Brick apartment houses will be badly damaged at these pressures, but not utterly demolished. Factories and commercial buildings will be collapsed by overpressures of 10-12 PSI or more. Heavily reinforced concrete construction has the most resistance, and, ironically, bridges tend to endure blast best of all. The issue of which American highways might still be usable after a nuclear exchange is controversial — the road is not apt to be destroyed more than a few miles from each blast, but the way may be blocked by fallen debris.

The blast effects of a nuclear weapon arrive some time after the light and thermal radiation, in the rough proportion that thunder follows lightning. The farther away the observer is from ground zero, the longer he may have to prepare for the arrival of the blast wave, and this time can be wisely used to seek whatever blast shelter may be available. The speed at which the blast waves travel is influenced in part by the yield of the weapon, but people living at the five PSI range, five to ten miles from ground zero, would generally have 20 to 30 seconds to react before the arrival of the blast. At a range of 15 miles from the center of the explosion, blast will not arrive until a full minute after the first light of the detonation. This interval, once known and remembered, can be used to calculate the rough distance of the observer from the explosion, along the lines of the artillery flash-and-sound technique for measuring distances. And the knowledge of the distance can aid in fallout planning, as indicated in the next chapter.

Like light and heat, blast effects can also be reflected by clouds and other weather phenomenon and can appear in odd places far from the explosion. Some Nevada test explosions of the 1950s were notorious for causing scattered clusters of window breakage in areas not expected to be affected.

LOCAL FALLOUT

If the fireball of a nuclear detonation has touched the ground, a very intense, localized fallout is apt to begin within a relatively short time after the blast. This fallout, which may reach extremely high levels and be difficult if not impossible to counter locally, comes from the stem of the now-familiar mushroom cloud, rather than from the cap of the formation. The area endangered by this local fallout is roughly the same that experiences any immediate damage from the blast itself, 25-30 miles for a high-yield weapon and five to ten miles for a one-megaton surface burst. Anyone who survives the blast in such areas is generally advised to flee, as swiftly as possible, in a direction away from the blast and at right angles to the prevailing wind.

The intensity of localized fallout can be such that seeking shelter-in-place is considered an insupportable concept by most nuclear scientists, if the area under consideration is within the one PSI overpressure ring of a modern weapon. Even pre-arranged fallout shelters in such areas are not likely to be sufficient to offer useful protection against this localized fallout.

Local fallout is likely to begin from ten minutes to one hour after the explosion, depending upon such factors as the weather and wind direction, the type, size, and altitude of the blast. The area of greatest danger from localized fallout can also be defined roughly as the maximum diameter of the cap of the mushroom cloud. For a one megaton weapon, the cloud will generally reach a height of 10-12 miles and a width of the same size. Larger weapons may cast debris particles as much as 20 miles into the sky shortly after the blast, and such weapons may have mushroom clouds with caps up to 50 miles wide.

SCENARIOS

The varying effects of modern nuclear weapons can perhaps best be understood by examining them against a real backdrop. For this purpose, we will consider the area of Westover Air Force Base in the western Massachusetts city of Chicopee. To see the varying effects in detail, we will examine the effects of three different forms of nuclear attack:

1. A one-megaton weapon, such as is mounted atop most Soviet land-based missiles and deployed on some U.S.S.R. submarines. This first example will be for such a weapon groundburst at Westover.
2. The same size weapon set to detonate at 6000-8000 feet above the base, producing an airburst.
3. A giant, 25-megaton warhead, such as those mounted on some Soviet SS-18 missiles, but fired at an altitude of 15000-16000 feet over the target area.

The information will be used by way of introduction to the topic of fallout that will be covered in the next chapter. Specifically, the fallout from these hypothetical explosions will be demonstrated to bring a potential hazard to the population centers around Boston, Massachusetts, and Providence, Rhode Island, both of which are far enough away to avoid damage from the immediate effects of any hypothetical attack on the western Massachusetts area around Westover AFB.

Within the range where they might be directly and immediately affected by a nuclear weapon targeted upon Westover reside more than one million people. The airbase itself, once a proud U.S. Air

Force facility, lies on a plain east of the Connecticut River, near the industrial cities of Chicopee, Holyoke, and the population center around Springfield, Massachusetts. Thirty miles to the south lies Hartford, Connecticut. The same distance to the east and slightly north lie the western outskirts of another fairly large city, Worcester, Massachusetts.

In the immediate area of the target is a rich and varied complex of industry, the venerable Springfield Armory that made the weapons of another era, communications, and culture. Due north of Westover AFB, for instance, lies the vast, densely populated campus of the University of Massachusetts at Amherst and a series of smaller institutions such as Smith College, Mount Holyoke College, and Amherst College. The area also serves as a major road and rail center. Two interstate highways, I-91 that runs along the Connecticut River from New Haven, Connecticut, to northern Vermont, and I-90, the Massachusetts Turnpike running from Boston to Albany, intersect roughly six miles from hypothetical ground zero. A local network of high-speed roads further serves to interconnect the main highways.

Other human resources abound in the immediate vicinity. The huge Quabbin Reservoir, which provides the drinking water for several million people in and around Boston, lies due northeast of Westover, at a range of 15 to 30 miles. Just five straight-line miles from ground zero is the large hydro-electric dam on the Connecticut River at Holyoke, the New England region's largest such facility. The area is served by several commercial, and one non-profit UHF, television stations, and a multitude of radio stations. Cable television hook-ups bring in more far-flung signals from Boston and New York. There are three daily newspapers in the immediate vicinity of Westover and others at Worcester and Hartford nearby.

Westover Air Force Base itself, officially de-activated since the Nixon administration, once served as the headquarters of the 8th Air Force of the U.S. Strategic Air Command during the 1950s and 1960s. This tradition-proud military organization traces its history back to England, during the days of World War II, when it was responsible for the daylight bombing of Nazi Germany.

In the late 1940s, Westover first came to some public note when it served as the major U.S. staging base for the famous Berlin Airlift. In the 1950s, in addition to its headquarters duties, Westover also served as the home of a B-52 bomb wing. In this role, it was widely considered one of the top military targets in the United States. Subsequent budget cutbacks, the national program to emphasize missiles rather than bombers, and, some say, the intentional desire of officials in the Nixon administrations to remove military facilities from Massachusetts, all led to a reduction in the status of the Westover base.

To this day, however, the chief facilities of the base, nuclear weapons handling and storage gear, runways long and strong enough to handle B-52s and other heavy military aircraft, all remain in workable condition, thanks to cooperative programs that allow the U.S. Navy to fly anti-submarine missions from the base and other branches of the military to use and maintain the facility. Today, if you drive by south of Westover on the Massachusetts Turnpike, you are apt to see a variety of low-flying aircraft in the immediate area, indicating that the base could be fully re-established in short order if the need to do so ever arose.

The First Case Scenario:
A One-Megaton Groundburst at Westover

This is the type of attack theoretically preferred for hardened, "point" targets such as missile silos. The groundburst of the weapon maximizes overpressures in a small, very selective area, so as to vaporize specific, hardened facilities. One school of thought holds that the Soviets are apt to have targeted any U.S. runway anywhere that is long enough to handle heavy bombers — runways more than 6000 feet in length — for groundbursts intended to vaporize those runways. Other nuclear war theoreticians, assuming that aircraft and trained personnel are more the target than the physical facilities, opine that the optimum weapon of choice against airbases are multiple airbursts, especially in arcs running outward from the base in which escaping aircraft might still be caught shortly after take-off.

A one-megaton groundburst upon the taxi aprons of the Westover runway system would create a large crater, more than 1000 feet wide and nearly 200 feet deep. For more than a half mile from the center of the explosion there would be nothing recognizable whatever after the blast, not runways, hangars, towers, or bomb dumps. Surrounding the lip of the crater itself would be a rim of highly radioactive soil running

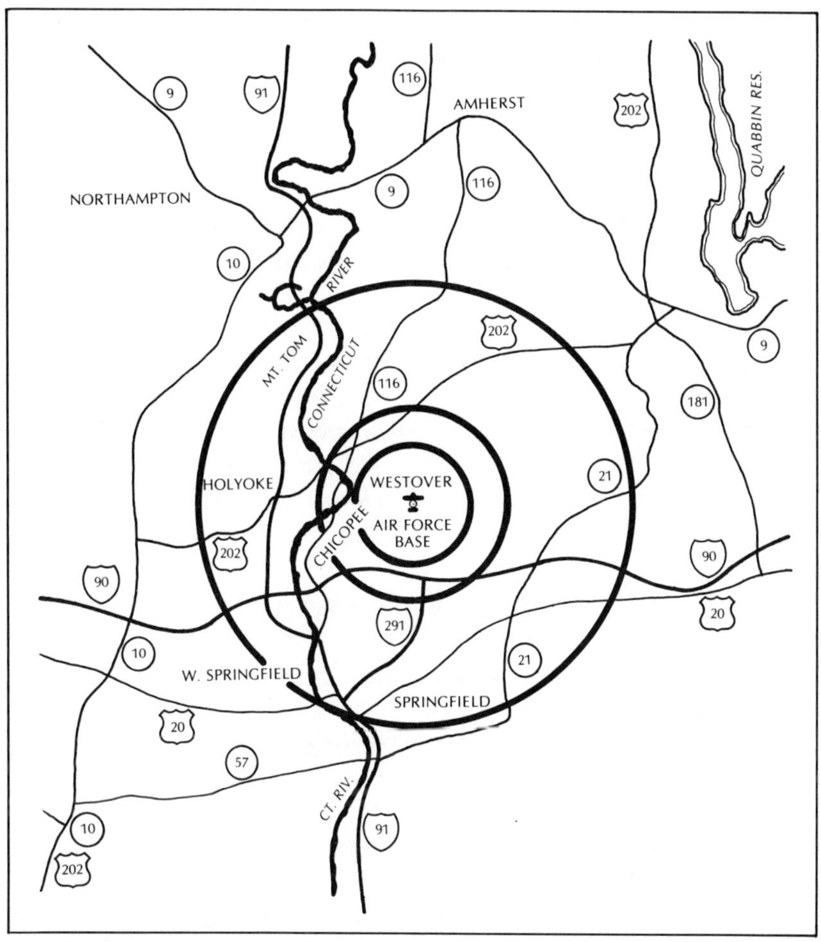

One megaton groundburst at Westover: The circles show the immediate effects of a one-megaton nuclear weapon detonated at ground level at the control tower at Westover. The inner circle covers the area of 12 pounds per square inch overpressure from blast, where 98% of the population would be killed instantly in the explosion. The middle circle is the 5 PSI ring, where 50% would die and most of the rest would be injured. The outer circle is the 2 PSI overpressure area, where one in twenty would be killed and half would be injured immediately.

out more than a mile from ground zero. No significant building or structure would be left standing anywhere within a mile and three quarters of ground zero of this hypothetical weapon, and no one in this three-square-mile area could possibly survive. Strongly built bridges that are part of the Massachusetts Turnpike a mile or so south of ground zero might conceivably remain standing, but would be badly damaged, and the highway itself would not likely be serviceable for evacuation or incoming help.

In the next ring around the core area of utter destruction, out to a distance of roughly five miles, virtually all homes and commercial dwellings would be flattened. One half the people in this area at the time of the explosion would be killed outright, mostly by blast and heat. Four of every five survivors in this area would be badly injured. Depending upon the time of day and other factors, such as the population density at time of the explosion, many thousands of people would be killed or hurt in such a hypothetical one-weapon attack. *This single event would be the largest disaster in the history of the United States.*

The area of five PSI for this burst extends westward throughout the city of Chicopee, which has a population of more than 60,000, down to the banks of the Connecticut River. Individual residences in this area and in the northeast section of nearby Springfield would be totally destroyed, only the foundations and cellars of each structure still recognizable. A rough estimate is that 35,000-50,000 people would be killed in this area alone, another 25,000 and perhaps more would be injured. Debris in the streets would make rescue work nearly impossible. Transportation would likely be shank's mare.

In the area from five to ten miles from ground zero, an area which incorporates the entire city of Holyoke, there would be severe damage. This is the area of two to five PSI for this type of weapon, and about one person in twenty would be killed instantly in the explosion and about one half of the people in this area would be injured in some way. Depending on a number of factors, this could mean an additional five to ten thousand immediate deaths and a casualty count approaching another 100,000 people, most of them in heavily damaged downtown and residential areas in Springfield and Holyoke. As many as one out of four people living in the next five-mile ring — nearly another 100,000 people — would become casualties as well, though with comparatively few immediate deaths. Only about one fourth of the area's hospitals and medical facilities would be left comparatively undamaged, leaving perhaps a few hundred available beds for more than 100,000 injured people.

Still farther away, the chief danger would be the outbreak of fires caused by the intense heat of the weapon or by blast damage to flammable facilities, such as pipelines and storage tanks. This particular type of attack would not necessarily damage the hydro-electric dam at Holyoke, but any such damage could threaten to release the impounded Connecticut River waters above Holyoke and inundate the Hartford area farther downriver. There would be a few immediate deaths from this singular attack as far away from Westover as Westfield and Northampton, Massachusetts, and, across the state line, the residential area around Enfield, Connecticut. Local blast effects throughout the area likely would be sufficient to cut all power and communications facilities instantly.

The chief concern of such an attack, if a priority can be assigned to such devastating events, would be the intense local fallout that would begin within a half hour of the attack. This localized fallout would be so heavy — it would be visible as a heavy powder or a dark-colored precipitation — that it would effectively eliminate the possiblity of helping any of the survivors of the blast for some time, probably days and weeks rather than hours. Those injured by the blast and heat would now be exposed to intense radiation caused by the relatively ''dirty'' groundburst of the warhead, and the radioactive mushroom cloud — the subject of the next chapter — would then drift downwind to endanger people far from the immediate blast zone.

Fallout, of course, behaves as the wind behaves. Assuming a steady, idealized 15 mile per hour westerly wind blowing across the devastation at Westover for one full week after the blast, fallout would arrive in the Greater Boston metropolitan area, roughly 75 miles east of Westover, about five hours after the attack, and it would remain very hazardous for at least the full week. In that initial seven-day period, for instance, the plume of the most intense fallout would cover a long, elliptical swath of the State of Massachusetts, from Westover to the coastline and as wide as 20 to 30 miles at its broadest. In the first week after the blast at Westover, the heavily populated Boston area would be apt to receive a dose of fallout radiation half again higher than the level considered typically lethal for unsheltered populations. Thus this single attack upon Westover would likely necessitate the evacuation of nearly three million people in eastern Massachusetts, within a few hours after the assault. All those who did not flee from the fallout plume — and the direction of this plume would be contingent upon the shifting winds of New England — or take sufficient expedient shelter against it, would be doomed to die.

The Second Case:
A One-Megaton Weapon Airburst over Westover

As a population-killer and city-buster, this type of attack is preferred by contemporary attack strategists. In contrast to the groundburst described above, it would generate comparatively little or no local fallout to add to the area's woes immediately after the attack, but the optimum-altitude at which the weapon is detonated tends to spread out the effects of heat and blast, causing relatively more damage to people, homes, and places of work.

In this second type of attack, the weather in the vicinity of Westover at the time of the explosion would be a major factor in determining the extent of human injuries, especially burns. If the air is clear (visibility of 10 miles or more), a one-megaton weapon may cause second-degree burns requiring competent medical treatment at distances of six miles from the explosion. Lower visibility reduces the range of this effect substantially.

Raising the point of detonation for this weapon has many effects that make the results different from the groundburst of the same size described above:

> There will be no crater at the epicenter of the explosion.
> There will be little or no local radioactivity or fallout.
> Some structures may still stand, even directly beneath the blast.
> The range of each PSI ring will be increased.
> Blast and fire damage will be extended farther outward from ground zero, thereby exposing more people to more danger and probably doubling the number of immediate casualties.

For the purpose of examining this second attack, we will assume a Soviet one-megaton warhead has been targeted to explode at an altitude of 6,000 feet over Westover. A few thousand feet higher would maximize the five PSI ring and widen the danger to humans in non-reinforced dwellings, but the 6,000 foot altitude also maximizes the 30 PSI circle directly beneath the blast to do the most damage to the Westover facilities, short of vaporizing them. The 6,000 foot altitude

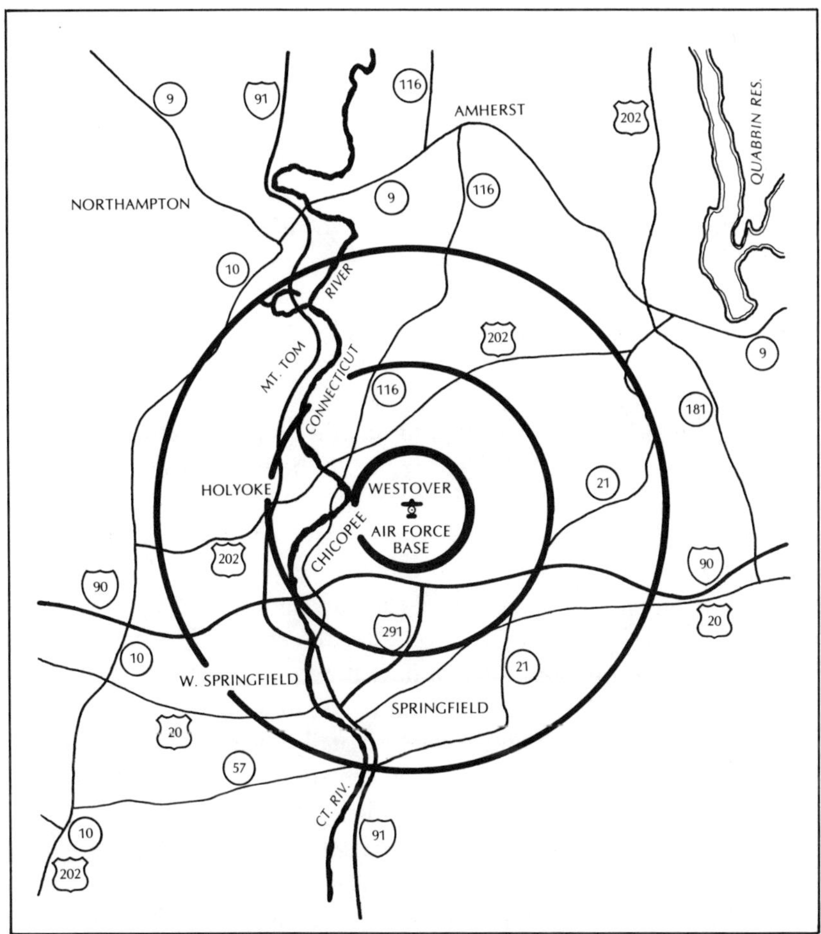

One megaton weapon airburst atop Westover at 8,000 feet: The circles show the immediate blast effects of a one megaton weapon airburst over Westover at an altitude of 8,000 feet. Virtually all those in the inner circle would die instantly, half of those in the middle area would be killed, and half of those in the outer ring injured. Setting the weapon off as an airburst extends the areas of blast damage.

also reduces the range of the five PSI ring by only 10 percent of its own maximum.

In this second case, the five PSI ring is apt to extend at least four miles from ground zero and may well reach something more than five miles, bringing larger areas of highly populated Holyoke and Springfield within range of lethal destruction. Many of the people who might survive the effects of the first-case surface burst would be less likely to survive the airburst, though they were the same distance from ground zero. Immediate effects in this area would likely claim more than 100,000 people in the general vicinity. The difference in altitudes in the first and second hypothetical cases means, literally, an increase of two-thirds or better in the size of the five PSI ring of severe damage.

The blast and damage effects are extended in corresponding fashion for all the various nuclear horrors. For instance, the first-case ground-burst would shatter windows and potentially harm people near them to a distance of eight miles from ground zero. But the same weapon would do the same damage at 11 miles distance if the warhead was designed for airburst. If seen from a satellite high in the sky, the visible area of damage would be far greater in the second case than in the first.

In particular, the airburst scenario would widen the area encompassed by the two PSI ring, where many people would be injured, a few killed, but where a major hazard from fires started by the heat of the weapon would rapidly develop after the attack. The two PSI ring would extend throughout most of downtown Holyoke and Springfield and would theoretically cover an area of roughly 70 square miles. Inside this 10-mile-diameter circle, virtually every residential building would be damaged severely or destroyed. The upper floors of lightly constructed office and apartment buildings would be blown into the streets, and only the interior frames of the heavier buildings would still be standing as one came closer to the center of the explosion. Many of the buildings on the outer edges of the damaged area would be set afire in the course of the attack. Where such buildings stand within 50 feet of one another, defense analysts assume the fires will spread for at least the first 24 hours after the attack, increasing the danger to any survivors.

A rough estimate is that one half or more of the 300,000-plus people living in the immediate vicinity of this blast would be killed in the first day of such an attack, a fatality count approaching 200,000, with most of the remaining survivors injured in some degree. In the *first day* of one single such attack, the nation would suffer about one half the fatalities it experienced during the entire duration of World War II.

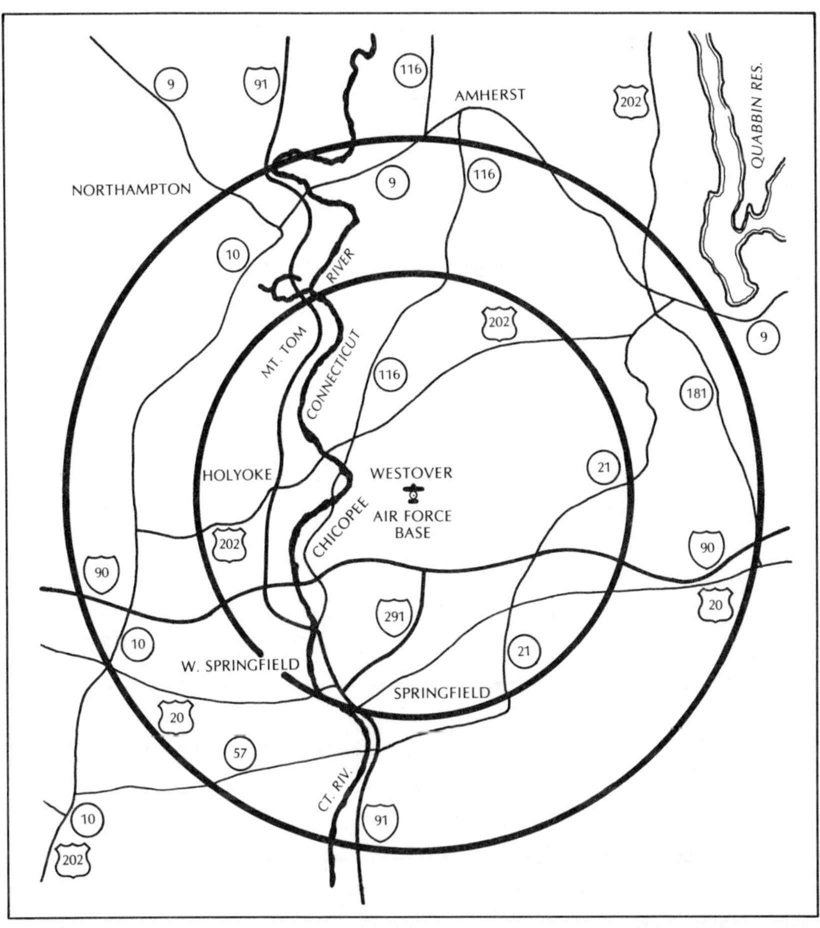

25 megaton weapon airburst over Westover: The circles demonstrate the huge area affected by blast from a giant 25 megaton Soviet weapon, such as those said to sit atop the Soviet SS-18 rockets. In this example, the warhead is detonated at an altitude of 16,000 feet, and there would be some immediate fatalities at ranges far off the map scale. Almost all of those in the inner, or 12 PSI ring, would die immediately. Half of those in the middle ring would also be killed, as would one in 20 of those in the outer ring.

The Third Case:
A Giant, 25-Megaton Warhead Airburst above Westover

Because the effects of nuclear weapons do not increase in linear fashion as the yield of the warhead increases, truly gigantic weapons are assumed to have little military purpose, other than to instill terror in the targeted population. A 25-megaton thermonuclear weapon, of the type known to sit atop some Soviet SS-18 missiles, is such a horrible weapon, but one whose chief nuclear facility is to obliterate a vast stretch of landscape and pound the remaining rubble into pieces.

In the case of a 25-megaton missile warhead designed to burst in the air 16,000 feet above Westover, the 12 PSI ring of utter destruction and 95 percent human fatalities extends to seven miles from ground zero, effectively obliterating all but a small fraction of the populations of the cities of Springfield, Holyoke, and Chicopee, along with most of the suburbs in the general area.

The five PSI ring of such a blast extends to roughly 11 miles, covering the entire urban area in this vicinity of western Massachusetts from a point near Northampton in the north to the suburbs of Agawam and Longmeadow to the south, from West Springfield and Easthampton on the west to beyond the town of Palmer to the east. No residential dwelling in this vast area would still be standing after such an attack, which would likely kill more than a quarter of a million people immediately and leave just small groups of lucky survivors with the impossible task of trying to help the thousands of injured.

One out of twenty people in the area north and east of downtown Hartford, Connecticut, would be injured by flying glass or other objects from such a blast, nearly 30 miles away. The same would hold true for the western environs of the city of Worcester, Massachusetts. The force of the explosion could conceivably be sufficient at the Holyoke Dam on the Connecticut River to endanger Hartford's population in a wholly new way, by threat of flooding. Virtually every building and residence inside a circle nearly 40 miles in diameter and centered around Westover would be damaged to some extent, and the total number of uninjured survivors in this area would be much smaller than the total count of dead and wounded. And all of this would occur in the first *minutes* of the 25-megaton blast.

If such an attack were the only one to take place upon the United States, help would be available, slowly, from surrounding areas, and the effect would be that of an awesome natural disaster striking a 400 square mile area. Some electrical power might be restored within a few days, and heavy equipment suitable for work in the rubble could slowly be moved along the main highways, especially those from the north and south, which would be a bit less affected in this particular

TABLE 4 Range of Prompt Effects of Nuclear Weapons

	40 kilotons	170 kilotons	one megaton	10 megatons
Damage:	Airburst, in miles			
12+psi over-pressure; 98% human fatalities	0.3	0.5	2.9	4.8
98% deaths of people in open	0.4	0.6	1.1	2.2
third degree burns 100%	1.5	2.6	3.8	5.8
5psi over-pressure; 50% deaths	1.2	2.0	4.6	9.0
lethal direct (neutron) radiation	0.7	0.8	0.9	1.0
no direct radiation harm	1.0	1.1	1.2	1.3
max. range for 2nd degree burns	3.2	4.0	6.1	11.8
max. range for 1st degree burns	2.8	4.7	7.0	13.6
up to 5% immediate lethality/casualties	2.7	4.7	7.0	13.2
broken windows, 25% injuries	5.0	6.7	10.4	19.8
max. range of temporary flash — blindness (daytime)	8.0	9.0	11.1	20.5

The header "YIELD OF WEAPON:" spans the four weapon columns.

Wide variations exist in the technical literature for the predicted range of most direct effects of nuclear weapons. The varying estimates stem from different assumptions used for each study. The most significant variables that affect the maximum range of nuclear weapons damage are, in order of priority (assuming similar yields), the altitude for which the weapon is fused, the weather at the target site, and the time of day at target. On balance, lethal hazards from the thermal (heat) effects have the greatest range. Direct radiation is not assumed to be much hazard from modern, high-yield weapons because most people within range of that effect would already have been killed by the blast and heat.

area. But if any such attack should ever happen as but one of several thousand such explosions on U.S. soil, help from outside would be literally impossible, and any survivors in the Westover area would be forced to rely on themselves and the resources that might be left in the vicinity to make any attempt at recovery.

Sources

Material in this chapter about the direct effects of nuclear weapons is drawn largely from various government documents and publications, the most widely available of which is the booklet *The Effect of Nuclear War* produced by the Congressional Office of Technology Assessment and cited previously. A standard reference on this subject, also sometimes available to the interested reader willing to undergo a diligent search, is *The Effects of Nuclear Weapons,* edited by Samuel Glasstone and published jointly by the U.S. Department of Defense and Department of Energy (third edition, Washington D.C., 1977).

The most comprehensive information on this subject is contained in the nine volumes of the *Attack Environment Manual,* produced by the Defense Civil Preparedness Agency of the U.S. Department of Defense (Government Publication CP G 2-1A, Washington D.C., 1973). Hard to obtain, this may sometimes be found with the help of local civil defense directors or by writing to the National Technical Information Services, U.S. Department of Commerce, 5285 Port Royal Road, Springfield, Virginia, 22161. Two other government publications were also used for the development of Chapter Three, "The Effects of High-Yield Nuclear Explosions," (U.S. Atomic Energy Commission, Washington D.C., 1955) and "The Effects of Nuclear War," by the U.S. Arms Control and Disarmament Agency (Washington D.C., 1975). Both of these may be available in the section on United States documents at most college and university libraries.

Comments concerning the predicted range of direct or neutron irradiation were drawn from a report of the U.S. National Academy of Sciences, "Pathologic Effects of Atomic Radiation" (N.A.S. Publication #452, 1955) and "A Summary of Accidents and Incidents Involving Radiation in Atomic Energy Activities, June 1945 through December 1955," by D.F. Hayes (U.S. Atomic Energy Commission document #TID-5360, 1956).

The description of the widespread and powerful effects of the electromagnetic pulse phenomenon (EMP) were drawn in part from Office of Technology Assessment study cited previously, with the addition of opinions of private researchers and scientists at such firms as Boston-based EG&G, a private concern that serves as a principal government contractor for studies involving the measurements of nuclear effects. There is some evidence that the United States has studied this effect far more extensively than is now known, including some tests of chemical explosives fired at high altitudes above the Arctic Circle, but little has been revealed thus far in public. The quotes on how to handle EMP effects are from the "Checklist Guide for Nuclear Emergency Operations Planning," (ALFA NEOP, U.S. Defense Civil Preparedness Agency, CP G 2-2A), a publication cited more extensively in Chapter Eight. This publication has never been widely distributed by the government, but copies may be obtainable through local civil defense directors or, perhaps, through the offices of the Federal Emergency Management Agency now officially responsible for U.S. civil defense.

Commentary in Chapter Three on the likelihood of widespread burns from any nuclear attack are extrapolations from the Office of Technology Assessment study cited previously, with additional material supplied by private medical sources in the Boston area, including physicians connected with the Shriner's Burn Center and the Massachusetts General Hospital. The occasional rebound effects of flash and heat are drawn from interviews with scientists who attended some of the U.S. tests in the Nevada desert during the 1950s. The projections of the effects of various weapons upon the area surrounding Westover Air Force Base in western Massachusetts are based upon the Glasstone textbook previously cited and the Office of Technology Assessment's studies of various nuclear war cases.

5 Long-Term Effects

When a man sees an animal dying, a horror comes over him. What he is himself — his essence, visibly before his eyes, perishes — ceases to exist. But when the dying creature is a man and a man dearly loved, then, besides the horror at the extinction of life, what is felt is a rending of the soul, a spiritual wound, which, like a physical wound, is sometimes mortal, sometimes healed, but always aches and shrinks from contact with the outer world that sets it smarting.

Leo Tolstoy, *War and Peace*

When a thermonuclear weapon is exploded, the heat of the reaction sears a volume of air in the vicinity to temperatures matched only in the interiors of stars. In ten seconds, the incandescent fireball of a one-megaton weapon has expanded until it is more than a mile across. Then it begins to move rapidly upward, at 300 feet or more per second, until it reaches an altitude of 25,000 feet. Depending on the yield of the weapon, this takes about one minute from the time of detonation. The fireball then cools and loses its glow. Films of weapons tests show that the fireball itself glows in a riot of colors, flashes, and lightning-like bolts of light during its early stages, usually taking on red/orange hues that are conventional when air is super-heated. Over the target, the mushroom cloud now grows.

LONG-RANGE FALLOUT

If, at any point in its development, the fireball comes in direct contact with the surface of the earth, the pulverized remnants of soil and tree and flesh and bone near the target are carried upward until they fall back again to earth with rain or snow or settling dust. This is what is known technically as fallout, and the phenomenon can reach a great many miles downwind from the immediate target area.

Fallout first came to general attention in March, 1954, when an American H-bomb test in the Pacific accidentally salted a Japanese fishing boat, the *Lucky Dragon Number Five,* nearly 100 miles downwind from the test site.

Fallout hazards had first been observed in the pioneering American nuclear test, "Trinity," at Alamagordo, New Mexico, on July 16, 1945. The fireball of this vaporized the test tower from which the bomb had been detonated. Radioactive dust from the tower, bearing microscopic bits of fission products, settled on the backs of cattle several dozen miles away, leaving burn-like scars on the hides. Evidence of fallout at Hiroshima and Nagasaki was not released until 1956, but the initial announcement at the time indicated that substantial doses of radiation would have been received by unsheltered persons up to 100 miles due east of Nagasaki.

All this, however, was but a mild foreshadowing of the truth about fallout and its hazards, and true public concern did not begin until the 23 Japanese fishermen, who had inadvertently wandered into the U.S. testing area near Bikini Atoll in the central Pacific, returned sick to their home ports with reports of a strange, irritating white ash that had fallen on their boat six hours after they had noticed a "second sun rising in the west early in the morning." Tests showed that all 23 men, their boat, and even the harvest of fish they had brought home were contaminated by fallout. One of the men subsequently died a few months later, though not necessarily or directly from fallout.

The test weapon that did the damage was known as the "Bravo" shot. It was a giant, 15-megaton weapon that had a fireball nearly three and a half miles wide. Its explosion vaporized and obliterated the small islet on which it had been sited, casting radioactive fission products over a huge area downwind and, as later evidence proved, contaminating nearly 7,000 square miles. In addition to the Japanese fishermen who had been contaminated, several hundred natives and 28 American service personnel had to be evacuated from tiny islands far downwind from the test site. Some of the contaminated areas were still uninhabitable by peacetime radiation standards more than three years after the test.

Today considerably more is known about the hazards of fallout, and it is now clear that certain types of weapons, especially those which rely in large part upon the fission process and those designed to explode at ground level, can render huge areas unusable and unsafe for human beings for many years. This judgment generally assumes the use of current peacetime standards as a yardstick for radiation danger. Such standards have been lowered several times since the early days of the nuclear age until, today, they are far more stringent than could conceivably be called realistic in the event of any nuclear war.

The chief concern of many U.S. defense analysts is the danger posed by fallout for heavily populated areas in the Midwest and along the East Coast. Source of that presumed fallout would be a massive Soviet atomic strike on American land-based missile silos west of the Mississippi River. It is likely that each silo would be the target of several Soviet warheads, as the nature of atomic warfare demands a "better safe than sorry" strategy. One estimate is that each U.S. missile complex, and the area around it, would receive up to 400 incoming warheads, each designed to detonate at ground level to maximize the damage to the hardened missile silos. Such groundbursts produce the maximum amount of fallout danger to areas downwind of the immediate target vicinity.

For this reason, many millions of people in the United States are at risk from any Soviet strike at U.S. missile fields, even if population centers are not targeted in the first wave of an assault. The fallout from U.S. silos would reach midwestern farming and industrial areas anywhere from a matter of hours to a few days after a Soviet attack. For those living in New England, or elsewhere along the East Coast, there would be a bit more time to prepare before the first arrival of fallout, but the danger would likely be high in any case.

If this theoretical Soviet strike happened to use strictly airbursts, the danger of fallout contamination downwind would be much lower, but this type of targeting is far from the most efficient way to destroy hardened, single-point targets. Even airbursts produce some degree of fallout, according to how much fission power is used to fire the weapon, and airbursts shoot their radioactive detritus high into the sky, allowing it to circle the entire earth at roughly the same latitude as the explosion. This earth-girdling phenomenon may last for some years, but the types of fallout resulting from it are, in the words of one U.S. government study, "comparatively trivial" when assessed against the levels of fallout that would result from a groundburst Soviet assault on U.S. missile fields. The radiation produced by airbursts consists principally of longer-lived radionuclides, or isotopes, such as strontium-90 and cesium-141. Both of these isotopes can be harmful, especially to young children and those born at the time the fallout was the heaviest — it reached a peak in the mid-1960s after the spate of nuclear weapons tests of earlier years.

Many nations had learned enough of this particular subject by the early 1960s to agree to the Nuclear Test Ban Treaty. Neither the U.S. nor U.S.S.R. have been known to violate the provisions of this treaty, which requires that all tests of new weapon designs be detonated in chambers far enough below the ground to ensure the containment of the resulting "fallout." In a few cases, vents and leaks have occurred during the tests, but neither side, perhaps recognizing its own accident-proneness, has been willing to accuse the other of bad faith.

Not quite 600 nuclear weapons had been fired by the time the Nuclear Test Ban Treaty took effect. Two of those, at Hiroshima and Nagasaki, had been used in war, and all the others as tests, the majority of the latter conducted as air or groundbursts. Long-term radioactivity from the testing alone is readily measurable and will remain so for several centuries. At latitudes of 20-40 degrees north of the equator, trace amounts of long-lived plutonium-239 can be measured, even at the bottom of the ocean. Depending upon which estimates are used, this residual radioactivity has increased the natural, background level of radiation by anywhere from 10 to 40 percent, enough to be readily detectable by instruments, but not high enough to lead a clear judgment of the human harm that has been caused. Many factors, including the precise nature of the radiation given off by various hot isotopes, cloud the issue.

Today, the U.S., U.S.S.R., and Britain conduct their tests in accordance with the provisions of the Nuclear Test Ban Treaty and generally attempt to keep residual radiation from leaking into the atmosphere. In contrast, France, India, and China have all demonstrated their willingness to continue testing weapons in the open atmosphere.

TYPES OF RADIATION

When the nucleus of an atom is split in a fission reaction, the resulting fragments can take the exact atomic form — so many neutrons and protons in each new nucleus — of virtually any element. Generally, this resulting element will be an unstable, or radioactive, isotope of the basic element. Fallout is produced when these tiny radioactive particles are attached to larger particles of dust and pulverized debris tossed into the sky by a groundburst. The larger particles then precipitate from the atomic cloud downwind from the explosion, with the heavier particles falling earliest and the lightest falling farther downwind. When it poses an immediate danger to human health, most fallout can actually be seen, as a fine dust, powder, or spray of ash, similar to that reported by the Japanese fishermen in 1954.

The various particles in fallout produce three distinct types of radiation, each of which has a specific effect on mammals.

Alpha Particles

These are relatively large particles, basically the nucleus of the helium atom. Alpha particles produce an intense radiation because the energy conveyed in the release of the particle is very strong. However, alpha particles can be deflected entirely by a mere sheet of paper. Hence this sort of radiation poses a very specific hazard to humans, who should avoid allowing any form of alpha-emitter into the body. Simple exposure to alpha radiation is not generally considered a major hazard, but ingestion of such particles, or inhalation into the lungs, is an entirely different story. Once inside the body, alpha-emitters are not easily removed, and set up a lingering radiation that affects a tiny area of flesh in a sphere around the site of the particle. The potential for cancer is clearcut. Unfortunately, most alpha-emitters are among the longest-lived of all radioactive isotopes. Plutonium, for example, is an intense alpha-emitter.

Beta Radiation

This type of radiation is half-particle, half-waveform. Beta radiation results from the stripping of free electrons from atoms during the fission process. These electrons are then emitted over short ranges to produce the hazard. Shielding from beta radiation is comparatively easy, since the energy is not great and the ability to penetrate the body is not strong. Beta radiation, in fact, is usually seen in the form of skin and surface burns. Examples have been seen among scientists and U.S. Air Force personnel who removed air-filters from the devices carried by high-altitude jets to monitor Soviet nuclear progress. In one instance, the workers removed the cumbersome gloves they had been supplied for their task and received beta burns on their hands as a consequence. In fallout, beta-type radiation produces essentially the mildest and least threatening hazard. Strontium-90, the element most often associated with fallout, is a beta-emitter.

Gamma Rays

These are true waveforms, very similar to conventional X-rays, and they result from the excess energy emitted by the fission process. Unlike alpha and beta irradiation, however, gamma waves are very energetic and are capable of penetrating deeply into the human body in the same way as X-rays. As a result, human beings exposed to gamma radiation must either be removed from the area or shielded behind some substance that has a high density, such as lead. Protective shielding against the hazards of gamma radiation can readily be seen in the thick lead vaults and walls that are used at nuclear power plants and similar atomic installations. Gamma rays also travel in a straight line, so it is not accidental that the corridors and walkways within an atomic facility are organized in zig-zag fashion. Against a high intensity of energetic gamma waves, the basic means of protection is thus to pile up something between people and the source of the radiation. The thicker and denser this material is the greater the protection offered. Recent evidence from studies at Hiroshima and Nagasaki seems to indicate that gamma radiation may actually be considerably more harmful than had previously been supposed.

MEDICAL EFFECTS

For proper medical therapy of radiation illness, the type of radiation, its intensity, the duration of the victim's exposure to it, and the organs of the patient's body most heavily exposed must be considered. Radiation is a form of gross injury to the human body, and its treatment is of a specialized kind not likely to be available to many people in the aftermath of any nuclear exchange. To accomodate generalizations about whole populations, rather than specific patients, modern analysts prefer to think in terms of the "whole body dose" when pondering the effects of intense fallout and massive radiation problems that would be natural *sequelae* in the event of war between the superpowers.

"Whole body dose" is a statistical misnomer that best applies to macroscopic speculations of what the world might be like in the aftermath of a major nuclear war. Its conceptual genesis lies in the rapidly expanding field of nuclear medicine, where scientists are learning how to measure harmless traces of radioactive elements in millionths and billionths per part of mortal flesh and bone. In the grossly contaminated world after a nuclear war, such measurements are far too fine. When no one can accurately foretell how many people might be standing or kneeling at the time the first bomb fell, how many awake or asleep, healthy or ill, the future must be predicted in only the most general terms. Hence, "whole body dose" becomes the only available measure applicable to the almost unimaginable human situation that would prevail after a nuclear war, when the few doctors still able to help could not possibly tell with accuracy the intensity of the radiation dosages received by myriads of individual patients. Whole body dose is best stated in terms of "rems," an acronym that means "roentgen equivalent man." The roentgen is a precisely defined term of nuclear physics. The "rem" is the essential effect a roentgen will have on human flesh. The two terms are almost, but not quite, identical in their mathematical meaning. But, as man has gradually learned to understand the implications of the nuclear age for the human species, the standard expressed by "rems" has come to be the more common usage.

By peacetime standards, doses of as little as five rems of radiation received per year are sufficient to require taking a worker off a job in a nuclear facility. Such low-level doses, however, are not apt to be the case in the event of nuclear war, when far more of the general population would likely be exposed to much higher amounts of whole-body radiation.

Because the human body is capable of slowly healing radiation damage, estimates of radiation dosages are established for comparatively short periods of time (acute doses that cannot be compensated for adequately by the body's defense mechanisms). One standard often used is to measure the whole-body dose received by the victim during a period of seven days. The seven-day dose can be used to predict likely outcomes according to the total dose received.

0 to 50 rems

This is a "sub-clinical" dose. The victim will not necessarily realize his exposure, will not present clinical symptoms, and will generally not be aware of the accumulation received. Doses of this magnitude can be determined by blood tests, but the change in blood count is actually quite similar to the effect produced by the common cold or other viral infections. Such a dosage might, however, be all too easy to accumulate in a nuclear war environment. Exposure to a radiation rate of five rems per hour without shielding will quickly produce an accumulation of this level. According to several American studies, if large populations were exposed to this radiation dosage, between one half of one percent to two and a half percent of the victims would be expected to develop a fatal cancer many years later. In view of the high likelihood of great human harm from the immediate effects of the use of nuclear weapons, this long-term hazard is considered too insignificant to call for advanced planning.

50-200 rems

At this level the victim may complain of nausea and general lassitude within a few hours of accumulating the exposure, but most people will recover. At the 100 rem dosage level, one in twenty will experience some vomiting, beginning about three hours after the cumulative exposure. (The time before onset of clinical symptoms is a good measure of the dosage level; the heavier the dose, the quicker the onset of illness.) At the 200-rem level, about half of those exposed will be sick, though virtually none will succumb to the effects of the radiation itself. Radiation exposure tends to lessen other bodily defenses, however, making victims at these dosage levels somewhat more susceptible to other maladies and infections. The recommended medical course is surveillance of the patient's blood, and reassurance. Assuming no complications from other infections or injuries, the prognosis for complete recovery is excellent.

200-300 rems

If a human population is exposed to a level of 300 rems accumulated in very rapid fashion, all the people in the group will begin to vomit roughly two hours after the first exposure. The tissues most affected by this level of radiation are the blood-forming organs, and illness manifests itself primarily as a blood-type malady. Good medical therapy is considered very effective at these levels, and the therapeutic regimen generally consists of blood transfusions and antibiotics to ward off other infections and aid the body's general defenses. The critical time for such victims is the first month after the exposure. One U.S. study suggests that about ten percent of a population exposed to a prompt dosage of 300 rems may die of the exposure within two months, but variables in the type of radiation and the availability of proper medical treatment make accurate predictions quite difficult.

300-600 rems

According to one U.S. study, ''The precise shape of the curve showing the death rate as a function of radiation dose is not known in the region between 300 and 600 rems, but a dose of 450 rems within a short time is estimated to create a fatal illness in half the people exposed to it.'' The other half of such a population would all get very ill, but most would recover, barring other complications or injuries. Of course, this does not include the long-term health effects from high levels of radiation. Above 300 rems, the clinical symptoms of radiation illness are quite marked: hair falls out, spontaneous bleeding will often occur, sperm counts drop radically, and the patient will be endangered by death from hemorrhage or infection. The critical period will generally be the first six weeks after exposure. Medical treatment at this level is nearly the same as for the 200-300 rem level: blood transfusions and massive use of antibiotics to ward off infections. The prognosis for eventual recovery is more guarded and extremely variable from case to case according to individual susceptibility. In the words of one character in Nevil Shute's famous *On The Beach*, as the world-ending fallout radiation first appears over Australia, ''It has to start somewhere, you know. We are not machines. We do not fall over in neat rows.''

600-1000 rems

In this range, medical management may conceivably save one out of five victims, but all those who cannot get proper treatment are doomed. Recent advances — bone marrow transplants in particular — suggest that careful handling of victims with this level of exposure might save some lives, but the procedures are complex, expensive, and not likely to be available in the event of nuclear war. Even with such medical help, the prognosis for most victims is very guarded, and the recovery period may be many months. Virtually all the exposed population will begin to get sick within an hour of any sudden dose at this level. All will lose their hair and show spontaneous bruises and other signs of hemorrhage, especially in the intestines. The chances of long-term survival drop precipitously as the 1000-rem level is reached.

1000 rems and more

At this level there is virtually no hope for the survival of the victim, and the illness will begin swiftly, usually within a half hour of exposure. Therapy is strictly palliative, an attempt to keep the patient as comfortable as possible before the end. A few, rare people with a strong non-susceptibility to radiation, might survive, but only after a prolonged and difficult course of illness. The vast majority will inevitably die, within two weeks after a 1000-rem dose, two days after dosages exceeding 5000 rems. At dosages between 1000 and 5000 rems, the gastrointestinal tract rather than the blood-forming organs becomes the primary system attacked by radiation. Above 5000 rems, such as the effects predicted for the American "neutron" bomb, the central nervous system of the victim will be severely damaged, leading to brain shock, unconsciousness, stupor, convulsions, and lethargy. The prognosis is hopeless.

FALLOUT

Fallout Distribution

Fallout is airborne, dependent on wind and weather, and therefore its exact course after any nuclear detonation is very difficult to predict. Fallout may literally behave as the wind behaves, brushing a mare's tail of death across the landscape according to its own whims. One area may be safe and another, nearby, deadly. Rainstorms may precipitate considerable fallout out of the cap of a mushroom cloud in one area, leaving other places farther downwind relatively unscathed. All that is essentially known, or can be known without experience with the matter, is that a major Soviet attack on U.S. missile silos in the west would pose great danger to heavily populated areas far from the sites of the multiple groundbursts.

U.S. government studies of the hazards of fallout generally take the form of idealized charts and maps. If, for instance, a steady 15 mile-per-hour wind were blowing from a particular direction at the site of a groundburst the area affected would be in the form of a long ellipse stretching downwind from the explosion for several hundred miles or more. Contours may then be plotted, in theory, to predict the areas that might be exposed to certain dosage levels in the first seven days after the attack. The assumption, of course, is that the wind blows at precisely that speed for the entire period of time while maintaining its direction about as precisely. In reality, especially in areas such as New England where the weather can be extremely variable, the pattern of fallout deposition would be considerably more complicated, perhaps taking the form of curls and arcs.

For a one-megaton groundburst, such as the one hypothesized at Westover AFB, the likely fallout distribution in the idealized conditions used for analysis would bring deadly dosages of radiation to a 30 to 50 mile swath across the entire heavily populated Boston area, 60 to 75 miles away from Westover, assuming only that the prevailing winds remained at 15 miles per hour from the west. Thus, in the first week after any such attack on Westover, virtually the whole area around Boston proper would receive a dose of 900 rems, enough to cause death to the vast majority of people who had no fallout sheltering or protection. If the prevailing wind happened to be stronger, the ellipse would be longer and narrower. If there were little wind, the fallout would be far more localized in the western Massachusetts vicinity around Westover, and its drift would be highly unpredictable. Local rain or snowstorms occurring in the first week after the assault would create wide variations in fallout deposition, as would all wind shifts which might temporarily alleviate the fallout upon Boston at the hazard of other areas lying in other directions.

The residents of the Boston area would also be handicapped in large measure by their general inability to know if fallout was a clear and present danger to their well-being. When fallout is heavy enough to provide immediate hazards to human health, it may usually be seen, but its proper measurement requires instruments not commonly available anywhere in the U.S.

For those people, the news of the attack upon Westover would precede the first arrival of fallout from the west by at least four hours, assuming a westerly wind of 15 miles per hour. The interval between the time of the blast and the first arrival of fallout, which is a function of the distance to ground zero in miles and the direction and speed of the wind, could well be used to produce some form of expedient fallout shelter. Conversely, because automobiles provide very little protection against fallout, any attempted evacuation of the Boston area that began after the first blast at Westover might be very ill-advised, for such a step would simply leave many people stranded in massive traffic jams on the highways at precisely the time fallout would be at its peak. For the people of Boston, it would probably be better to seek shelter near their homes and places of work, rather than to flee. In Part II of this book, several types of expedient shelters will be described, all of them requiring only common sense and little in the way of mechanical aptitude.

Even in this instance, however, useful data would be missing, for few would have the equipment to measure the actual rate of fallout. This information would be invaluable in the event of nuclear attack, for it would serve to determine when shelter should be taken, how much the shelter must be beefed up, who must take shelter first, who may leave on necessary missions, and when it might again be safe to come out for any length of time. In reality, in the event of nuclear war, radiation rates at any given point might vary widely from hour to hour and day to day, as the winds aloft carried the radioactive particles to and fro.

Civil defense planning books distributed to local officials by the U.S. Defense Civil Preparedness Agency state that a fallout rate of 50 rems per hour is very high; high enough, indeed, to require immediate sheltering of all personnel until the rate has fallen below that level. Should it rise again from a new blast or from changes in weather or wind, people would again be required to seek shelter.

The length of time people would have to endure shelter conditions is also in considerable dispute. American studies generally suggest that two weeks to a month would be required to shelter sizable populations along the East Coast in the event of a massive Soviet first-strike at U.S. missile silos alone. If the Soviets chose to attack population centers as well as military targets, the sheltering period could readily be a month or more, depending on a host of local factors. During this time, it might be possible for people to undertake short trips outside the shelter, in periods when the fallout rate had been diminished for whatever reason. Life in the event of true nuclear holocaust — all-out nuclear war — would clearly be a matter of going to ground and staying there.

The principles behind theories of fallout sheltering and fallout "protection factors" will be discussed in detail in Part II. Here it is enough to know that the predicted 900-rem dose near the Boston area from a groundburst attack upon the runways at Westover could not conceivably be handled without some form of fallout sheltering of the population in the Boston area. Even so simple a step as taking up residence in the cellar of an undamaged house in the Boston suburbs — New England is considered fortunate as a region in this respect, since full basements are traditional and commonplace — could cut the dosage received in the first week after a Westover-type blast by one half or even more, perhaps down to one tenth. This step alone could, thus, reduce the exposure dose to 450 rems or as little as 90 rems — a subclinical dose — if the shelter were well built.

Actual fallout would begin near Westover shortly after the hypothetical groundburst surmised in the last chapter, at roughly the two PSI circle around the blast. Assuming the 15 miles per hour westerly wind, the fallout would begin on the side opposite the wind direction — east of Westover, in other words — within minutes after the blast. The area in this direction to a distance of 20 to 30 miles from ground zero would theoretically be exposed to a seven-day fallout accumulation on the order of 3000 rems or more, an insupportable total. People in this general area would be better advised to flee at a right angle to the wind, rather than seek local shelter.

Fallout in the western suburbs of Worcester, Massachusetts, for instance, roughly due east of Westover and a bit more than 30 miles away, would begin to be measurable within two hours of the explosion, assuming the 15 mile per hour wind. Boston would have roughly four or five hours warning time, enough to construct reasonable shelters, given the distance from the target. Here the preferred course of action, assuming there are no subsequent attacks upon American population centers, would probably be to go to ground close to home and family. However, if there were such subsequent Soviet attacks, the Boston area population would then suffer more from any weapon targeted in that particular vicinity.

Fallout Decay

Fallout decays and loses its radioactivity at a predictable rate: as a general rule, weapons fallout is reduced in its virulence by a factor of ten for every seven units of time that go by after the explosion. In short, after seven hours, fallout should drop to one tenth of its peak level. After 49 hours, it would diminish to one-hundredth of its top intensity. On the seventh day, fallout, in theory, would be at a level of one tenth what it was on the first day after the blast.

This rule is again idealized, as it gives no weight whatever to variations in fallout rates caused by wind and weather or to the possibility that more than one burst might be the fallout source. In reality, in the event of a first-strike type of nuclear exchange, the fallout rates at most population centers along the U.S. East Coast would be apt to vary widely from hour to hour and day to day before diminishing. Again, the means to measure the rate of fallout would be an invaluable tool for any who hoped to plan some rational course for survival.

Nuclear Power Plants

A common question at this stage of all such analyses is "What happens if a nuclear power plant happens to be hit?" The answer, for the short-term, is that there would be little difference in the observed effects of the weapons fallout alone versus that fallout combined with the radioactive debris released into the environment by the rupture of the containment built into a nuclear power plant, at least for the first week or two. In that early period after the attack, fallout rates and depositions would be more influenced by the "traditional" factors governing their spread. But, because the processes involved in a nuclear weapon and a nuclear power plant are considerably different from one another, the areas affected by the additional radiation spewed from the demolished power facility would be hazardous for a much longer period of time, on the order of years rather than weeks or months.

In addition, nuclear power plants are quite strongly constructed, a factor which tends to make them a target more resembling the hardened missile silo than a sprawling city. If the purpose of a Soviet attack was to lay waste to the United States and leave the largest possible land areas uninhabitable for prolonged periods of time, there are essentially more efficient means available to Soviet nuclear strategists — designing all weapons for groundburst, increasing the proportion of the fission yield, wrapping the weapon itself in a coating of some material such as cobalt that can readily be rendered radioactive — than to include on the priority target list all the American civilian nuclear power plants. A nuclear plant is, in fact, a small, hardened target generally located far from population centers, of little military value, and poses little threat to Soviet soil. This makes nuclear power plants unlikely targets for the first wave of any presumed Soviet assault. Should such a plant be damaged in the course of other, more militarily meaningful forms of nuclear attack, then the result is generally considered to be a targeting bonus in modern strategic thought.

In the general area of fallout planning America and its people appear to have been somewhat remiss in their thinking for several decades, compared to their Soviet counterparts. In the Soviet Union, some reports hold, a comprehensive program to educate the public about the hazards of fallout and how to lessen those dangers has been in force for some time. In theory, every Soviet citizen has already graduated from a locally-taught course in emergency nuclear war procedures.

Fallout Sheltering

In the United States, by comparison, even the notion of fallout sheltering was dismissed in the early 1960s, though a comprehensive program along these lines could clearly aid millions of people in the event of nuclear attack. The U.S. system of blast and fallout shelter identifications, begun in the 1950s but halted for 20 years now, still exists in the form of building signs that mark such shelters. But supplies in most have not been checked for years, and the vast majority of such previously-inspected shelters have long since been abandoned in public thought and deed.

Particular to the U.S., there is a virtual absence of the technical equipment that might be used to measure fallout rates and provide extremely valuable survival information. Without such equipment — described in detail in Part II — no one who successfully reaches shelter can know his own fallout circumstances, and this lack of good information could be very costly indeed. For example, most radiation detection equipment is scaled for industrial use, where the rate of radioactivity is generally quite low. Such instruments, even if available, would be virtually useless to measure the much higher intensities of radiation produced by the fallout of modern nuclear weaponry. Without the precise data available only from the proper instruments, almost any shelter or evacuation plan is apt to be extremely limited in its rationality and usefulness.

Sources

Reasonably accurate information about radiation is widely available to the general public. Some of the earlier works remain among the most useful. In this category, the reader is referred to a fairly simple book, *Radiation — What It Is and How It Affects You*, written by two well-known scientists of the 1950s, Jack Schubert and Ralph E. Lapp (Viking Press, New York, 1957). This particular book also provides a brief and readable account of the ill-fated voyage of the Japanese fishing boat *Lucky Dragon Number Five*, which had the misfortune of being something less than lucky for the Japanese crew it brought too close to an American H-bomb test in the Pacific.

For the most part, the radiation standards referred to in this chapter are those published by the "handbooks" of the National Bureau of Standards, U.S. Department of Commerce, and the broader-based International Commission on Radiation Units and Measurement. Additional medical information on the clinical results of radiation and on the therapeutic approach to the treatment of radiation sickness was obtained from physicians in the Boston area.

The best, and longest, recap of the hazards of radioactive fallout may be found in several volumes of Congressional testimony produced in the late 1950s, nearly 5,000 pages worth, in fact. The two published papers resulting from these hearings were issued in 1957 and 1959 and entitled, respectively, "The Nature of Radioactive Fallout and Its Effects on Man," and (three complete volumes) "Fallout from Nuclear Weapons Tests." Both may still be available from the Superintendent of Documents, Government Printing Office, Washington, D.C. 20402. These two massive testimonials cover the entire spectrum of radiation subjects, and both resulted from hearings conducted at the time by the Special Subcommittee on Radiation of the U.S. Joint Congressional Committee on Atomic Energy. This particular committee, incidentally, had by far the strongest legislative influence on nuclear matters for the better part of the first quarter century of the nuclear age.

Material on the present-day residues of radioactive material still measured in our northerly latitudes was derived from another useful book, *Radioactive Fallout, Soils, Plants, Food, Man,* a series of technical papers edited by a Los Alamos scientist, Eric B. Fowler (Elsevier Publishing Company, New York, 1965). Some additional material used in the shaping of Chapter Five may be found in two additional technical papers, "Beta Radiation Lesion of the Skin," by R.A. Conrad and C.F. Tessmer, (American Medical Association Archives of Dermatology, Volume 74, 1956) and, by the same authors and additional colleagues, "Skin Lesions, Epilation, and Nail Pigmentation in Marshallese and Americans Accidentally Contaminated with Radioactive Fallout," (Naval Medical Research Institute Report, 1955). The latter report covers other people harmed by fallout from the same test that damaged the Japanese fishermen aboard the *Lucky Dragon Number Five,* though the coverage is far more technical.

An excellent textbook used for reference in this chapter and subsequently in this book is *Fundamentals of Radiation Protection,* by Hugh F. Henry (Wiley Interscience Division of John Wiley & Sons, New York, 1969). This text provides technical information that is not necessarily beyond the average untutored reader.

6 Modern Targeting

By contemporary standards, the first-generation atomic bombs dropped on Japan were the Model T's of nuclear weaponry. "Little Boy," the bomb dropped on Hiroshima, was a black cylinder, ten and a half feet long, two and a half feet in diameter, and it looked like the public's general idea of a bomb.

FISSION BOMB DESIGN

"Little Boy" worked on the principle of the nuclear fissioning of the rare uranium-235 metal in a container whose size and weight could be carried in the bomb bay of the propeller-driven B-29 bomber. The limitations of size produced a design that worked like a gun: a precisely machined plug of uranium-235 was fixed to a conventional explosive charge at one end of a tube resembling the interior of a gun barrel. When the charge was fired, the plug of U-235 was propelled into another slug of U-235 positioned as a target at the other end of the barrel. Kept apart, the two pieces of enriched uranium were essentially harmless, but when fit perfectly together, they produced what scientists call a super-critical mass and produced a fission explosion. There was no test of this design before its first use on August 6, 1945. There was no need for a test, the scientists had determined mathematically. The principle was certain.

The gun-type design could not be used with the other known fissionable material, plutonium. Plutonium was a then-new man-made element produced when ordinary uranium-238, the kind of uranium most commonly found in the natural environment, was bombarded with neutrons from a fission reaction. As a material with great war potential, plutonium could be manufactured in huge plants that used first-generation reactors to create the necessary controlled-fission reaction. Well into 1944, American atomic researchers worked hard on trying to design a gun-type plutonium firing mechanism, one similar to that of the uranium bomb, but it was discovered that no such design would be possible with plutonium. The discovery came so late in the Manhattan Project, the A-bomb building program, that it essentially precluded any possible use of atomic weapons upon Hitler in Europe.

The flaw of the gun-type design for a plutonium bomb was inherent in the physics of the event. The plutonium that was produced by the nation's secret plants contained two chemically identical forms, plutonium-239 and plutonium-241. The two would be nearly impossible to separate industrially because of their chemical identity. But plutonium-241 was so inherently unstable that it would begin to fission even as it was propelled down the barrel of the gun-type bomb, long before, in atomic time, the projectile had reached its target mass. The result was a kind of fizzle with considerable local radiation from the release of neutrons, but not much explosive force.

The American researchers then threw their scientific all into the design of a plutonium bomb that could be triggered by means of implosion, or inward direction of force toward the core of a sphere. This was a more difficult design, because the several pieces of plutonium had to be slammed together at precisely the same instant, and it was difficult to fire all the explosive charges simultaneously. Research concentrated on experimental shapes of conventional explosives — pie-shaped wedges were finally chosen — and their electrical firing circuits. The final design called for a hollowed sphere of plutonium centered around a neutron-initiating source. Around the plutonium sphere were wrapped the wedge-like "lenses" of conventional explosives. The entire assembly was further enclosed in neutron-reflecting material that served as a kind of tamper and rebounded escaping neutrons back into the critical mass at the core of the sphere. When the chemical explosives were fired, the plutonium was crushed by the inward force produced, and it then went super-critical and caused the atomic explosion.

The bomb that resulted from this design was nicknamed "Fat Man" for its bulbous shape. Wrapped in its outer casing, Fat Man resembled a giant black egg, 11 feet long and five feet thick at its widest girth. A bomb of this type was the first nuclear weapon to be fired on earth, during the American "Trinity" test at Alamagordo, New Mexico, on July 16, 1945, three weeks before the atomic bombing of Japan. The second implosion-type plutonium bomb in history was the one dropped on Nagasaki. Ironically, this design, because of its comparative nuclear efficiency, was the principle subject of Soviet espionage into the American A-bomb program. The secrets stolen did not concern nuclear matters or materials, but the shape of the triggering lenses of chemical explosives.

Since the end of World War II, the design of nuclear weaponry has undergone several technical advances, most of them having to do with making the bombs smaller, cheaper, and more powerful. During the entire time of nuclear-enforced peace of the post-war era, there has been a series of significant breakthroughs.

The earliest of these came at the very dawn of the nuclear age, in the days just after World War II. It was discovered at the American atomic laboratory at Los Alamos, New Mexico, that the element beryllium should be used as the external wrapper of each bomb. Beryllium is a light, gray-colored metal most often found in the natural environment in combination with another element. In itself, beryllium is brittle and hard to machine, and it is highly toxic chemically. (This discovery, a feat of medical science, was made when researchers investigated an unusual outbreak of lung disease near a Nazi beryllium plant that had operated during the war.) The property of beryllium that attracted weapon designers was its ability to reflect neutrons; its atomic reflectivity, in effect. When used in the outer wrapper of a fission weapon, beryllium reflects escaping neutrons from the beginning of the reaction directly back into the critical mass in sufficient numbers that the reaction may be boosted. Had the United States used beryllium in the wrapper of the Hiroshima uranium bomb, the explosion would have been four to ten times more powerful.

Thus, by the late 1940s, weapon designers could maximize the blast effect of the A-bomb or, if they chose, could use smaller amounts of the rare and expensive fissionable materials to produce the same effect as the first-generation bombs. Today, a good assumption is that nuclear weapon miniaturization has progressed to the point that a fission weapon could be loaded into a spherical geometry roughly the size of a grapefruit. For the experienced designer of nuclear weapons, it is said to be easy to build a bomb that could fit in a briefcase or shoebox.

FUSION BOMB DESIGN

The other major development in nuclear weaponry, a step not taken by the United States until after the revelation that the Soviets had also developed a workable A-bomb in 1949, was the introduction and advancement of design of the thermonuclear device, the H-bomb. In terms of its power, the H-bomb was colossal. A large conventional bomb of the World War II era yielded a force equivalent to several tons of high explosive. An A-bomb has yields measured in thousands of tons. But an H-bomb yields forces that are measured only in terms of millions of tons of TNT. The difference in size between the H-bomb and A-bomb was actually much greater than the difference between an A-bomb and a conventional weapon. In the whole of World War II, for instance, Allied forces had sent the equivalent of 2.5 million *tons* of explosive force hurtling toward Nazi Germany in one form or another. Now, with the H-bomb, a single weapon could carry the equivalent explosive force, or much more.

From the start, the search for an H-bomb was also a matter of design. Ruminating on the possibility of a super-bomb — the principle had been demonstrated mathematically, but not yet in reality — a Los Alamos scientist in 1945 likened the problem to trying to ignite a large piece of petrified wood with a paper match. The target material was too large, too inert, and too difficult to ignite with a puny trigger that could not bring the mass to combustion temperatures. Using an A-bomb trigger to create the requisite heat was an obvious possibility. The question was one of design, how to make the necessary staging mechanisms work in a bomb-like form.

The mathematical answer to the question of how to design an H-bomb was solved for the first time in the spring of 1951, at Princeton, New Jersey, by Edward Teller — a Hungarian scientist who had escaped the Nazi invasion of Europe and subsequently worked on the A-bomb at Los Alamos — and Stanley Ulam, a Pole. In the patent application for their discovery, the two men are described as the "inventors" of the hydrogen bomb. Even today, Teller, an outspoken critic of all ban-the-bomb movements, is considered to be the man who invented thermonuclear fire.

The Teller and Ulam design was produced in 18 months and first test-fired on the tiny island of Elugelab, at the northern end of what was then called Eniwetok Atoll in the Pacific, in November, 1952. The device, code-named "Mike," was not a deliverable weapon, because of its size and huge weight. It incorporated a form of liquid hydrogen that required heavy refrigeration machinery. Ensconced in a 50-foot building on Elugelab, Mike was actually a huge steel cylinder resembling a large water or chemical tank lying on its side. It weighed 21 tons and contained at least one fission-type weapon in its mechanisms. Scientists had predicted that the device would yield not much more than several thousand kilotons, but Mike surprised all those who observed its firing. The yield was more than ten *megatons,* and Mike's fireball was so great that it vaporized the entire island on which it had sat. Quoting nuclear weapons designer Ted Taylor, John McPhee says in his superb *The Curve of Binding Energy,* "When the heat reached the observers, it stayed and stayed and stayed, not for seconds but for minutes." The sheer power of the device stunned veterans of atomic tests. Thought was given in the high echelons of the American scientific community to withholding information of the development. The principle was simply too horrifying.

The following spring, the Soviet Union fired its first hydrogen bomb. Tests soon revealed that it had contained lithium deuteride, a dry form of the hydrogen material that could be fused but required no heavy refrigeration machinery, which meant that it was a weapon that could be carried by an airplane. No one knows to this day whether the Soviet design principle was the same as that of the Americans, for there are just a few thousand people on the face of the earth today who know the secret of H-bomb design, and there is a clear stricture against revelation of the principles.

This awesome nuclear firepower changed the course of history, and determined modern man's uneasy thinking about contemporary war. By the mid-1950s, computers had already predicted that either the United States or Soviet Union, despite their large geographic size, could be utterly, completely, destroyed, its population eradicated, if brought beneath 50,000 megatons worth of thermonuclear force. The monstrous power of the H-bomb also introduced the age of greater interest in rocketry as a means of delivery. Prior to the H-bomb, the smaller atom bomb had not had sufficient explosive force to overcome the aiming error likely in the rockets of the 1950s. The H-bomb, however, could destroy an area of several hundred square miles, even if its missile was a clear miss.

Significant advances in the design of thermonuclear weaponry have continued ever since. In the mid-1950s, discoveries at the Livermore Laboratories in California greatly reduced the size and weight of H-weaponry and made it possible for a megaton-yield weapon to be fitted atop a rocket small enough to fit inside the new atomic submarines then coming into service. At that point, it became possible to produce a near-megaton yield in a device weighing less than a ton, just one-twentieth of the Mike device that was fired in the Pacific in 1952.

An H-bomb is generally believed to take the shape of a long cylinder, a geometry that aids in the firing of the weapon. Photographs of the American H-bombs recovered from the depths of the Mediterranean in 1966, after a B-52 bomber exploded in mid-air over Palomares, Spain, indicate that the four bombs lost were of the Mark 61 design, with multi-megaton yields packed into brushed-metal cylinders about 12 feet long and a foot in diameter. Hydrogen weapons — or their shells — are on public view at the National Atomic Museum at Albuquerque, New Mexico. The H-bombs there generally take the form of cylinders, or pipe-like objects, some just a few feet long and mere inches across.

About 30,000 of these monstrous devices will be deployed by the U.S. and U.S.S.R. by the mid-1980s, more if the American defense build-up is carried out. They will be stored in nearly 3,000 dumps and depots, watched over by coveralled acolytes who tend them and see to their safe-keeping and maintenance. Officially, the United States makes no comment whatever about the presence or absence of nuclear weapons in any given place, but a reasonable assumption is that thousands of the weapons lay like dormant monsters, silent and inert, atop intercontinental rockets in land silos and submarine chambers, and in their war bunkers at the bomber bases, watched over by a specialized priesthood of young people, none of them knowing a bit more than their particular job requires them to know. The disposal of all this nuclear firepower will one day come either by a decision to dismantle or by use in war.

TARGETING STUDIES

In the autumn of 1950, a year after confirmation of the first Soviet A-bomb test and several years before the H-bomb was exploded, the United States began the first formal targeting study of the Soviet Union. At the time, the nation had fewer than 500 nuclear weapons, all of them fission bombs with yields of less than 100 kilotons. Earlier that year, a secret technical assessment of the relative military positions of the U.S. and U.S.S.R. had made American political and military leadership apprehensive. It appeared, in that assessment, that Russia could do considerable damage to the United States if it chose to attack American soil with atomically armed bombers, after which the Red Army could seize western Europe with impunity. We had the strength, on paper, to deter any such assault by means of World War II era aircraft such as the original B-29 and its advanced successor, the B-50. But the U.S. war-contingency plan largely assumed that target planning would be accomplished by air staffs after hostilities had begun. This was clearly insufficient, given the high stakes. With new bombing aircraft on the drawing boards or beginning deployment — the hybrid, half-jet, half-propeller-driven B-36, the medium-range all-jet B-47, and the new intercontinental B-52 — it would clearly be better for the United States to have an idea of what Russian targets to hit well in advance of war. With atomic weaponry, World-War-II-style mobilization was obviously out of date as a military concept. The object now was to forestall attack by conveying the impression that the bombers could be over Soviet targets within a matter of hours, not months, after any assult on the U.S. The atom bomb had made war something that would happen in hours or days, not months and years.

For that first targeting study in the autumn of 1950, however, the U.S. hearkened back to strategic bombing concepts of World War II. Specialists in nuclear weapons from Los Alamos were brought to the Pentagon to spend weeks poring over aerial photographs of potential targets in Russia — specific military bases, oil refineries, naval facilities, ball-bearing plants, cities. The question in each case was what level of atomic force would be required to obliterate such targets, one by one, or all at once. Nuclear weapons technology, even in 1950, had already progressed so that it might be possible to design a specific weapon for a specific target, taking all the target's characteristics into consideration in the process. The analysts looked at the heights of hills around Moscow, the flow of a river near a Russian armaments factory. Many of the photographs used in the study had been made by the Luftwaffe, the Nazi air force, during World War II. They had been brought to the United States after the war in programs so secret that they are only now becoming public.

The development of much more powerful thermonuclear weapons brought a new dimension to the entire subject. If anything, the sheer ferocity of the weapons about to become available made it even more critical that an advanced targeting plan be ready at all times. Moreover, all such plans would henceforth have as their purpose the survival of the United States as a political entity, not just the deterrence of any attack on some far-flung battlefield. The H-bomb quite clearly had the power to degrade or destroy the core institutions of even such large geopolitical entities as the United States. Nations such as Britain and Germany, weaker and much smaller in area, literally had no chance in the event of H-bomb attack. The new weaponry made it virtually certain that nothing would be left on the surface of a small area such as the British Isles in the event of an all-out H-bomb attack. A nation of the size of the United States might conceivably survive, but only if its military forces could strike back against an assault so swiftly that they might limit the general damage done to the nation by disabling some of the enemy's attack potential. Deterrence, damage limitation, and retaliatory punishment became the keynotes of an American policy that persists in essentially the same form today.

There is considerable evidence that the "massive retaliation" policy of John Foster Dulles in the 1950s involved American targeting of a substantial portion of the Soviet citizenry at that time, since it made little sense to vaporize Soviet military installations that had been emptied by an opening Russian assault. Well into the 1980s, the assumption of many defense analysts is that American nuclear submarine missiles are aimed mostly at Soviet cities and population centers and not the military facilities of the U.S.S.R. The reasoning is twofold: first, the missiles themselves are only now becoming accurate enough to be targeted upon small, hardened sites such as missile silos, and, second, the launching vehicles themselves, the submarines, still remain relatively invulnerable to Soviet attack — the sea is a vast area, and advances in anti-submarine technology have still not allowed either side to keep perfect track of the other's subs. This means that such missiles could be launched at any time, even long after an initial Soviet attack had obliterated other American retaliatory forces.

The realization of the awesome power of thermonuclear weapons — and the awful responsibility vested in anyone who must decide upon their use — brought a new wave of serious thought about the unthinkable. For one, it was obvious that any American President, faced with a split-second decision on whether or not to retaliate, required hard, confirmed information that a Soviet attack had indeed taken place. The United States began, in the 1950s, to construct the military system that, to this day, must confirm or deny the presence of an attack upon the nation. Much of the United States was wired with secret sensors that could detect the seismic shocks of nuclear weapon bursts; this system, known as NUDETS (for "nuclear detection system") provides positive confirmation of one or more nuclear explosions upon American soil. If data from NUDETS is positive, then America is clearly at war and must respond accordingly. Anything short of this leaves room for doubt.

Moreover, beginning in the 1950s, responsibility for advance warning of attack, in contrast to authority to retaliate, was vested in two separate military bodies. Defense of the North American continent against nuclear attack, which includes providing as much early warning as possible, is vested in the North American Air Defense Command, or NORAD, with headquarters in the huge underground chambers within Cheyenne Mountain, near Colorado Springs, Colorado. NORAD keeps track of *all* manmade hardware in space, uses its radars and visual sensors to track the various devices, predict their future orbits, or their potential targets on the earth's surface, and is responsible for warning U.S. officials of impending Soviet assault. By contrast, the American Strategic Air Command, or SAC, is responsible for much of the retaliatory response, if any is to be made. Thus no single group or individual, with the exception of the President, can decide to go to war at its sole discretion. Even the centers of command are kept in separate places in Colorado, Nebraska, and Washington, D.C.

As far as can be determined, Soviet nuclear doctrine is quite similar, despite the fact that the U.S.S.R. is faced with potential threats from locations other than the United States. (Britain and France openly announced that their relatively small nuclear forces are aimed at Soviet cities, Moscow in particular, because they do not feel that an American President would necessarily be willing to trade Washington and Boston for London and Paris. The Chinese have most likely targeted the U.S.S.R., also. In fact, the French openly say that their land-based missile sites are intentionally located in eastern France, where fallout from any attack upon them would most likely drift eastward into the Soviet Union.) The most reliable Western reports place Soviet air defense headquarters, where any attack would have to be assessed, near the city of Omsk. Soviet strike headquarters are said to be located far away, near Tutaev.

THINKING THE UNTHINKABLE

As the horrible potential of modern thermonuclear weaponry became evident in the 1950s, a new kind of cold-blooded strategic analysis was born, the professional process of "thinking about the unthinkable," typified in the writings of such commentators as Herman Kahn, whose *On Thermonuclear War*, published in 1959, still stands today as a kind of bible of modern thought about when and how to think about the use of nuclear weapons in war. As bizarre as such ideas may seem, analysts of Kahn's persuasion insist that, if man is to survive at all in the face of imminent nuclear peril, it is probably best to give serious and rational, if difficult, thought to the subject of nuclear war and to think through its eventualities with a level of common sense that is, at the least, "not insane." To do anything less, these critics say, is to lose sight of obvious self-interest and to risk disaster by pure accident.

Popular conceptions, such as the current concern about Soviet first-strike capabilities, do not concern such analysts as much as other factors of the nuclear equation, such as the nominal value of the threat perceived by one side or another. A broad working assumption is that, although the attacker is not necessarily suicidal, he may nevertheless be willing to rattle nuclear sabers and threaten an attack, while not intending to carry out the threat, simply to achieve some desired political goal. For example, in this intellectual context, the credibility of an aggressor's first-strike *threat* may be far more significant, in real-world terms, than his intention to act on his threat. Faced with Soviet intervention in some Middle East oil crisis, for instance, an American President might be reluctant to take action, not necessarily *knowing* the extent of Soviet willingness to begin a nuclear war, but believing the U.S.S.R. capable of such a step. The perceived threat alone may be sufficient to accomplish the goals of the Soviet Union.

Conversely, in a world in which both superpowers should acknowledge the other's ability to do intolerable damage no matter who strikes first, a violation of the long-standing prohibition against the use of nuclear weapons might, in itself, demonstrate to the other side that the first felt its most vital interests were at stake. In such circumstances, one side could be construed as telling the other: "Listen carefully. We regard the attainment of our goals so important to our continued existence that we are willing to use nuclear weaponry, with all the horror that it entails. You should stop resisting us. To do otherwise in the present circumstances is to risk something neither of us want, but we are willing to take the risk in the face of the danger we already perceive to ourselves."

Nuclear war, then, might not begin with an all-out assault and world holocaust. It might begin, instead, relatively slowly, with clearcut gradations and escalating levels of intensity, with all-out war taking place only in the last stages of prolonged conflict. After all, if neither side can be certain that it could eradicate the entire threat to itself from the other it might nevertheless be willing to go part of the way in an attempt to achieve something it considers of significance to its own plans and desires.

In this way, many forms of nuclear war might be plausible and possible, assuming only that the first use of the weaponry did not, in itself, set off an irrevocable and totally reflexive response on the part of the opponent.

The issue here lies at the very heart of what is considered modern strategic thought. Is the object of war, any war, simply to commit suicide? Hardly, say the proponents of thinking about the unthinkable. The object of war is to attain goals otherwise unattainable, not to poison the very atmosphere of the earth and render all "victory" meaningless. The easier such goals might be realized, the better the strategy, especially if a show of strength at a critical moment of international tension renders the other side incapable of an effective response.

To select, as a first option, an all-out attack upon the population and cities of the opponent is irrational and senseless, if there is a high probability that the enemy's remaining military power is sufficient to do intolerable damage in return. Better, perhaps, to provide the opponent with some way to back down at a critical moment, and to use only sufficient force to paralyze the opposition and prevent it from taking the final, fatal step.

The principle of gradually escalated nuclear war is also apparent when it comes to the allocation of resources — what *should* be on the priority-target list as opposed to what might be in theory. The question here is how to stage a nuclear attack and limit the possibilities of damage to oneself. Ironically, in this context, the sheer power of nuclear weaponry tends to highlight and increase enlightened self-interest. If you have only so many offensive rockets to launch, it is clearly more prudent to aim most of them at the enemy's ability to respond militarily, at his rockets, rather than at his cities and people. The latter will not hurt the attacker swiftly and surely. But the destruction of the enemy's cities and people without the simultaneous degradation of his ability to strike back is a sure and certain way to assure that he will strike back with all available nuclear force.

TARGETING STRATEGIES

Contemporary strategic analysts widely assume that the forces of the U.S. and U.S.S.R. are targeted in this way:

United States

The working assumption here is that the majority of U.S. land-based missiles, such as Minuteman and Titan, are aimed at Soviet military targets — airbases, re-loadable missile silos, nuclear submarine facilities. There is no other plausible explanation for Minuteman's widely acknowledged accuracy, which is far more than enough to hit a particular street corner in a Soviet city. Because American command, control, and communications facilities are known to be extremely flexible, the planned targeting could readily be changed. But, at current levels of force, the best available estimate is that a significant portion of the American land-based missile force is intended to reduce the ability of the U.S.S.R. to damage the United States.

By contrast, American bombers and sea-launched missiles are commonly assumed to be aimed at Russian cities and the Soviet population, particularly its leadership. Clusters of thermonuclear warheads atop American Trident and Poseidon sea-launched missiles are known to be especially effective city killers, any of which might be launched long after the U.S. had ceased to exist as a nation.

Soviet Union

The recent development of huge, extremely accurate rockets such as the SS-18 is assumed to pose a threat to the American land-based missile force, which is presumably growing increasingly vulnerable to a Soviet pre-emptive strike. However, even this is not necessarily enough to prompt the U.S.S.R. to strike first at such missile sites in the continental U.S., since roughly two-thirds of the American force would survive any such assault. One recent estimate, for instance, is that the U.S.S.R. maintains sufficient land-based force to allow it to try to hunt down American missile-firing submarines by saturation-like shelling of huge areas of the open sea, where U.S. submarines might be lurking beneath the waves.

In fact, the standing land-based missile force of the U.S.S.R. at the present time, and for the foreseeable future, is large enough to allow the targeting of virtually every American city and town over 50,000 in population. Such targets might or might not be hit in any first assault, but the most important consideration in assessing the likelihood that fairly small American population centers might be hit fairly early in any nuclear exchange is the degree of Soviet certainty that the first wave of missiles would catch the entire American Minuteman force in its silos before any retaliation could be launched. Because none of this ''certainty'' has ever been, or can be, tested, short of war, the assumption is that most of the Soviet initial assault would be aimed strictly at Minuteman and Titan silos and control points, American bomber bases, and the areas and bases near which U.S. Trident and Poseidon-carrying submarines might be found.

Although the sheer numbers available to the U.S.S.R. seem extremely high when compared to the American position today, a working assumption is that the Soviets must also plan some type of targeting of western Europe and the Chinese mainland. These requirements may substantially reduce the force available to be targeted upon American cities. As with the American submarines, Soviet *Delta* and *Yankee* class missile-launching submarines are also assumed to be aimed principally at American cities because this force is clearly a "second-strike" organization capable of attack long after the outbreak of war.

KINDS OF NUCLEAR WAR

With these factors in mind, let us look at four different kinds of nuclear war.

Case One The use of one or more nuclear weapons as a demonstration of force.

Imagine, if you will, some international circumstance in which the U.S.S.R. wishes to convince the United States that it is deadly serious about its goals and that the intensity of its beliefs is worth some form of nuclear demonstration.

In these circumstances, it is conceivable that the U.S.S.R. might be willing to use nuclear weapons far in space or, in small numbers, at high altitudes over the continental United States, to maximize the EMP effect of the weaponry.

Such an "attack" would do considerable economic damage to the U.S. in prompt fashion, while causing an absolute minimum of human casualties in the process. The damage done would be largely limited to a kind of latter-day property damage to the entire American electrical grid. Communications and electrical power in the U.S. would be devastated for some time by anywhere from one to three modern thermonuclear weapons detonated at altitudes of roughly 100,000 feet over American soil, at precisely determined points. The resulting damage would be limited to power facilities, communications antennas, electrical wiring, and the entire American computer system network. The implication of such an attack would be that the U.S.S.R. is so intent upon its goals that it is willing to violate the unspoken agreement against the use of nuclear weapons. The Soviet Union would have crossed a significant line of international behavior in the modern world, while simultaneously demonstrating that its general discipline had remained intact. Any American response to this form of nuclear assault would have to be measured in kind, for to act otherwise would be to invite escalation to the next-higher step of nuclear exchange, at the least.

The economic impact on the United States would be both significant and instantaneous. Gone would be our customary radio and television communications, the electric power in much of the country, much of the nation's telephone system, with collateral damage to transportation and daily life. Recovery time would vary from place to place and might range from a few days, for those places where the basic source of power is, say, hydroelectric, to many months for those areas that rely upon single line extensions of the electric grid.

The cost to the United States of such a Soviet demonstration attack might be measured in billions, including lost productivity, disruption of the economy and of the daily life of millions of people. Yet no more than two or three Soviet warheads would be required. And because no lives were lost directly, the American response to this form of Soviet demonstration would be problematical.

Case Two   A nuclear attack specifically designed to do a maximum amount of economic harm and to prolong recovery time.

Technically speaking, this form of nuclear attack would be quite simple for either superpower to inflict upon the other, as it requires no more than 100 warheads to drive the opponent's economy into complete disrepair for many years. Despite the many formal attack studies commissioned by the American government over the years, this particular case has rarely been assessed by the executive or legislative branches, probably because, by definition, this kind of attack leaves the victim's entire retaliatory force intact and capable of a massive response. Knowing this, neither superpower would be apt to select such a targeting procedure as its sole option, though this form of assault can readily be combined with other attacks designed to minimize damage to the nation that happened to strike first.

Despite the comparative paucity of solid information, this type of nuclear attack might, in fact, be conducted by a second or third rate nuclear power embroiled in a dispute with either of the nuclear giants. The number of warheads required is well within the means of such secondary nuclear powers such as Great Britain, France, and China, and quite probably available also to the two supposedly secret atomic powers, Israel and South Africa. If nuclear weapons continue to proliferate as they have thus far, this particular form of economic attack might also be the targeting scheme of choice for any small, unstable country, such as Libya, intent upon doing maximum damage to one of the superpowers. The retaliatory response would be apt to eradicate the original attacker, but would itself be likely to raise international tensions to the boiling point. Thus the plan of attack outlined here for Case Two could well serve as a stepping stone to a much wider nuclear exchange.

Only one American study of this particular case has ever been made public, an analysis conducted at the request of Congress by the U.S. Office of Technology Assessment in 1979 and 1980. This study points out that the optimum way to cause profound damage to an advanced, heavily industrialized, modern state is to wage nuclear war upon its energy supplies. Results of the study, not widely publicized in this country, indicate that oil refineries and storage facilities are the preferred targets in both the United States and the Soviet Union. According to published figures of the American oil industry — comparable data for the Soviet Union is not made public and must be obtained from private sources — the U.S. maintains nearly 300 oil refineries within its borders and in the territories over which it has control. By comparison, the Soviet Union, with an oil refining capacity roughly two-thirds that of the U.S., operates fewer than 100 refining complexes, most of them very large and widely scattered and sited fairly far from Soviet centers of population.

The study of this kind of nuclear attack highlights the potential differences in the vulnerability of the U.S. and U.S.S.R. It is not that one nation is necessarily more susceptible; the two are simply different in major ways.

To establish a basis for study, the Office of Technology Assessment made several basic assumptions. For one, it assumed that only 80 warheads would be used, about the number that might readily be available to a smaller nuclear power bent on attacking one of the giants. In addition, the study assumed considerable advance warning, enough for some population centers to be evacuated and for some resident populations to take shelter. Estimates of the damage — the theoretical attack gives no thought either to minimizing or maximizing the human casualties — are also influenced, of course, by such factors as time of day, season of the year, and wind and weather conditions.

To develop the model for such a study, analysts assumed that the Soviets might use no more than 10 of their giant SS-18 land-based rockets, each with eight one-megaton warheads aimed independently. For a comparable attack on the U.S.S.R., the United States is assumed to assign seven submarine-launched Poseidon missiles, each with up to 14 relatively small, independent warheads, plus three Minuteman III missiles with three MIRVed warheads apiece. The reason for this mix of weaponry is that some Soviet refineries lie beyond the range of the sea-borne Poseidon and require the use of the longer-ranged Minuteman III.

This type of weaponry may generally be targeted with high accuracy, but all the warheads of each individual missile must be aimed at an oval-shaped area, a kind of "footprint" on the surface of the earth. The restrictions on the total number of missiles used built into the study assumptions mean that neither nation could entirely obliterate the oil refining capacity of the other, though severe damage would be done with such a "small" nuclear attack. Other assumptions of the study are that each warhead is designed for airburst over its target, each hits its target very precisely, and each explodes as expected. Variations in these factors would cause significant differences in the predicted results of the study. It is assumed that target planners on both sides would single out the largest refineries accessible to the missiles, given the restrictions on numbers of rockets available.

The contrasts in results show both the asymmetries between the U.S. and U.S.S.R. and the varying effects of the weaponry upon differing regions of each country. New England, for instance, would be spared any immediate damage from the prompt effects of such an attack, since the region has no refineries that might appear on any Soviet targeting list. However, other sections of the nation, particularly the Gulf Coast regions and the California coastline, would suffer immeasurably more. From three to five million Americans would die in such an assault, with nearly as many badly injured. Most of these casualties would occur in the vicinity of the refinery targets, and comparatively few would result from the less hazardous fallout produced by airbursts. The comparable U.S. attack on Soviet refineries would kill between one million and a million and a half Soviet citizens, with another two million people badly injured by the immediate effects of the assault. The hypothetical attack would destroy two-thirds of America's oil refining capacity — the facilities are easily damaged by nuclear airbursts — and the comparable attack on the Soviet Union would eradicate approximately three-fourths of the oil capacity of the U.S.S.R. Neither nation would likely recover swiftly from such an attack, since refineries take a considerable period to build and many of the needed technical specialists would be killed in the attack.

The damage would clearly be worse for the U.S. than for the U.S.S.R., because unlike Soviet refineries, most American oil facilities are located close to, if not within population centers. American cities within the footprints of the 10 Soviet SS-18s assigned to this type of targeting strategy include virtually all population centers along the U.S. Gulf Coast, from Texas into Alabama, the heavy concentrations of people along the California coast, the industrial heartland of America south of the Great Lakes, and a significant portion of the population corridor in the northeast, ranging from the southwest corner of Connecticut down into Virginia. To single out New England again, virtually no population center would be targeted, but the entire region would swiftly feel the effects of the eight SS-18 warheads that would fall on oil refineries in New Jersey and around Philadelphia, Pennsylvania. Depending upon the wind, New England could suffer a few fallout casualties, but the region would otherwise be spared much of the nuclear horror.

Not so the Gulf Coast. Four of the 10 Soviet missiles would be targeted upon the many refineries in that region. For the targeting required by this hypothetical attack, two SS-18s would be aimed at California, two for the area south of Lake Michigan, and single missiles would fall in the area around Kansas City, the refineries in New Jersey, and within the city of Philadelphia. Six of the ten largest American oil refineries are in Texas, which would mean that the cities of Houston, Dallas, and their surrounding areas would be under nuclear fire. That particular danger zone would extend eastward past Shreveport and New Orleans, Louisiana, to as far north as Arkansas. The entire California coast would be in danger, with the exception of the region 100 miles north of San Francisco and a smaller area near Santa Barbara. Major cities, each with more than half a million residents that would be endangered by this relatively small-scale nuclear attack, would include Houston, Dallas, New Orleans, San Francisco, Los Angeles, Chicago, Detroit, Kansas City, Washington, Baltimore, Philadelphia, and New York. In contrast, only Moscow would be in direct danger, though people in the vicinity of Minsk, Gorki, and Kalingrad would also be endangered immediately. In the northeastern United States, Philadelphia would suffer the most because it contains two major oil refineries, which together supply much of the oil and gas for the entire northeast. Both these targets lie within the city limits of Philadelphia. New York would be in considerable danger from four or more Soviet warheads from the single SS-18 targetted in this region, with each warhead aimed at one of the four major refineries in nearby New Jersey.

In essence, any such attack, small as it is compared to an all-out Soviet effort, might kill five percent of the current U.S. population, injure a similar number of citizens, and leave behind an outraged American public, most of whom would survive the assault but whose lives would be changed, immediately, for years to come. For a nation so reliant upon oil and so geared to the automobile for transport and communications, the attack would instantly bring back many conditions of the Great Depression, or worse. No help to the badly damaged areas would be likely until people were certain that the attack was over and no further assaults could be expected. Extreme rationing of gasoline and oil would be required, and would last for years, with only the most essential industries and agriculture receiving the minimum necessary to operate.

It would take years, according to the government study, for even a semblance of normalcy to return, and no one who survived the limited attack could reasonably expect to see today's style of American life again in his lifetime. For people in the colder climes, such as New England, only an austere level of heating oil could be expected for at least 20 years. Survival over the long term would require major adaptations in lifestyle and profound adjustments in the present-day American economy. Beyond that, such an attack would clearly be the worst disaster in U.S. history, and the longer-term effects would be extremely disruptive to the lives of the majority of the survivors.

Overnight, the American economy would be shattered. In the regions directly affected by the attack, there would likely be conflagrations produced by gasoline and petrochemical fires, and considerable release of toxic chemicals and carcinogens could be expected in the vicinity. Suburban living, far from the workplace, would become untenable, and the service and vacation industries typified by shopping malls and fast-food restaurants would become a thing of the past. New markets would have to be developed for many products, and the trickle-down effect of the attack would continue in a host of ways for years to come. Major changes could be expected in society for decades as most of the American population began to establish new population centers and ways of life. Courts would be overwhelmed by litigation and local governments, whose tax rates are based upon current standards of population distribution, would become nearly inoperative in many areas. Such a relatively "small" nuclear attack, even if launched by a power other than the Soviet Union, would have the capacity to create profound changes in America. It is noteworthy to point out that, if the adversary were indeed the Soviet Union, *less than one percent* of the U.S.S.R.'s land-based missile force would be required to cause this extent of damage.

Case Three   A "counterforce" attack waged by the Soviet Union on U.S. land-based missile facilities and military commands.

This is the most oft-studied nuclear attack case in American history, because it represents the "most rational" way for the U.S.S.R. to attack the U.S. while minimizing the damage done in retaliation upon itself. Most formal studies of this case have been conducted at the behest of various agencies of the Executive branch of government, notably the U.S. Department of Defense. The subject has, over the years, received considerable attention in the public press, though the American citizenry probably does not yet realize precisely what is involved and how such an attack would affect the future of American life.

The scenario in Case Three involves a major attack by the U.S.S.R. and requires several thousand Soviet warheads, most of them ground-bursts and therefore producing massive amounts of fallout. There are two basic forms of such an attack, one that is aimed only at American land-based missile silos and their control facilities — this is a subset of the general counterforce attack — and the other adding bomber bases and submarine ports to the list. At first glance it would appear that an attack limited to the far-flung Minuteman and Titan silos might prove less damaging overall than the larger scale assault. In reality, variations caused by other factors — size and type of the warheads, the altitude of the explosion, the prevailing winds — have more influence on the damage estimates than does the simple inclusion of American cities in the vicinity of military bases to the target list. In the words of one such technical study, "available data is too coarse to support a believable differentiation between the civilian effects of each attack."

For the purpose of this kind of attack, the Soviet Union is presumed to target every one of the 1,053 American land-based missile silos with one or more groundburst warheads, using its new and massive SS-18 missiles as the launch vehicles. There are presumed to be slightly more than 300 SS-18s available to the U.S.S.R. target planners in the mid-1980s, with perhaps one out of six of those deployed devoted to the carrying of a single, large, 25-megaton warhead. Each of the remaining 250-plus SS-18s could carry as many as 10 one-megaton warheads, each of which is thought to be more than accurate enough to land within 600 feet of a missile silo on the other side of the world — close enough to vaporize the installation. In effect, by firing its entire SS-18 force, the Soviet Union could theoretically target virtually every American missile silo with two separate warheads, yet still have nearly 500 such warheads to spare for targeting of the American missile command centers in the vicinity of the silos. The Soviet SS-19 and particularly the SS-17 may also have sufficient accuracy to constitute a back-up force for any such counterforce assault.

The technical proficiency to allow this form of massive nuclear attack is possible today, at least on paper, though the problems involved are very large. Most, if not all, of the attacking missiles must pass over the earth's north magnetic pole, where unusual magnetic effects might serve to throw the rockets off course. No missile in history has been fired with this precise trajectory, and so a question remains whether such an assault could, in fact, succeed. Moreover, recent evidence indicates that each warhead would have to detonate within five seconds of the other at the target site, a very difficult time-on-target feat from half a planet away. If the second warhead is late in arriving, the explosion of the first might, in theory, vaporize the late arrival, producing what scientists call "fratricide" among the assault force and reducing the effectiveness of the attack. Finally, the overall accuracy of the majority of the missiles has not been tested. Tests of specially fitted missiles, each fired singly, may not prove out fully for hosts of missiles fired from operational silos in a salvo. Yet the theory behind such a potential attack is enough to make American officials apprehensive in the 1980s.

The blast damage from any Soviet counterforce attack on the United States would largely be confined to the immediate vicinities of American military bases, assuming that no additional missiles were simultaneously launched toward U.S. cities and population centers. Most of the civilian damage done to the U.S. population, other than the destruction of those populated areas near bomber and submarine facilities, would result from the massive amounts of fallout produced as a by-product of the attack. Groundbursts are a more effective way to destroy hardened missile silos than are airbursts, and groundbursts, of course, produce excessive fallout when the fireball of the weapon comes in contact with the surface of the earth. In the Case Three scenario, several thousand Soviet warheads are presumed to explode on American soil, the vast majority of them in the missile fields west of the Mississippi River, but up to 50 more atop the four dozen bomber airfields and submarine ports in the contiguous 48 states.

It is this particular scenario that has given rise to the great debate about how to protect the American population best in the event of nuclear war. One government organization, the Federal Emergency Management Agency, which is responsible for organizing the national response to civil disasters, has developed an outline of a plan to evacuate the populations of American cities to presumably safer places in the countryside. Much of this agency's thinking is based on the assumption that any further attack aimed at American population centers, beyond the assault on military facilities, might best be ameliorated by evacuation, despite the recognized threat of fallout. The purpose of evacuation, this agency states, is to reduce the huge casualties that would result from the direct effects of nuclear airbursts over the heavily populated sections of the nation. However, by way of contradiction, virtually all studies of results from any Soviet counter-force-type attack — which is the scenario of Case Three — indicate that the fallout from the area of the western American missile fields would pose a major hazard to the heavily populated eastern half of the nation within a few days of the start of nuclear war. In the words of one counterforce study, "Evacuation would probably be a poor choice, since it would be difficult or impossible to predict which would be the safe areas and which the hotspots, and since a car in a traffic jam would offer poor shelter indeed."

In all such studies of major Soviet attacks on the U.S., variations in assumptions about the time of day, time of year, the type of weapons used, and their targets create wide variations in projections of probable American casualties. If the assault were limited to a military-counterforce attack, shelter of some kind would be available to the majority of the American population, but the time available to seek or improve shelters would be relatively short. Worse still, most people would not know what to do, how long they had, or what their own hazards and prospects were. The Case Three scenario points out the short-sightedness of the official American policy of the past two decades, which has done little or nothing to make the U.S. population aware of the hazards and what to do about them.

After a nuclear attack on American military facilities, fallout would descend upon the heavily populated sections of the nation in intensities and degrees according to the nature of the Soviet attack and the weather. Those without adequate shelter — and in some areas fairly close to the missile fields, notably in the midwest, the fallout intensity would almost be beyond sheltering at all — would die from radiation. Others would be sickened if not lethally injured, but few would be apt to know, at the time, into which category they and their families fell. The almost total absence of effective measuring instruments would be a major factor contributing to the damage done and the panic caused.

Because of the multitude of factors involved, casualty projections for a Soviet counterforce attack range very widely, anywhere from two million deaths at best to 22 million at worst. The higher figures generally assume that people had little or no warning and no more protection from fallout than that provided on average in daily life. The lowest estimates result from assumptions that the population has been evacuated, not just to another place, but to shelters capable of reducing fallout hazards to a 20th or less of what they would be without such sheltering. Even the seasonal winds have a profound influence on such casualty estimates. The two worst months for a Case Three attack would be March and November, when prevailing westerlies are at their strongest and would bring fallout from the missile fields rapidly eastward. July, December, and January would be the three "best" months, because the high-altitude winds are then generally at their calmest, and storms are apt to be more local. The average estimate of fatalities from a Soviet-first strike at American missile fields is 14 million.

For local areas near bomber and submarine bases, the issues are considerably more complex, because all such areas are endangered as much by the direct effects of nuclear weapons — blast and heat — as by later-arriving fallout. In these areas, evacuation might, indeed, be a better alternative than going to ground near home, provided that there was sufficient advance warning to allow for flight.

Another important factor is the degree to which the public could be educated about how to protect itself against fallout in the period before the hazard arrived. Fallout comes like a fine beach sand raining down from the skies. It is at its most intense at the time it is deposited, and its intensity diminishes fairly rapidly, provided that no new fallout is deposited by perverse winds in a given area.

Assuming no follow-up attacks after the initial assault upon military targets, the economic vitality of the nation would not be as threatened in this instance as it was in Case Two, the form of attack designed specifically to prolong economic hardship. In most areas, the required sheltering period would vary from a few days to a few weeks at most, and survivors would emerge to a landscape still hot by peacetime standards but not so radioactive as to present a lethal threat. Some areas, however, would clearly be more dangerous than others, depending on the idiosyncracies of fallout deposition. After the fact, public health standards would be much lower than in peacetime, and it would be virtually impossible to estimate the psychological impact on the population, for there is no previous experience of such kind on which to base any reasonable judgment. The closest approximation in our national history is perhaps the case of the suffering undergone by the South in the decades after the Civil War, which has not yet fully healed after more than a century.

More than anything else, Case Three points out the inadequacy of advanced planning the United States. That proper education of the public about fallout protection could conceivably reduce casualties from this form of nuclear attack, which is presumed to be the most likely type to occur, is a clear sign that our government and people have not given sufficient thought to the problem.

Case Four   Nuclear holocaust, all-out modern war between the super-powers.

This is the case that might threaten the entire planet. The presumption of all such studies is that both the U.S. and U.S.S.R. fire virtually all their nuclear missiles at each other and at other targets in the world, aiming a sizable percentage of the firepower at cities and people. For most such formal studies of this case, an assumption is that the weaponry would not necessarily be used in its entirety in the first hours or first days of war. In fact, given the ability of nuclear submarines to remain safe beneath the sea for prolonged periods of time, subsequent attacks on cities and surviving clusters of population might come months and perhaps even years after the outbreak of hostilities. Nothing in human experience remotely matches the remorseless consequences of this form of war.

To see how such a terrible course of events might develop, simply assume that war might start, after a period of visible international tension, with the economic kind of nuclear assault by a relatively small nuclear power upon one of the two nuclear giants. Badly damaged by this assault, the victim responds in kind against his attacker, obliterating the entire surface area of the perpetrator within days of the initial attack, despite clear warning from the other superpower that retaliation might mean all-out war. In the course of his reflexive retaliatory response against the smaller nation, an ally of the undamaged superpower, the original victim also fires an EMP demonstration above the territory of the opposite nuclear giant, to indicate the seriousness of the situation. The second giant nuclear power then launches what it understands to be a necessary pre-emptive attack upon the military forces of the original victim. The additional damage brings with it further escalation, over hours or days, weeks or months, until the entire planet is embroiled in the most stupendous event in human history. Such a war might conceivably take place in a matter of hours. More likely, however, it would develop more slowly and might continue for months, as each of the superpower's invulnerable submarines seek out surviving remnants of the other's population and infrastructure.

Virtually all formal studies of this full-scale kind of nuclear war admit to great uncertainties about its effects. The sheer size and horrible power of thousands of nuclear weapons fired upon the surface of the planet make it nearly impossible to predict the outcome with any accuracy. But new factors quickly emerge.

For one, the scope of the conflict would bring into question major long-term damage in genetic terms and from the possible depletion of critical portions of the earth's atmosphere, most notably the ozone layer. In the first instance, the most recent scientific evidence available appears to diminish the human risks of genetic damage, caused by radiation, from necessarily being transmitted to many future generations. Though there would still be cause for major concern about the issue, the latest available evidence seems to indicate that the so-called "doubling dose" of radiation required to cause genetic damage — the exposure level at which twice as many genetic mutations can be expected in a given population — is considerably higher than first feared. This now is estimated to be something more than 200 rems, a level not likely to be reached by a majority of the surviving population of the earth, even after nuclear holocaust. This estimate assumes that what is left of humankind would live in the southern hemisphere or in places far removed from major fallout hazards.

By contrast, concern for possible depletion of the ozone layer of the earth itself has increased in recent years. Estimates of this particular hazard have risen and fallen for the past two decades, as new scientific evidence has been developed, and each new assessment has seemed to contradict the last. The worrisome world-wide effect is presumed to be caused by multiple bursts of thermonuclear weapons, each of which could produce massive amounts of nitrogen oxide — akin to the smog caused by auto exhausts — and yet be powerful enough to inject these high into the earth's stratosphere, where their presence might serve to deplete the protective layer of ozone high in the earth's atmosphere. The ozone layer serves to absorb ultraviolet radiation from the sun, and any reduction in its thickness or density would allow more ultraviolet light to reach the surface of the planet, potentially causing major climactic changes on earth and creating conditions in which danger from a kind of profound "sunburn" might force entire populations to shun the daylight hours and become nocturnal. The potential effect on animals and crops as well as people is speculative, but the latest available indications are that ozone-layer depletion could conceivably prove a true hazard in the aftermath of a major nuclear war.

In 1975, the American National Academy of Sciences first formally called attention to possible reduction in the depth of the earth's ozone layer on the order of 30 to 70 percent in the wake of nuclear holocaust. Since then, further analyses leading to a better understanding of the complex chemistry governing the earth's upper atmosphere — the best direct evidence still comes from the results of the atmospheric H-bomb tests of two decades ago — have provided seemingly contradictory indications about the plausibility of this bizarre effect. To some scientists, the general reduction in the yield of modern weapons occasioned by the introduction of MIRVed weapons (each warhead is smaller, though there are more of them) has served to reduce the potential hazard of ozone layer depletion. But changes in the estimates for this particular effect are commonplace in current scientific thought, and the odds are that the judgment will change several more times as new evidence is developed.

Whatever the longer-term effects of a nuclear holocaust are on the ecosystem of the planet, the obvious truth is that any such major nuclear exchange would mean, for all practical purposes, the utter destruction of both the Soviet Union and the United States as working, organized societies. A major nuclear war might kill 160 million Americans in the first month after hostilities began, and the remainder, still subject to subsequent nuclear attack from Soviet submarine-launched missiles, would be injured and susceptible to all the consequences of the breakdown of modern life. Contemporary society, as we know it now, would literally cease to exist. The few remaining survivors, a year later, would be most apt to be widely scattered in little groups, organized in local fiefdoms, a small community here, another there. Man has no prior experience with such utter devastation on so vast a scale, and the contemplation of who ''won'' or who ''lost'' would be immersed in the awful daily problems of continued survival.

It would not necessarily happen swiftly. It could take years, and there would be no guarantee that those who might survive the earliest of the onslaughts would not again be brought under nuclear fire. The ultimate test of the wisdom of the human spirit, of the resilience of life itself, would begin on the second day of this new, man-made genesis. The awful fire would be momentarily visible, like the light from the stars themselves, throughout the emptiness of space, as if man's final message was one of denial. We are the only known possessors of that infinitely precious spark, the gift of life. To risk nuclear war is to risk the suppression of that eternal gift.

The rest of this book will be devoted to the region of New England, to the hills and the lovely country side I have known from birth, where my family and I live today. Hopefully, it will be a practical guide, something useful, even optimistic, something to keep the spark of life alive on earth, in my own tiny corner of eternity, no matter what circumstances man may one day bring down upon himself.

Sources

Much of the discussion in this chapter is based on Herman Kahn's *On Thermo-Nuclear War*, cited previously, and upon the author's private sources at such government think-tanks as the RAND Corporation and the Stanford Research Institute. The opening sections of the chapter, describing the events involved in the development of the first atom bombs, were derived from *City of Fire — Los Alamos and the Birth of the Atomic Age — 1943/1945*, an excellent review of the period by the son of one of the scientists present, James W. Kunetka (Prentice-Hall, Inc., publishers, Englewood Cliffs, New Jersey, 1978). There are many available references, in addition, to the peculiarities of plutonium-239 and plutonium-241 in declassified technical literature today. The descriptions of the first atom bombs are derived from government literature available at the historical museum now established at Los Alamos. The descriptions of the H-bomb are derived from widely published press photographs of the presumed thermonuclear weapons recovered from the bottom of the Mediterranean Sea after an aircraft accident over Palomares, Spain, in 1966.

The comments about the use of beryllium in the design of

nuclear weapons are based on the author's private sources at M.I.T. and the various national atomic research facilities, such as those at Oak Ridge, Tennessee, and Los Alamos. Material in this chapter about the presumed Soviet system of command and control are similarly based on the author's private sources, who must remain nameless in this case, at such facilities as the Stanford Research Institute and the Institute for Defense Analysis.

Some of the best material on limited nuclear war is available in testimony published by the Subcommittee on Arms Control, International Organizations and Security Agreements of the U.S. Senate Committee on Foreign Relations. Of particular interest is the public testimony incorporated in "Analysis of the Effects of Limited Nuclear War," available from the Government Printing Office, cited previously, in Washington. The material includes testimony by then-Secretary of Defense James R. Schlesinger before this Subcommittee on 11 September 1974, covering various aspects of counterforce-type attacks, such as the one cited in this chapter.

The comments about the doubling dose of radiation necessary to produce hereditary damage in future human generations and on the hypothetical effects of multiple nuclear detonations on the earth's ozone layer are taken from interviews by the author with various personnel connected with the National Academy of Sciences surveys of these subjects. Recommended to the reader here especially are the several reports of the Committee on the Biological Effects of Ionizing Radiation, known as the "BEIR Reports."

Of the various case studies of different kinds of nuclear war, the first, an EMP-demonstration attack, is solely the author's own, based on many conversations with government and private industry scientists and researchers.

The second case, that of an attack intentionally aimed at producing maximum economic damage, is derived from a study contracted for by the Congressional Office of Technology Assessment with the Sante Fe Corporation. The contractor's report, entitled "Small Attacks on U.S. and Soviet Energy Production and Distribution Systems," is separately available by writing the National Technical Information Service, U.S. Department of Commerce, 5285 Port Royal Road, Springfield, Virginia 22161. An additional source of material on this type of limited nuclear attack may be found in a paper by M.M. Stephens, "Vulnerability of Total Petroleum Systems," published by the Office of Oil and Gas, U.S. Department of the Interior, in 1973.

The third and fourth cases presented in Chapter Six, counterforce nuclear attacks and all-out nuclear war between the superpowers, have been the subject of literally hundreds of studies by various U.S. government agencies, from the Defense Civil Preparedness Agency of the U.S. Department of Defense to the numerous private firms contracted by the government to produce such studies. Of particular value here is the aforementioned testimony of Secretary Schlesinger before Congress in 1974.

These studies differ widely in their predictions of effects, recovery times, and total casualties, according to the assumptions used for each study. Studies useful for the development of Chapter Six that can be found in both classified and unclassified versions included "Examination of the Direct Effects of Nuclear War," (General Research Corporation, 1979) and "The Effects of Nuclear War: Economic Damage" (Analytical Assessment Corporation, 1978).

Several individual study papers from the Stanford Research Institute were also helpful in the development of Chapter Six. In particular, the following reports from this institution were used for background: "Analysis of National Entity Survival," (1967); "Critical Factors Affecting National Survival," (1965); and "Potential Vulnerabilities Affecting National Survival," (1970), which is useful for more detailed analysis of the asymmetries between the U.S. and U.S.S.R. All these papers were produced by R. Goen and colleagues. Another prolific technical writer on these subjects is W.M. Brown, whose work includes "Emergency Mobilization for Postattack Reorganization," (Hudson Institute, paper number HI-874/2, 1968).

Other studies recommended to the interested reader in these areas would include "Economic and Social Consequences of Nuclear Attacks on the United States," a report issued by the U.S. Senate Committee on Banking, Housing, and Urban Affairs (Government Printing Office, 1979); and "Industrial Survival and Recovery after Nuclear Attack: A Report to the Joint Committee On Defense Production," by T.K. Jones of the Boeing Company, Seattle, Washington, 1976. Mr. Jones, who now works for the Federal government, is the analyst whose public testimony that nuclear war is survivable has become the focus of public outcry by anti-nuclear activists in the United States in the early 1980s.

PART II

Surviving Nuclear War

7 New England Targets

And in those days men will seek death and will not find it; they will long to die, and death flies from them.

Revelations, Ch. 9 v. 6

To assess the risks you and those you care for face from the perils of nuclear war, you must first think strategically, in the manner of generals, admirals, and target planners. This is less difficult than it might seem, provided that you are willing, in the most cold-blooded and grisly fashion, to think of what *must* be done in any nuclear exchange, not what *may* be done.

TARGETING VARIABLES

From the outset, it is important to remember that limiting the potential damage to yourself — the power of modern nuclear weapons requires this — is the first goal. To protect your own people, you must strike first at the opponent's ability to wage war. Hence your first targets must be those that, if left unstruck, would present a clear and immediate danger to your own homeland. In practice, this means all those facilities, installations, and places that have the potential to strike back in the first minutes, hours, and days after the opening of hostilities. A target that represents a danger to your country and your people three years from now does not properly belong on your list of priority targets. It is not, as they say, "time sensitive." If you succeed in diminishing your enemy's power of response in the first few hours, then you will have the option of striking other places much later, at your leisure, or of holding them in a state of nuclear blackmail. After all, even in the nuclear era, it makes little sense for a conqueror to lay waste to and irradiate the conquered if anything useful belonging to the victims might otherwise be saved.

This brings about something of a quandary, even in a profligate age, when there would seem to be an abundance of nuclear firepower available, enough perhaps to make a target of virtually any location in your enemy's homeland. The question always comes down to how much is enough. If, for instance, you have a reserve of intercontinental rockets, but each of these rockets has only a 50/50 chance of hitting its target accurately enough to assure a kill, then you should plan to allocate more than one rocket to each target with the potential for nuclear retaliation. How many to allot for each such critical, time-sensitive target? If you aim two of your rockets at each critical target, and each missile has a 50 percent killing efficiency, then there is still one chance out of four that both rockets will miss. If you target four missiles for the same critical area, there is still a one-in-sixteen chance that all your weaponry will miss, and that the target may survive long enough to inflict considerable damage. It is an elusive chase, the pursuit of nuclear certainty.

In short, force allocation and targeting, even in an era when the inventory of firepower reaches into the many thousands of nuclear warheads, still depends mostly upon the target itself.

Now consider a particular region of the United States, such as New England. The six northeastern states that comprise the region, when taken together, present a coherent picture of rough, jumbled, hilly terrain. Except for a few places, the topsoil is thin and the underlying ground very rocky in nature. There is a relative abundance of water, but very few places where the terrain is flat for more than a mile in any direction. Seen from a satellite, the Vermont hills closely resemble the hillocky region of the Ardennes Forest in Luxembourg and Belgium where Hitler's Germany gave out its last aggressive spasms, during the Battle of the Bulge in World War II. New England is not good tank country because the terrain, despite the excellent road network, is best suited to defense, not offense. Except for the coastal plain, there is precious little flat ground. There are comparatively few military targets that require assault in the early rounds of any nuclear exchange. There are no oil refineries, no economic targets whose destruction might incapacitate the United States. There are, instead, colleges, woods, and hills; people in fair-sized cities and in small, white-steepled villages; a few ports and airbases; manufacturing and technology concerns that may be threatened later but require no immediate action on the part of an attacker who must be certain to husband his own resources carefully. It is almost, but not quite, possible to consider New England an area that may be bypassed in the opening stages of any nuclear war, left for later threat, or simply abandoned to its own devices, to wither away on the vine, so to speak, once a larger national destruction has been accomplished.

In terms of the four kinds of nuclear war outlined previously, New England is apt to be endangered no more, and perhaps less, than other regions within the United States.

In the first instance, a Soviet show of nuclear force employing the electromagnetic pulse phenomenon to signify its seriousness, the region would suffer no more and no less than any other general area in the United States.

In the second case, a Soviet economic attack on the United States with a specific focus on oil refining capacity, New England would directly suffer considerably less than other major areas of the nation. The same absence of oil refineries that makes the region vulnerable to ever-rising costs for the heating of winter homes, in this instance, would help keep it safe from the direct effects of modern nuclear weaponry.

True targets begin to appear in the New England region only when the third classic case of nuclear war is considered, a Soviet counterforce attack on United States military facilities. There are no missile silos in New England, which means that the region would not necessarily be targeted by the U.S.S.R. for the kind of salvo fire of nuclear rockets likely for the Minuteman fields of the western United States. But there are military targets in the New England region, if somewhat fewer today than there were two decades ago. And there are other targets as well, communications nerve centers, State capitals, all of which might come under the nuclear gun at some point, but in a series of gradations of relative strategic importance so fine that it does not directly correspond to the classic case studies of nuclear warfare.

The following pages present a list of the "most likely" targets in New England, from the point of view of a Soviet target planner. The targets are presented in order of relative priority to the Soviet Union, though the list is not likely to coincide with prevailing conventional wisdom. Cities and concentrations of people are listed, but not given critical priority, for the reasons cited above. They can, after all, always be hit later. In this sense, the Massachusetts Institute of Technology might be considered a target, for its ability to concentrate technical brainpower, but the school poses no threat to the U.S.S.R. in the first days, weeks, or months of war.

The judgments expressed here are based on numerous sources of information, including some ostensibly classified material rarely discussed openly in public. There is disagreement, of course, even among planners. The target groupings are organized into various categories, according to the certainty that they would be hit in any nuclear war. The list is not at all what the general public and the daily press think, for places that would seem safe are, in fact, deadly dangerous today, and others that would seem primary targets are comparatively safe.

At least for a little while.

PRIMARY TARGETS

All of the target areas listed in this category are military in nature, and in some the work is highly classified. The location of one of them cannot, for reasons of national security, be given precisely.

1. The U.S. Air Force Pave/Paws radar station on Cape Cod, Massachusetts.

Why: Because it is one of three major coastal radar sites in the U.S., all of them devoted to detecting and tracking missiles coming in from the sea after launch by ships or submarines. There is one site in California to cover the Pacific and its coast. There is another in Florida, to cover the Caribbean. The third is just east of the Cape Cod Canal. Its job is to cover the entire Atlantic, from Greenland to the Carolina Capes and beyond. Its radars are very powerful, and it is the subject of local environmental debate for that reason. It is, however, an instrument of national policy, and so the environmentalists are quickly put down. To the Soviet Union, the reduction of this site to rubble would mean a grave lessening of U.S. capabilities to track down Soviet submarines in the Atlantic, to provide warning of probable impact areas for incoming sea-launched missiles, and to determine the precise nature of any Soviet attack on the U.S. East Coast. Nobody will ever tell you very much about this Air Force facility, which does not have an official name per se. If you enlist, a USAF recruiting sergeant cannot guarantee that you could be stationed there, because, in theory, he does not know the place exists. All personnel are specialists who are carefully screened. There is no attainable phone number for the installation. Mail is received at a post office box in a nearby town. The radars are large and their construction is robust. But, by the nature of their job, they must be sited above ground, which makes them relatively vulnerable to nuclear assault.

How: By clandestine assault, by a missile fired from very close in, probably by "fishing vessel" or submarine, or by land-based missile coming in over northern Greenland. The last is the poorest Soviet choice, since the attacking rocket would likely be spotted by the U.S. ballistic-missile-early-warning radar at Thule, Greenland; until that radar itself was hit. The weapon is likely to be of one to five megatons in yield, depending on the type of launcher. This target is sufficiently important to justify the use of more than one warhead.

Targeting strategy: Probably an airburst below 5,000 feet in altitude, to maximize the air over-pressure in a small area below the fireball. Second and/or third incomers would likely be groundburst, to pulverize the rubble.

One targeting attraction from the Soviet point of view is the presence nearby of the Cape Cod Canal, whose destruction would impair some coastal traffic and add a dollop of economic damage. There is also a nuclear power plant at Plymouth, Massachusetts, less than 25 miles away as the neutron flies. That is okay, from the standpoint of a Russian targeter; but, despite public opinion to the contrary, nuclear power plants are not necessarily top-priority targets. Such plants are usually chock full to the very brim with all sorts of nasty and very long-lived radioactive poisons, but the facilities themselves are small targets, hard to hit, and usually quite hard. To destroy one, the Soviets would probably try to vaporize it with a groundburst, but this is still a waste of first-round weaponry. With nuclear warheads, you are apt to do more damage with the weapons themselves, despite the relatively short-lived nature of the resulting radioactivity compared to the long-lived radioactive waste that might be scattered in a breech of the protective containment of a nuclear power plant. In modern strategic thinking, you don't aim at a nuclear plant in the first half hour, though it is fine if you happen to notch one up in the course of other destructive work. The only advantage is that the long-lived isotopes in the power plant, once let loose, might tend to make the local area literally unusable for a few centuries, compared to a few years.

2. Nantucket Island, Massachusetts.

Why: Although few know it, this pristine vacation area happens also to be the site of a secret U.S. Navy communications facility that allows contact with deep-running atomic submarines throughout the Atlantic. Water, of course, obliterates normal radio waves, and so such submerged vessels — both hunter/killers that would be engaged in anti-Soviet-submarine work and missile carriers — must be reached by means of extremely low-frequency signals sent forth by specialized equipment. For some years, the Navy has had a proposal to modernize the submarine communications system by wiring up a large portion of the bedrock of the State of Wisconsin and thus making its key communications links harder to hit. Local opposition in the midwestern state and resistance from Congress have kept the Navy proposal on the shelf for a decade, however. As a result, as it has in the past, Nantucket will just have to do. The circumstances of this facility are similar to those of the USAF radar installation on Cape Cod. In theory, the place does not exist, but it would be an early target to reduce U.S. combat capabilities throughout the North Atlantic.

How: Nantucket is an island and it does not move, which gives a strategist all sorts of attack options. A sea-launched missile is the probable choice, particularly if launched from close-in to minimize warning time. People who live there will have less than 10 minutes warning, at best.

Targeting Strategy: Important enough target for more than one incoming weapon. A series of groundbursts on the island is likely.

3. ''Cutler's/Hunter's'' Island, off the coast of Maine.

Why: More secret than the first two top-priority targets in New England, it is sometimes called ''Cutler's Island,'' and sometimes ''Hunter's Island,'' depending on the source. Little is known about it. Its precise location cannot be given. Its job is to send the go-code for a nuclear attack by American submarines upon the U.S.S.R. It does this via both radio to aircraft and an extremely long wavelength signal directly through the ocean.

In this way, this site is more specialized than Nantucket. The communications gear is run by the Navy and tends toward more specialized versions of the extra-low-frequency submarine system. Nantucket handles both routine and war-measure communications, down to and including daily housekeeping and message traffic. The Maine facility tells American submarines when to go to war and destroy Moscow. There are satellite hook-ups and secure communications with what we Americans called the "National Command Authorities," who might be deep underground or high in the air.

How: Again, the island nature of the place makes it vulnerable to close-in missile launch, with little or no warning. Groundbursts would be preferred, but follow-up airbursts might help. The launcher might be a submarine, an aircraft ostensibly on the routine patrol route from Moscow to Havana, something that looks like a fishing or research vessel, or a small canoe with a computer-guided weapon.

Targeting Strategy: This might be one of the highest priority targets on the North American continent. Then again, it might prove to be one of the safest places on earth, at least for the first few hours or days of any nuclear conflict. It all depends on what you think the American system for command and control of missile-launching submarines is, as classified a subject as there is in modern American life. The set-up is known to be far more flexible than its Soviet counterpart in the freedom of final action given to the sub commander. But what authorizes a launch on Russia? Does such a communications station, charged with the responsibility of emitting the war signal, stay silent entirely until the time comes? Or, instead, should it send out a constant signal composed of certain components measurable by the submarine's electronic gear? If the signal and all its components are there, then we are at peace, and the nuclear warheads aboard the sub remain locked up electronically. But should the signal suddenly cease, or some component of it change, then that alone is the signal for release of weapons. If the latter is the case — and the Soviets would dearly love to know — then there is every chance that they would avoid hitting this Maine island like the plague, for deep-running American submarines might thus not know for hours or days that the nation had been attacked and that it was time, in turn, to attack the U.S.S.R.

Cutler's/Hunter's Island is the best spot in New England for a commando raid rather than a nuclear assault. Should it be seized by an enemy at the start of a war, at least one analyst suggests, it might then become a target for an *American* missile, to ensure that U.S. retaliation begins.

4. The entire vicinity around Loring Air Force Base, near Presque Isle, Maine.

Why: Because Loring is the home of a B-52 bomber wing of the U.S. Strategic Air Command. Given advanced Soviet air defenses in the 1980s, these aging aircraft from Maine might find it difficult to penetrate Russian air space, but the current U.S. plan is to equip them with stand-off missiles that may be fired at the target from hundreds of miles away.

Some bombers are kept in the air at all times, the number depending on the alert status of U.S. forces, but this is an expensive way to run an air force, and the majority of the planes are usually on the ground. This is an important point for the U.S.S.R. because it is far easier to destroy aircraft still on the ground, or just after take off, than by interception over Soviet air space. Hence Loring, and all such U.S. bases, are time-sensitive targets, which fall higher on the target priority list.

How: A relatively low altitude, high-yield airburst over the base to cause damage, perhaps a groundburst to vaporize runways and facilities, and a series of airbursts in a fan-shaped pattern running 50 to 100 miles from the base, from northwest to northeast. The airbursts closest to the base, from five to 10 miles, will be detonated anywhere from 6,000 to 10,000 feet, to catch bombers climbing to their operating altitudes. Those airbursts farther away will be set higher. Anyone living within this fan-shaped area is in imminent danger from the direct effects of the weaponry, from the moment of the attack. A major intercontinental bomber base today can count on being targeted for three to 12 warheads or more, which makes a vast area north of Loring very dangerous. If the attacker is profligate in the use of his weapons, then the airbursts may be extended in a full circle of 50 to 100 miles in radius, in all directions from the base. Should any of the base remain operational despite the onslaught, the immediate vicinity can count upon being targeted for a subsequent groundburst to finish the job, and this may happen days, weeks, or months after the outbreak of war.

Targeting Strategy: One of the more spectacular forms of nuclear attack. To disrupt a bomber stream, you attack the base itself and simultaneously set off a series of airbursts in a fan-shaped area extending outward from the base along the escape lanes the bombers would fly. At a bet, the Soviets have long since studied the departure lanes for Loring B-52s bound for the far north.

Loring is close enough to the coast to suggest that the optimum attack would be from a Soviet submarine in the Gulf of Maine. Land-based missiles, arcing in over the North Pole, take half an hour to reach Loring. Sea-launched missiles would arrive over Presque Isle within 10 minutes at most, minimizing warning time and making it easier to time the opening sequence of any Soviet attack with utmost precision.

In June, you could attack at any time of day, since the sun never really sets at latitude 70 degrees north, where your fighters might first be able to engage incoming B-52s. Winter is different. Moscow, for instance, does not reach full daylight during Christmas week in December until after nine in the morning. In the earliest interception areas, still farther north, the sun may not rise until 10:30, and it will set by one in the afternoon. At this time of year, you must time your attack precisely to give yourself maximum tactical advantage.

Loring AFB is a little more than 4,000 miles from Moscow. A B-52 bomber cruises at approximately 500-550 miles per hour. It may take retaliation-bound B-52s from American bases like Loring up to six hours flight-time to reach the first interception zones in the far north. As a Soviet planner, you will wish this arrival to coincide with the rising of the sun at roughly 70 degrees north latitude, which means 10:30 A.M. To reach that point at that time, the bombers should have taken to the air at four or five in the morning, Moscow time. Moscow time is eight hours ahead of Loring AFB, meaning that the B-52s should have been forced into the air just after dusk the previous day, Maine time.

For the vicinity of Loring AFB, the month of June could bring attack at any time of day, but the window of optimum timing narrows considerably at all other seasons of the year. If you were a Soviet general, you would plan to hit Loring just after dusk, for instance, Loring time, if you wished to attack at Christmas, when the days are very short. In fact, you would be apt to hit Loring at that season between 8:30 and 10 in the evening, U.S. time. On a clear Christmas night, with much snow on the ground, the spectacular display of airbursts involved in any Soviet attack on Loring AFB might be visible as far south as Portland, at mid-evening.

5. The entire area around Pease AFB in New Hampshire and for 100 miles north.

Why: Because Pease is an operational base serving FB-111 bombers, which can fly at twice the speed of sound and potentially carry nuclear weapons over the U.S.S.R. Designed as fighters in the McNamara era, these rugged planes have now become medium bombers. Officially speaking, Pease is to serve as a possible staging base through which F-111s could be funneled to Great Britain to help repel any Soviet land assault upon western Europe. The range of the planes makes them dangerous to the U.S.S.R. directly, however, and their speed extends the required fan-shaped area of airbursts designed to knock down escaping aircraft to a full 100 miles, enough to cover most of the population centers of southern Maine.

How: Three more missiles from the same submarine targeted upon Loring, in the first moments of a counterforce attack. If Loring is hit, Pease will be, too, at the same time. You either get such speedy aircraft quickly, or not at all.

6. Other primary targets that could affect the New England region.

Two major U.S. bases in upstate New York, one at Griffiss AFB near Rome, (location of the only operational B-52 cruise-equipped wing) and the other at Plattsburg, west of Lake Champlain, are in the military time-sensitive category but would pose no immediate threat to New England from blast, fire, and heat. But their destruction in the early stages of a nuclear war would add some radioactive salt to the national wound in the New England region because the prevailing winds would bring their nuclear detritus down as fallout upon the heads of New Englanders anywhere from three hours to a day after the initial Soviet attack.

In addition, there is continuing rumor, unconfirmable through official channels, of the existence of a Federal shelter for the National Command Authorities somewhere in the foothills of the Berkshires, in the area of Massachusetts that lies west of the Connecticut River. The precise location of this site, which is said to serve as a back-up evacuation point for high Federal officials and to assist in the maintenance of national and state communications in the event of nuclear war, cannot be determined here.

In theory, the President, if he were to survive, might go to this place at some point after the initial Soviet assault, to proceed with the war. If it exists, the site will be known by local rumor, but it will be a major target for any attacker. The area would otherwise be comparatively free of immediate danger. The Soviets are apt to know more about this place than the American people do.

SECONDARY TARGETS

These targets include non-operational military bases and centers of population. Any direct assault upon them implies an ever-widening nuclear war.

To nuclear strategists, the idea of modern war means that nations will fight largely with stocks and inventories on hand. Although both the U.S. and U.S.S.R. organized their industries and made massive quantities of new war materiel over several years during World War II, a working assumption is that hitting factories and industries will prove less important for the early stages of any nuclear war.

In addition, because most major industries in both countries are located near large centers of population, there is the spectre that attacks on background, non-military areas would produce so many casualties as to compel the attacked side, in turn, to assault the opponent's population. Casualties will rise into the many millions. The largest human catastrophe in history will be near at hand.

If any of the New England targets listed below is ever hit, then the war has grown much more intense, and Armageddon approaches. There will be far fewer survivors in this situation, all-out war.

1. The area around Westover AFB in Chicopee, Massachusetts.

Why: This is the base that served as the model for the hypothetical nuclear attacks described in Part I. Once a proud facility that housed the headquarters of the U.S. 8th Air Force, of World War II fame, the base was shorn of this title, and its wing of B-52 bombers, in Nixon's time. The runways are still just as long as they ever were, though, and capable of handling large aircraft. There are specialized equipment, nuclear weapons dumps and arming pits, secure communications gear. The U.S. government maintains the base and its gear in reasonable shape. With a smart war-response plan, Westover might become fully operational within 24 hours after the outbreak of hostilities. That is the danger to the area.

How: This depends primarily on when the base was hit. If immediately, or at the same time as the operational facility at Loring, the job could probably be done with a single ground or low-level airburst, something big enough to crater the runways. If hit later, when bombers might be operating from it, the pattern of warheads would resemble that of Loring AFB in Maine, combining ground and airbursts to knock down aircraft in the entire area. The latter type of attack would endanger, immediately, populations still in the region as far south as Hartford, Connecticut, and as far east as Worcester, Massachusetts.

Targeting strategy: If Westover is a top Soviet target priority, it will get hit in the first assault upon the nation, and the very same Soviet submarine in the Gulf of Maine could do the job neatly. If the attack comes later, within a day or a week of the outbreak of war, Westover will be in danger from a Soviet missile from over the North Pole or, still later, from aircraft.

An added attraction to the Soviet targeter is one of New England's largest hydroelectric facilities, located in Holyoke on the Connecticut River. Further, the presence nearby of a highly concentrated civilian population, well over a million people, could lead to many casualties if that is the Soviet objective.

On the other hand, in an attack limited to military targets, the presence of large numbers of civilians may serve to make the Russians think twice about hitting Westover.

Of special note is the fact that Westover may, as a result of this unique situation, be a bellweather of Soviet intentions. If it goes early in a war, say within the first day, then the war is very serious, for the Russians are willing to cause huge casualties to make their point.

2. The vicinity of New London, Connecticut.

Why: This was once home base for American nuclear-missile-firing submarines assigned to the Atlantic. This honor has been moved south to Charleston, South Carolina, for political reasons, and to get farther away from incoming land-based missiles. The area still contains excellent submarine facilities and could well serve as a temporary refuge for American Poseidon subs. This makes it a target, though not necessarily a high priority. Like Westover, the presence of throngs of civilians nearby might give the Soviets some pause, unless they were willing to cause massive casualties from the outset.

When: Not as quickly as Westover, or top-priority military targets in New England, but probably within a week or a month or more.

How: Sea-launched missile or any of the early-generation Soviet land-based rockets that might have survived American counterstrikes. Neither type of launcher is extremely accurate, and so there is a chance that this area could get hit once or several times later, at intervals, if the first few shots do not finish the job.

Targeting Strategy: The base contains equipment fairly hard to destroy, so likely a groundburst, in an attempt to vaporize the installation. If the war goes on long enough, and the Soviets miss New London at first, they will probably try again and again. If, conversely, New London goes very early, within the first day or two, then the Soviet attack is massive and without conscience.

3. Boston, Framingham, and South Weymouth, Massachusetts.

Why: The main target is a major U.S. population center, state capital, communications center; a road, rail and shipping point; one of the very essential nerve centers of American society. A strike here means every city in the nation is at stake, as is the rest of the world.

At Framingham, roughly 30 miles due west of Boston, there is a hardened, blast-resistant bunker designed to house up to 300 high officials, who might attempt to keep some semblance of regional order in the event of nuclear attack.

At South Weymouth there is a major airbase used for anti-submarine warfare work.

There are more than three million people in this small area.

How: To kill a city, which is a soft but sprawling target, detonations are set for airbursts at roughly 6,000 to 8,000 feet, maximizing the range of air overpressures that destroy buildings. For Boston, a predictable pattern might be two or three thermonuclear warheads of about a megaton and a half apiece, probably from Soviet SS-19 or SS-11 missiles, if the event occurs in the early 1980s. Sea-launched missiles could also do the job, especially from subs at sea a week, a month, or more after the beginning of hostilities. Boston will be targeted at the intersection of, say, the Massachusetts Turnpike and Route I-95/128. A second warhead would be appropriate, aimed at the inner harbor area of the city marked by, say, the intersection of the Expressway and the Sumner/Callahan Tunnels downtown. Road intersections are convenient aiming points from half a world away because they are readily discernible and easily mapped with great accuracy by satellite reconnaissance.

Framingham, with its hardened bunker, would suffer a groundburst aimed at the intersection of state Routes 9 and 126.

South Weymouth would buy its nuclear farm differently. A cluster of four warheads in the nosecone of a newer SS-17 Soviet missile, each with 600 kilotons of power, would be aimed at the town and the adjoining Naval Air Station. One or two would groundburst, the others atop the missile set for airburst to approximate the effect created by nuclear weapons over bomber bases.

Targeting Strategy: The matter is more a question of nuclear geopolitics than of military necessity. Boston would not likely be hit at the outset, despite the large local populace. But, if the war continued into the meaner levels of human nature, it might be devastated an hour, a day, a week, a month, or as much as several years after the war began.

4. Barnes Airfield, Westfield, Massachusetts.

Why: A potential fighter base and staging area for combat aircraft headed for Europe. It would be hit in the later rounds of any nuclear exchange, to eliminate its possible utility as an interceptor base against Soviet bombers.

How: Sub-megaton class in a cluster from a Soviet SS-17, one set to go off at ground level at Barnes. Possibly, depending upon when in the 1980s or 1990s, a 1.5 megaton warhead from an SS-11 arcing in over the north polar cap of the earth from Siberia. The aiming point is the intersection of the Massachusetts Turnpike (Exit Four) and state highway 10.

5. Otis Airbase, Cape Cod, Massachusetts.

This assumes that this facility survived the early assault on the nearby Pave/Paws early-warning radar station.

Why: Because Otis is the only operational fighter-interceptor base in the New England region. Its elimination would allow Soviet manned aircraft to penetrate at will, scouting for unhit targets, in the later stages of a war.

How: The same formula as for Barnes Airfield.

6. The area around Hartford, Connecticut.

Why: A state capital, major transportation intersection, and near to a civilian airport (Bradley Field in nearby Wethersfield) that has runways long enough to service the largest jet aircraft in the world. If you target Hartford, you risk causing many deaths, but gain the chance to wipe out crucial jet engine factories, just in case the war turns out to be a long one.

How: Hartford is a small city with a core of concrete, heavily reinforced buildings occupying a small downtown area. The city rises out of the Connecticut River flood plain, in a wide valley rimmed by distant hills. The Soviet weapon of choice available to it in its, say, 1985 nuclear arsenal would be a one to 1.5 megaton thermonuclear warhead, detonated about 6,000 feet over the intersection of Interstates 84 and 91, just to the west of the Connecticut River. The flatness of the immediate surroundings would seem to indicate that flash and thermal effects would be widely spread in the wooden framed suburban dwellings.

Targeting Strategy: Hartford is close enough to the sea to be within range of a submarine missile. It can be gotten to, if an attack comes during earlier stages of any war, by means of a land-based Soviet missile from Asia, if necessary. Hartford can also be attacked by manned aircraft at any later, mop-up stage of a prolonged nuclear war. There is no real hurry, and an attack here will cause grave harm while accomplishing nothing much more, necessarily, than re-routing the course of the Connecticut River for the rest of history.

7. The area of Providence and the State of Rhode Island.

Why: Because it is a state capital, whose destruction would degrade America's system of government, and because the home state is so small that an attack on its nerve center will instantly paralyze, or harm, almost everyone else in the state. There is a waggish argument about the presumed need for the use of another weapon on nearby Newport, the site of the graduate Naval War College in the U.S. Among some U.S. admirals, there is the belief that the Soviets might save the war college intentionally, so that the U.S. can continue to breed the kind of admiral that got us into all the trouble in the first place.

How: There is no reason for the Soviets to target Providence, short of some desire on their part to kill people for the sake of killing. This is apt to happen only if the war is prolonged, with the attack coming perhaps weeks or months after the war has begun.

Targeting Strategy: Airburst, at about 6,000 to 8,000 feet over the point where Interstate I-195 branches eastward from I-95. The intersection makes a handy, visible target. If Providence ever goes, it will likely go late. The agent of its execution might even be a Soviet Bear bomber, ostensibly flying back toward Russia from Havana, approaching Narragansett Bay unexpectedly from the south.

8, 9, and 10. Concord, New Hampshire; Augusta, Maine; and Montpelier, Vermont.

Why: State Capitals.

Because all these places are state capitals, their destruction, by whatever means, would eradicate the best-organized local authority, contribute to panic and disruption.

How: At the pick and choose of the nuclear assailant. One bomb each, airburst, will accomplish the task, even by airplane.

11. The area of Bangor, Maine.

Why: Because of the former Dow AFB, a former Strategic Air Command base with runways long enough to handle heavy jet bombers. Unlike the Westover case in Massachusetts, the military capability of the former Dow AFB has been left to rust. So Bangor becomes a target, just in case. Presuming the prior destruction of Loring, Pease, and Westover, and the big civil runways near Boston, Hartford, and Providence, the former Dow runways are all that is left in New England.

How: With or after all the other long runways in the region. A single, heavy groundburst near the base, probably from a plane.

TERTIARY TARGETS

The Soviet Union still has, and will probably continue to deploy, 330 or so SS-11, second generation land-based missiles. They are slow to send on their way, since they are liquid-fueled. They cannot carry more than one warhead in their nosecone. The single warhead atop each will average a yield of 1.5 megatons. The SS-11s are not especially accurate, as modern missiles go, and, like the American Titan missiles, their volatile fuels may pose some danger for their handlers and for the area immediately surrounding the silos.

The Soviet SS-11s are generally accurate to within a mile or so of their targets at intercontinental ranges, which is sufficient to assure the destruction of small cities, villages and towns, or other congested areas. Assuming that the American counter-blows did not degrade the

Soviet SS-11's capabilities, the U.S.S.R. would have the capacity in these missiles themselves — not to mention any remaining nuclear submarines or SS-16s kept dismantled in storage — to target virtually every village and town in New England with a population above 25-30,000. Many such places might have been hit much earlier in any nuclear war or been damaged from strikes at more significant targets nearby. Subsequent attacks on such areas might come weeks, months, or even years after the war began, for a war between the United States and the Soviet Union that reaches so deep as to threaten small towns directly has long since grown past the point of nuclear holocaust for the planet. A complete list of these targets is too long to print. Some of the more important targets are listed below.

1. Worcester, Massachusetts. People. The free world's largest and most powerful forging press in nearby Grafton. Factories. More punishment.

2. New Haven, Connecticut. People again. Yale? An airburst or three.

3. Bridgeport, Stamford, Waterbury, the whole of the southern Connecticut shoreline. Still more people, including some fleeing from New York. A dozen or two airbursts, long after the war starts.

4. Springfield, Massachusetts. To break the road network further. To kill people. An airburst some time after the destruction of Westover AFB not far away. This is something of a matter of pounding the rubble.

5. Portland, Maine. A port. Even an atomic torpedo would do it for the major facilities downtown.

6. Lexington, Wayland, Sudbury, and Bedford, Massachusetts. Already damaged by proximity to Boston. For involvement in missile manufacture. Series of airbursts.

7. Portsmouth, New Hampshire. Small Navy base.

8. Bath, Maine. A destroyer-construction town, but possible Navy port.

9. Nashua, New Hampshire, Some defense-industry knowledge. People again. Late in the game, this area, plus Lowell, Lawrence, and Andover, Massachusetts; and anything that might be left of southern New Hampshire; and southern Maine. The FAA radar and control station in this area has some possible military utility for the U.S.

SAFEST PLACES IN NEW ENGLAND

This category consists of all places in the region that are more than 250 miles, straight-line distance, upwind, from all the other places mentioned above. There are essentially no such places anywhere in the region. A few places might be spared direct, immediate damage from the prompt effects of modern nuclear weaponry in as small a region as New England, but they would owe their continued existence strictly to mistakes and errors made in the course of the attack(s) — a missile gone off target, a warhead that does not detonate — and the pattern of their distribution would be impossible to predict in advance. The only general hope is that the war would have been brought to some sensible conclusion long before this ultimate level of hostilities had been reached.

Sources

The list of New England targets, and the priority in which they might be struck by the Soviet Union, is strictly the opinion of the author. Information used to compile it was derived from extensive interviews with professional personnel formerly connected with the Navy Department, the Office of the Secretary of the Air Force, and officers of the U.S. Air Force Strategic Air Command. Additional material was suggested by analysts and consultants for the Federal Emergency Management Agency (FEMA).

The priority in which the presumed targets are listed follows, accordingly, the most common analytical assumptions on the likelihood of nuclear war in various forms. For example, because counterforce attacks aimed at degrading the nation's retaliatory capabilities are widely assumed to be the "least irrational" form of nuclear war, military targets in the region, especially those with a counter-attack potential, are ranked first in priority. Those specific areas that are considered time-sensitive in the military sense (that is, they give warning of impending attack or launch immediate counter-attack) have received highest priority. Estimates for the presumed method of attack for each target and for the time of day that would be optimum from the Soviet point of view are strictly the author's own.

The listing of Nantucket Island high on the list is at the suggestion of Federal Emergency Management Agency personnel. By contrast, ''Cutler's/Hunter's Island'' off the coast of Maine has occasionally received a minor spate of local publicity, but the facility is scheduled to be replaced in the course of the U.S. Navy's progress with its ''Project Sanguine.'' This particular project, hotly debated since the late 1960s, involves a Navy proposal to arrange extra-low frequency communications with its submarines by way of wiring a substantial portion of the bedrock underlying the state of Wisconsin to generate the required pulses. The project is strongly opposed in the Wisconsin area, but is currently scheduled for completion in the mid-1980s, after which the character of the New England targets would presumably change.

In reviewing the manuscript, several people have questioned the author's omission of specific areas encompassing valuable national resources, such as certain industrial facilities at various points throughout New England and the high-technology brain-trust to be found in the Route 128 area in the suburbs ringing Boston to the westward. While these contentions might certainly have some validity in Soviet thinking, the obvious truth is that such areas would not represent an immediate threat of prompt retaliation to any attacker, but could be called into play by the U.S. only after a considerable period of wartime mobilization of resources. In addition, the areas in question also lie quite close to other targets apt to be on any list of the Soviet Union in the first place and would, therefore, likely suffer considerable destruction in the event of war.

New England is, after all, a regrettably small place.

8 Nuclear Survival

What a piece of work is man! How noble in reason! How infinite in faculty! in form and moving how express and admirable! in action how like an angel! in apprehension how like a god! the beauty of the world! the paragon of animals! And yet, to me, what is this quintessence of dust?

William Shakespeare, *Hamlet*

The conventional wisdom in the United States today, nearly made into a code by the recently renewed public interest in nuclear war, is that any use whatever of nuclear weapons must inevitably lead to the virtual incineration of the earth and the inevitable extinction of all life on the planet. This may or may not be true. Most likely it is not. Yet no one can be certain, for there is simply no experience on which to base judgment. Hopefully, there never will be.

SURVIVAL VARIABLES

In far more practical terms, the likelihood for survival of any individual or group caught in near proximity to a modern nuclear weapon is determined by a number of factors, not least of which are the physics of the event and human nature. Advance warning, technical knowledge, level of preparation, ability to apply training to the situation at hand, distance from the explosion, the interval of time between the blast and the moment of maximum exposure — all these factors act as major determinants of survival. A well-trained and knowledgeable person trapped at ground zero at the time of the burst will be incinerated, will literally cease to exist, in the billionths of a second required for atoms to form the fireball of a small new star. The same person caught ten miles from ground zero at that same moment has almost infinitely better chances of staying alive. Even the exact position of the victim's body can make a difference, as it did at Hiroshima and Nagasaki.

As a rule, the most direct effects of nuclear weapons — the blast and searing heat — pose the gravest danger, and rapidly diminish with distance in an inverse ratio. Simply stated, this means that if you are twice as far away from the explosion, your chances of living through it go up by a factor of four. In the nuclear age, time and distance provide the major safety factors, for a nuclear explosion strongly resembles an awesome natural disaster, but one that spreads outward from an epicenter. Those caught at the focal point will die instantly. Those farther away may survive, with the prospects for survival increasing with the distance from ground zero.

Complicating factors are the amount of advance warning and the knowledgeability of the probable victims. The second factor weighs heavily against the population of the United States today, because our culture tends to over-simplify complex phenomena and reduce them to terms that may be fathomed with an absolute minimum of effort. A good estimate is that the citizenry of many other nations, including the Soviet Union, China, Switzerland, and Sweden, are better trained, more knowledgeable, and more realistic-of-assumption than we Americans. Our national unwillingness to face facts may be related in some obscure way to our sense of authorship for the troubles facing the world. It is not, however, likely to stand us in good national stead in the event of any future nuclear emergency.

Those whose profession it is to study the amount of advance warning possible in the event of nuclear war seem to agree universally that nuclear weapons are today so powerful that no one but the ultimate madman would cause their use without an incentive built up over time. To most contemporary strategic analysts, therefore, a nuclear war is most likely to develop over a considerable period of time, rather than a sudden spasm, a final paroxysm of human history on earth. The assumption for most formal studies is that a nuclear exchange between the superpowers is most likely to take place only after a prolonged period of palpable international tension. The average American who watches television, listens to the radio, or is exposed to the newspapers could not easily escape noticing the trend of the news. The early warning would prove very useful, provided that people knew what to do.

That the American public does not, in fact, know what to do in the event of a national nuclear emergency is the fault of the government, which has seen fit to avoid frightening the populace at the risk of creating much worse circumstances should the awful events ever occur. No greater bureaucratic malfeasance has ever been perpetrated upon the American public, for no other in U.S. history has had the potential for as much human harm. This chapter is an attempt to rectify that situation, in part.

SURVIVING IMMEDIATE EFFECTS

The greatest danger posed by nuclear weapons to the average individual in the United States today comes from the immediate effects, the blast and heat released at the moment of detonation. If you are trapped in the fireball, which subtends as much as two miles from ground zero, you will die immediately. If you are within, say, five miles of the focal point, your chances of surviving the mechanical injuries caused by blast are not good. If you are within 12 to 15 miles of ground zero, and you remain exposed throughout the thermal pulse, you risk life-threatening burns. These factors lie at the root of the often laughable government plan to evacuate large cities in the event of genuine nuclear threat. As unworkable as such plans might seem, the giant Federal computers insist their implementaion at the time of impending war might save millions of Americans.

The second set of hazards that occur after a nuclear blast are fire and fallout. The amount of time that might pass before these factors become significant is contingent upon a host of variables, such as distance from the blast, the characteristics of the weapon itself, and the weather in the immediate vicinity. Still, it is impossible to combat fire and fallout unless you have survived the effects of blast and heat. Even in the hostile environment of a nuclear war, first things must still come first.

In essence, this means that the first rule for assessing the best course of action is to determine the average distance from the individual to the target in question. If you live and work, for instance, anywhere within 25 miles of one of the top two categories of U.S. targets outlined in the last chapter, the basic decision you will face in the event of the outbreak of nuclear hostilities is whether to stay or to flee. *Your decision should be influenced by the amount of warning you may receive before the onslaught begins.*

For those who live within 10 miles of a time-sensitive military target, the distance should be measured, as a straight line from the core of the facility (a mile or two, either way, makes little difference in terms of planning). If you, like most Americans today, believe that population centers would be hit swiftly in a nuclear war, then you should measure the distances involved from the point of intersection of two or more major highways. Examples would be the intersection of Routes 93 and I-87 in the vicinity of Concord, New Hampshire, interstate I-95 and I-90 in the suburbs west of Boston, or the junction of I-91 and I-95 at New Haven. Modern nuclear weapons fired at such points will destroy the general area around these junctions, and the intersections themselves are handy for strategic planners because they do not move and can be located to within a few feet's accuracy with modern technology. A good map of your area can provide help in making any such assessment.

Those who live within five nautical miles — slightly longer than conventional, statute miles — of major targets do so at high risk from any nuclear weapon accurately detonated upon the presumed target. (A necessary assumption for such planning is that an enemy's weapons would, in fact, work as they were designed to do; if the weaponry misfires or becomes inaccurate in the heat of battle, it becomes impossible to estimate the variables.)

An essential consideration in assessing the hazards nuclear war presents to you and yours is to remember that people do not stay in one place throughout the average American's day. Children go to school, parents travel to work, sometimes over distances much greater than the radii of nuclear weapons effects. To come to a reliable assessment that fits you and your family, you must consider all such factors in your personal equations.

The chance that those who live within an area of five to 10 miles from ground zero will be killed in the first instant of a nuclear blast fall sharply, according to the distance involved, to approximately 50 percent. This may not sound too bad, but all those in such areas run a severe risk. If people in these areas have any advanced warning at all they should take a chance upon evacuation as a first choice. The hazards in such areas immediately after the blast are so great that they outweigh the risks of being caught exposed elsewhere, in flight.

For the most part, the immediate danger of nuclear weapons falls even more sharply in areas 10 to 25 miles from ground zero. The hazards will continue to be reduced rapidly as the distance grows greater. People in such areas have essentially the most difficult decision: whether to flee or to hunker down and seek local shelter, and the decision should be strongly influenced by the extent of advance warning of the event. If you live in such a place, and you think you have had enough warning to provide you with several hours to escape — you must consider your means of flight, as well, and estimate your chances of avoiding tie-ups — then it might be more prudent to flee. Yet if, in balanced judgment, you live in the more remote regions of the area around the target, where immediate fatalities are less likely to occur, any warning time might best be spent seeking and improving some kind of local shelter. Remember also that you may be able to take flight at some later time, when family, friends, and those important to you have been gathered into a group.

Beyond 25 miles from a primary nuclear target, you are better advised to stay put, unless there is very ample warning, and unless the location to which you might flee is as secure as you could make your own residence in the time available. The principal issue here, as it is in all such analyses, is to know your own particular situation, to know the targets and hazards of your own particular area, and to know yourself and the people for whom you are responsible.

WARNING SIGNS

There will be, the experts say, omens of warning before the outbreak of any nuclear war, as sure and certain as are the stars above on a clear winter's night.

Foremost among these will be the prevailing world situation. With the presence of space sensors, there is little likelihood that the preparations for a nuclear assault by one superpower upon the other can conceivably go undetected. This means that each side is likely to be aware of the other's military alert status; in fact, the *absence* of key information is considered reason for raising the alert status of military forces, automatically.

The second major sign of trouble, beyond severe and building international tension, would be evacuation. Movements of large groups of people should today be assumed to presage much worse trouble indeed. The official U.S. plan to evacuate major cities when threatened by nuclear war might be precisely the kind of thing that would set off the war, rather than deter it. It is a commonplace assumption of contemporary defense strategists that civil defense may be useful only after the outbreak of war, not before, when its implementation might be construed as a further heightening of tension.

Many of the other signs of impending nuclear catastrophe would be noticeable locally. The absence of power and/or communications is one such bad omen. If everything goes out at once, and none of the normal receivers can receive a signal, then there may be trouble afoot.

Those who live closest to priority military targets may sense a change in the rhythm of activity at the facility. American B-52s, for instance, create an unmistakable roar and bring the surrounding countryside to a palpable tremble when very many of the aircraft approach the flightline at the same time, and the effect is noticeable for miles. Are there more airmen on a Saturday night near Presque Isle than there should be? If so, then there is probably no cause for alarm. Are military families alert? If so, it is not necessarily a good sign for the future of the world.

The absence of activity may be as significant as its presence. Is a military base sealed tight? Have personnel been called back to the base suddenly? Are the phone lines jammed even before the President goes on television to address the people?

Not all the warning signs are official. In point of fact, an assumption that communications might be intentionally interrupted or delayed or completely absent is something to consider. Bizarre atmospheric conditions are still another sign. Is there too much glow in the night sky? Does your CB radio work? Your shortwave? Are familiar television stations on the air? Radio? Telephone? Have the local police gone home suddenly to tend home and hearth instead of the community?

There are no sure and certain signs, just a collection of impressions conveying a whole. The average American citizen may, in fact, never again hear from his government once nuclear war looms. There does not seem to be, for instance, any prepared plan in the United States by which the authorities would convey vital information to the populace during times of international crisis. There is, of course, the so-called ''Emergency Broadcast System,'' by which commercial radio and television stations are to rotate their signals, so that enemy bombers can not use them to home in on their targets. Then again, enemy bombers have not had to home in on such radio signals, thanks to modern technology, since the Japanese attacked Pearl Harbor in 1941.

Better then to take stock of what news might be available in advance, to listen well, to watch for local signs and signals. Nothing else may provide any useful warning of nuclear war.

ALFA NEOP

In the late 1970s, the United States government provided to selected local authorities an official battle plan for nuclear war entitled ''Checklist Guide For Nuclear Emergency Operations Planning.'' The anonymous authors of this checklist did their work at the behest of the Defense Civil Preparedness Agency, an organization that is part of the U.S. Department of Defense. The guidelines they prepared take the form of a booklet, ring-bound at the top so that you must read it along its horizontal axis. The top cover of the booklet is red. The material inside refers from time to time to previously published civil defense handbooks. The plan is officially called ''ALFA NEOP,'' a term which signifies that its distribution is intended only for the lowest-level of secure personnel. In bureaucratic parlance, the guideline is public document ''CPG2-2A.'' You might or might not be able to obtain a copy from your local civil defense director, assuming that appointed or elected official knows of its existence in the first place. The pages inside are divided left and right, so that various fire and fallout conditions may be matched against the prevailing war conditions described in the left-hand pages. The document assumes that its reader is a person who has access to privileged information about national security, has had some training in the minimal plan by which the United States hopes to respond to nuclear war, and is already safely ensconced in some form of shelter that is blast resistant and protected against fallout. The guidelines assume the reader's shelter is equipped with some means of communicating both with the general public and with the next higher level of official authority in the state, a personnage nicknamed, in governmentese, "Nextup." There is no mention anywhere of the wildly controversial government plan to evacuate the populations of major cities in the event of nuclear war. ALFA NEOP is, despite these presumptive drawbacks, the single best guideline ever published by the United States to cover the awful eventuality of nuclear war.

ALFA NEOP, for instance, outlines the precise order of succession in the event that "Nextup" is destroyed by a nuclear blast. (The succession is to be, as could be expected, pre-arranged in 1, 2, 3, and 4 sequence, the numbers representing outlying shelters that presumably report ordinarily to an official approximating the local mayor of the city or town.) The left-hand pages of ALFA NEOP present a series of readily discernible events that might be observed from the local, hardened shelter — attack warning, distant-weapon-detonation-observed-or-reported, movement-to-shelter-is-completed, significant-damage-and/or-fires reported-in-zone, or escape-to-better-shelter. All the events are portrayed against a backdrop of local conditions to be determined by fire and fallout hazards present or observed in the vicinity of the local shelter. Those conditions, typified in 58 separate action steps outlined on the right-hand pages of the document, override all considerations of larger events in the world outside the local shelter. There are, in addition, a maximum of 46 "action" steps that might be taken, depending upon the general condition of the outside world. The combination of variables, all neatly outlined in the basic battle plan of ALFA NEOP, represent a nearly limitless number of possibilities for human behavior under the nuclear gun. The plan requires its reader to report to Nextup any objective evidence received from the national NUDETS, or nuclear detection system. In all cases fire and fallout are the precedent conditions, and the very worst case is "fire black" and "fallout red," which means that the local shelter must be evacuated to a safer place because of the threat of uncontrollable fires while fallout is greater than 50 rems per hour at the same time. Such conditions call for, automatically, the abandonment of the local shelter, even if such a step involves the dissolution of vital communications.

It should be noted that, in contrast to the large-scale evacuation plan made public by the government, ALFA NEOP assumes that the observer — its reader — has stayed put. The plan assumes that the individual has reached some form of pre-arranged shelter, after a period of advanced warning, but that such warnings are not apt to be given the general public by the government. ALFA NEOP then goes on to give, in considerable detail, required and recommended courses of specific action, depending upon what the sheltered observer is told of the world outside his own shelter and, more importantly, by the local conditions that prevail in the immediate vicinity of that particular shelter. If local fires are uncontrollable, for instance, the reader of ALFA NEOP is advised to escape as soon as possible, even if Nextup is then advising everyone to take cover against further attacks. The reason for this is sheer common sense and a much better acknowledgement of the facts of nuclear physics than the government otherwise admits: additional attacks might kill or injure those in the shelter at some future moment, but fire will kill them surely and certainly long before subsequent enemy missiles strike.

In its sense of doing-the-expedient in the basic operational situation, ALFA NEOP stands as a much better guideline about how to survive nuclear war than do most of the more widely discussed government plans for evacuation. Its assumptions are basic reactions to the known effects of nuclear weapons.

Blast and Heat   Unlike the official government evacuation plan, ALFA NEOP assumes that little can be done to protect against the blast effects of a moden nuclear weapon if the device happens to fall directly upon the shelter or quite close to it, within a mile or two. There is simply no way known to "harden" any shelter against this kind of vaporization. But any shelter at all, particularly one underground, provides at least some protection from the concussive effects of a nuclear blast. The principle is not essentially different from that used to construct bomb shelters during World War II. If any shelter happens to be at ground zero, or within a mile or two of it, then the shelter and its occupants will be destroyed. But the shelter itself can provide at least some protection against damaging concussion, overpressures, and the nuclear wind that comes with modern weaponry. If a particular shelter is destroyed by blast, then its functions and assignments are automatically to be taken over by another shelter in the system. Short of complete saturation attack, the system in some form should still exist, even after the blasts of a nuclear war.

Thermal Effects and Heat   ALFA NEOP assumes that simply taking shelter will provide some degree of protection against the burn hazards of a weapon's thermal pulse. Such effects are, in fact, the longest-ranged of all nuclear effects (with the exception of long range fallout), but ALFA NEOP is probably correct, as weapons tests have proved, that anything at all placed between the human body and the thermal pulse will reduce the likelihood of dangerous burns. Even shutting the blinds or drawing the drapes in the typical living room aids the cause of survival in this instance, as does placing anything at all — a wall, a tree, a building — between the individual and the thermal pulse. To survive the thermal pulse, even if you are caught out in the open, take cover immediately, even if only behind a small hillock or in a ditch. The intense light and heat of a weapon's burst are among its most profound killing effects, and shelter is the best answer.

Fire   The heat of the thermal pulse, combined with the blast damage, will tend to ignite local fires. Within five or ten miles, these fires may coalesce to form a giant conflagration, a wall of fire that is an immediate threat to survival. The best time to counteract such fires is in the first moments after the blast wave has passed, when local action may do much to reduce the danger. But, if the fires cannot be controlled in the immediate vicinity, escape becomes absolutely mandatory. This is a local condition the status of which is at all times precedent to all other needs of survival. If you cannot control and cannot escape fire, you will not live long enough to worry about later hazards.

Fallout   This is the other precedent condition that governs all local actions, regardless of the condition of the rest of the world outside the shelter. ALFA NEOP assumes that the privileged individual in the shelter has some means by which the rate of local fallout may be measured, which means that the shelter has the proper equipment in advance. Because fallout decays comparatively swiftly after its deposit, ALFA NEOP stresses the determination of the peak fallout rate, which can then be used to predict how long people must remain inside their shelters. The case is a simple one if only one upwind blast has occurred, for then fallout will begin at some time after the blast has cleared, peak rapidly, then decline to the extent that some minimal amount of necessary work might be done outside the shelter for short periods of time. Later, radiation risks from fallout will diminish to the extent that longer intervals may be allowed outside the shelter. But, if there are many blasts and hence many different sources of fallout, the fallout rate at any given point downwind may fluctuate up and down for some time, until each cloud has passed by and left behind its deposit of radioactive dust and sand. Hence ALFA NEOP provides instructions for varying conditions at the shelter site. For example, if a relatively low fallout rate prevails, but the intensity begins to increase, it is time to take shelter again until this latest arriving radioactive cloud has passed and the radiation intensity again diminishes to the point where useful outside work may be done.

ALFA NEOP suggests certain key gradients in the fallout rate. One is the rems-per-hour level. Fallout rates below one-half rem per hour are considered negligible hazards in wartime conditions, though such rates greatly exceed prevailing peacetime standards. At such rates of fallout, however, valuable work might be done even if the workers are necessarily exposed. Between one-half rem per hour to 50 rems per hour, the fallout rate is deemed "moderate," and care must be taken to note whether the rate is rising or falling. Increasing intensity of fallout requires the individual to insist on compulsory shelter for everyone. Those working outside should be rotated periodically so that no one individual is exposed too much. In this way, it may be possible to conduct life-saving operations outdoors even as the major fallout hazard approaches. But any time the fallout rate exceeds 50 rems per hour, compulsory shelter for all is an immediate action required by the ALFA NEOP plan.

SHELTER SUPPLIES

If ALFA NEOP is right in many respects concerning the hazards of nuclear weapons, it may not necessarily be appropriate for untrained and untutored civilians who have not prepared to take shelter in advance. The plan, for instance, is absolutely correct in pointing out that the visible effects of a nuclear blast are so phenomenal that they simply cannot be overlooked. But ALFA NEOP also assumes that the shelter has been very well equipped in advance and that considerable planning has been devoted to providing fallout protection, fire-fighting equipment and training in its use, communications with the outside world, emergency light and heat, food, water, medical supplies, and sanitation. None of these things is beyond the average American today, though the government persists in explaining away the hazards by proposing evacuation of huge segments of the population to places ill prepared to receive the incoming hordes.

For any individual trying to discover an intelligent approach to increasing his own prospects of survival in the event of nuclear war, ALFA NEOP best serves as a kind of guideline for the planning that must be done in advance. It will be too late to seek appropriate equipment or to begin learning how to construct expedient shelter against fallout once the event has happened. In particular, consideration must be given to a variety of advance requirements, many of which resemble the kind of preparations necessary for any kind of major emergency, including natural disasters such as hurricane, flood, or fire. But some items are specifics against nuclear war and have no other possible purpose. A basic advance checklist would look something like this:

Shelter This should offer some protection against blast and immediate heat, but, more importantly for anyone on the East Coast, it must be constructed in such a way to give the maximum possible protection against the hazards of fallout (the next chapter will provide greater detail). Ironically, steps taken to provide fallout protection are essentially the same as those required to combat the dangers of leakage from a nuclear power plant. The hazards are technically similar. But the "fallout" from a damaged nuclear power plant, because it comes from a different kind of fission process, is much longer-lived and therefore considerably nastier.

Who will take shelter What are certain individual's medical requirements in time of peace? Does anyone wear glasses? What would they do if the glasses were lost? Is there a diabetic requiring insulin, which must be refrigerated? Is anyone under the care of a physician and taking prescribed medicines? And what is the age of the people to be protected? Even small doses of radiation pose a greater hazard to children and youngsters, because they may live long enough to suffer from the extended effects that might appear later in life. Older people may be able to risk higher dosages.

Light and heat Inability to move about in the dark is frightening and can contribute to panic. Light is essential for any kind of shelter, and it should be safe light, not something apt to start a fire that drives everyone outside. There must be a considerable supply of light sources and a reserve against heavy usage. In the northern climes, such as New England, it may be important to provide as much protection against the cold of winter as possible.

Water You can live for weeks without food, but no one can survive without water. The water must be pure and be available in adequate supply, or some means must be found to produce more of it. The civil defense adages of the 1950s that advised people to fill up their bathtubs, sinks, and every available bucket with water are still useful advice. In a nuclear war environment, water supplies may be disrupted for a long time, especially in the cities, where water pipes will be destroyed. Hence steps should be taken in advance to provide ways of purifying any extra supplies against chemical and bacteriological hazards, since water itself is not apt to pose great radiation hazards, even if it has been exposed to fallout.

Medical supplies and the knowledge to use them This goes beyond mere first aid. People should have had CPR training and, ideally, there should be someone with some knowledge of what to do to assuage pain, treat burns, diagnose a condition properly. The medical requirements for nuclear war situations are vastly more extensive than those for normal kinds of natural hazards. These too will be covered in more detail in the next chapter.

Sanitation One of the obvious effects of nuclear war is that it is apt to lower standards of living drastically, which means that disease will become the major enemy. Prevention of disease begins with proper sanitation in potentially crowded conditions.

Tools and materials to improve shelter This may be nothing more than a few shovels, a place to dig sand, and pillow cases, which happen to double nicely for sandbags. Time spent in adding density and bulk to cut down on fallout hazards within the shelter can be very useful, as the next chapter will point out.

Special equipment to reduce radiation intake Gamma emitters must be protected against by providing as dense a shielding as possible for people caught in a dangerous area. The best and simplest way is to get below the ground on which gamma-emitting particles may fall. Beta emitters should be washed away by some means of decontamination. This sounds complicated, but it really only requires some planning to allow for the brushing off or washing down of new arrivals to the shelter, lest they track beta-emitting particles in with them. Alpha particles must be kept out of the human body at all costs. Ingestion is a danger, and so food sources should be washed thoroughly before consumption. (The food itself is not radioactive.) Inhalation of alpha-emitting particles is an even greater danger, for, once in the lungs, they are not readily removed from the body and may do major damage. The best way to keep alpha-emitters out of people's airways is with surgical masks, available without prescription from a medical supply house. If these are not available, dampened handkerchiefs, rags, or light towels may be used. This precaution is especially advised for any people caught downwind from an accident at a nuclear power plant.

Equipment to monitor radiation rates   Standard gear now on the civilian market would be almost useless in the aftermath of nuclear war or a nuclear power plant accident because it is calibrated far too low to provide useful information in such high-intensity environments. There is more information in the next chapter, but it is sufficient to say here that both rate meters, such as geiger and scintillation counters, and total-dosage indicators, cumulative exposure devices, are preferred. Without this equipment, which is rare in the U.S. today, vital information will be totally lacking, and this will clearly contribute to hardship. If people are aware of the potential hazards of radiation, but do not know how threatened they are, panic may result. Unfortunately, many of the obvious signs of both panic and radiation sickness closely resemble each other — vomiting, extreme agitation, anxiety. Better to know what is what than to guess. Without radiation monitoring gear, no one will know when it might be safe to leave shelter, or for how long.

Communications equipment   In practice, this means receivers that have been protected against the EMP effect and, hopefully, working transmitters as well, such as CB radios or ham radio stations. Knowledge of the outside world and conditions is a key ingredient in the prospects of survival. Yet the best available evidence indicates that little planning has been done in the U.S. to provide the public with adequate information in a war-emergency situation. Communications gear is placed last on this list because it is quite likely that the average American citizen may not hear in any way from the government for years after the opening rounds of a nuclear war.

Sources

Technical information and recommendations in this chapter are derived mainly from the three sources cited previously: The Congressional Office Of Technology Assessment's booklet on "The Effects of Nuclear War" (available through the Government Printing Office); Glasstone's textbook on the same subject (harder to find, as described previously); and the nine-volume *DCPA Attack Environment Manual,* published in 1973 by the Defense Civil Preparedness Agency of the Department of Defense. The ALFA NEOP booklet and guidelines are also the product of the latter organization. The DCPA material may be hard to locate, but an effort to do so is recommended for all those who wish to get more thorough grounding in the kind of cold-blooded and objective thinking required of all those who would wish to increase their chances of survival in a nuclear war environment. Try the local civil defense office, good local librarians, the libraries of colleges and universities and local government representatives for copies. The ALFA NEOP guidelines, extrapolated to cover the individual case, are especially useful.

The Federal Emergency Management Agency also can provide useful information in the form of easy-to-read booklets, although the organization's recent efforts have been strongly oriented to help sell the "crisis relocation" concept to the public in place of local civil defense efforts involving any attempt to stay near home. The reader is here cautioned to be quite wary of locally-announced FEMA plans for evacuation of people from the cities, as this material tends to be leaked in somewhat haphazard fashion, without corroborating detail or useful planning guides. Many of the civil defense pamphlets of the 1950s are considerably more useful for emergency planning.

9 Personal Civil Defense

Last October, hunting grouse, I met a red fox at a blind barway. At twenty yards, he was a gone goose, had I chosen to fire — and I think he knew it. Kill him? His pelt would have been far from prime, worth little and I require no trophies for wall or ego.

For a long moment, his strange, yellow eyes blazed into mine. Then he turned, slowly, disdainfully, and floated away with that wonderful fox gait that is the next thing to levitation.

I let him go. There is a time to kill, and another time to be a conscientious objector.

From *My New England,* by Frank Woolner,
official historian of the U.S. 3rd Armored
Division, the first U.S. force to enter Nazi
Germany in World War II.

Most manuals that purport to provide guidelines on how to survive a nuclear war contain a chapter on guns. Some go into elaborate detail in describing recommendations for specific firearms — so many grains of powder driving a particular kind of projectile at so many feet per second, with such and such a trajectory and a particular number of foot-pounds of energy. Some of these manuals delve into paramilitary subjects, such as how to organize a patrol, the techniques of small-unit infantry tactics, defense of a fixed position, and the well-armed squad in assault. There will be no such recommendations here. If you are interested in such subjects, you can readily find out about them for yourself, elsewhere. Here the assumption will be that you cannot shoot a germ, cannot force a gamma ray to hold up its hands. *In the awful environment of any post-nuclear-war society, starvation, radiation, and disease are apt to be far more dangerous to any survivors than the survivors are to each other.*

The assumption of this book is that, given leadership and equipped with knowledge, people trapped together in a disaster are as likely to pull together and cooperate as they are to revert to animal instincts. As there is clearly room in the human heart for evil, there is as much for good, and, in the environment likely after any major nuclear war, there will already have been enough killing to go around.

ADVANCE PLANNING

What is recommended here is a state of mind best termed "passive civil defense." This is a metaphorical notion, a way of describing an awareness-of-circumstance that should be developed well in advance. Passive civil defense costs little or nothing, beyond some study and some forethought. If, in its practice, you become more aware of your own daily circumstances, then it will already have done some good for you and those for whom you care most. It just takes a bit of daily practice.

Begin by noticing the weather around your home each morning. From which direction does the wind most often blow? Where do storms come from and which way does the wind blow then? At what season? How much snow does your area receive each winter? Snow can be important, because it may increase the rate of fallout deposition in your area after a nuclear blast, yet collect it on the ground. In Maine, for instance, radon gas naturally released as the snow melts in early spring traditionally raises the background radiation count each year.

Once you have acquired a more detailed sense of the weather near your home, consider what plans you and your family may have arranged for handling sudden emergencies. (There *should* be such plans.) The proper plan for nighttime fire in the house, for instance, should call for everyone, first, to escape from the house, then meet at some pre-arranged spot — the apple tree in the garden, the corner of your street or lot — so that you may count noses and see what must be done next. The basic principles of this plan are just as applicable, by extension, to times when a nuclear war might threaten. You and your family should all know where to go in an emergency and roughly what to do. A few minutes advanced planning for such contingencies can bring peace of mind and may save lives. You will function better, will serve as a better organizer, if you know that your people are as safe as possible in the circumstances. Useless worry about a missing person serves only to contribute to confusion and potential panic.

The next basic step is to check the emergency equipment you may already have on hand. Does your home have fire extinguishers? If not, it would be a wise idea to get some. There should be at least one in the kitchen, and another somewhere along the way to your heating source. Everyone who lives in the house should know how to use them and where to find them, even in the dark.

What about other emergency gear? How many flashlights do you have and where are they? In what condition are they? Are there extra bulbs and batteries? Where are these stored? If you live close to water, where there might be occasional danger from flood, what is the plan of escape? Do you have a boat? Life preservers? The world may, after all, not necessarily die by fire, and nearness to water might be a big plus in a nuclear emergency. There may be food in that water, and ways to supply potable water itself.

If you live in the country, do you have a well? How does it work and what happens to it if and when power goes out? What about septic tanks and sewer lines? Are these susceptible to breakage and disruption? If so, might they create a health problem if you had to remain in or near your home? And what would you do for water if the normal sources of supply were cut off?

What about winter clothing, blankets, footwear? People who frequent the outdoors often have an excellent supply of war emergency gear, probably without realizing it. Is there a useful first-aid kit in the home? Where is it and what does it contain? Most likely, it alone would not prove adequate for a nuclear emergency, but it is a starting point and an occasional review of its contents and recommended uses will serve you in good stead, regardless of circumstances. It will do you no good, however, if you cannot find it or cannot reach it in an emergency.

Who is your family doctor and what is the general state of health of your family? Has everyone been kept up-to-date on preventive shots? In recent years, Americans have become lax about innoculations and the prevention of disease that requires little time, effort, or money to accomplish, and this is a grave mistake, bad enough in peacetime, but worse in a post-nuclear war environment. Children should have had their shots against diphtheria, whooping cough, and tetanus (the DPT vaccine). In fact, everyone should have had a tetanus booster within the past five years, because this reduces the long-term danger from mechanical injuries and wounds. In the first winter after the outbreak of any nuclear war, diphtheria alone will present a danger not often contemplated in peacetime, when medical help is no more than a phone call away.

Is there someone in your home who requires prescription medication on a regular basis? If so, what are the storage requirements and might these be modified in the face of a much harsher environment? For all such medical considerations, you might consider a private chat with your personal physician. You may or may not choose to tell the doctor that you are growing increasingly concerned about nuclear war. (And if you do, you may find a more receptive audience than you might expect, for the American medical profession has become increasingly aware of the hazards that could be engendered by a nuclear exchange.) Whatever the case, your doctor can help and may even contribute to your stock of useful medical supplies. Most of the drugs that would prove most helpful in the event of a major nuclear emergency are prescription items, but few are of the type for which an underground market exists. Talk to your doctor frankly, express your concerns and demonstrate your stability willingly. These simple steps could go a long way toward increasing your chances of survival in the event of nuclear war.

As you acquire the habit of thinking simply and practically about so seemingly complex and frightening a subject as nuclear war, go back to basics to develop your own version of passive civil defense. Do you live in a private home or an apartment? Of what construction? A larger, strongly constructed building in a city may increase the danger from the standpoint of target potential, but the middle of one of its lower floors may offer some protection against blast or fallout, to offset the disadvantage. Are there subways near your home? The city may be more of a target than the suburbs, but subways must be strongly built by definition and, better still, they are below ground, where, again, there may be some protection against blast, heat, and fallout. And have you ever thought to examine the storm drains or manholes near your city environment? It may seem bizarre, but such odd places may provide ready-made blast and fallout shelters. You can lift off a manhole cover with a crowbar — the neighbors will perhaps consider you daft — or with two strong bolts of different size connected by hefty wire. The smaller bolt goes down the hole in the center of the roadway cover, then a tug on the larger bolt, which serves as a handle, can lift the cover. Beware, however, of toxic gases, which may still exist in such locations, especially in the smaller, older cities. Larger, newer cities have usually solved such problems for the benefit of their work crews.

In major metropolitan areas, existing subway systems can provide a reasonable degree of protection against the initial fire and blast of a thermonuclear weapon. Against airbursts, the preferred weapons-option for city destruction, the heavily reinforced roofs and walls of subway tunnels can provide more than enough protection against blast over-pressures and could conceivably serve in the same ways that the tunnels of London did during the Blitz of World War II, to shelter some of the civilian population. While they may be higher on the target list than most countryside locations, cities nevertheless provide an abundance of local sheltering sites for those willing to think about the unthinkable and to review their urban locations with an eye to spotting useful shelters.

Such steps begin to reach into the arcane world of the specialized requirements for protection against blast, heat, and radiation, but more mundane considerations are still appropriate. Do you have a cellar? If so, where is the access to it and could it be made into an expedient fallout shelter in a relatively short time? Go downstairs and look around, checking the next chapter of this book as well for ideas on expedient shelter construction. Even the simple step of getting below ground can offer some protection against fallout, whether the threat comes from nuclear war or from a nuclear power plant upwind of your home. When you stand on the surface of the earth, the gamma radiation from fallout particles lying on the ground has nothing to stop it from reaching you except air, which is not an efficient shielding substance. If, however, you can get below ground level, even in a shallow ditch, the soil can shield you from all gamma rays except those closest to you.

For those concerned with the safety of nearby nuclear power plants, especially those upwind of your location, the specialized steps required to establish some relatively efficient shielding against radiation can be a practical, daily concern that goes beyond the even less likely hazards to be faced from the radiation of a nuclear war. Before you begin to study these more specialized requirements of passive civil defense, be sure first to review the basics themselves, as they apply in your own specific case. Even at this early stage, simply thinking ahead has already increased your chances of survival.

MEDICAL IMPLICATIONS

In Nevil Shute's *On The Beach* — these lines do not appear in the now-famous movie — a character describes the time of waiting-for-the-end as "a period of grace." What he means is, in the simplest possible terms, hard times bring out the very best in the human species. The advice given here is that, if a "period of grace" is to befall us all, then it is best to think in the most practical terms possible. Nuclear war, if it ever happens, is not apt to arrive in the guise of springtime teas or the sailing races of summer. It would be hard, brutal in fact. It would have specialized requirements. The best rational course for civilized human beings is not to put heads-in-sand, but to think, to think clearly, as far in advance as possible.

If you have already assessed your personal situation, then you should now think through the implications of modern nuclear war. Medical matters are the first case. The best available medical help in human history exists today in America, but the bulk of it exists in cities. Not much would be apt to survive intact through a modern nuclear war. If you wish to go beyond just counting tonight's noses in your household, for instance, then you must also face the fact that the medical support to which we have all become accustomed is not likely to be available in the aftermath of nuclear war. This is the first specialized requirement of learning how to live in the nuclear age.

Officially speaking, the U.S. government, through one of its civil defense agencies, recommends that the following professional personnel be sought out if a physician is no longer available:

- a dentist
- a veterinarian

- a registered nurse
- a pharmacist
- a licensed practical nurse
- military-trained corpsmen or civilian-trained emergency medical technicians
- a podiatrist
- any student of any of these disciplines.

Strictly speaking, the U.S. government, for once, is perfectly right on this score, for any form of self-treatment or self-medication not only does not come recommended anywhere in these pages, but may be dangerous, period.

There *are* certain references you can consult, however. Among the best is a government pamphlet, titled *Austere Medical Care for Disaster,* which may be obtained through the nearest office of the United States Public Health Service. Essentially the same text, under a different title, is theoretically available through government civil defense organizations, which have largely been in disarray since the U.S. decided that there could be no possible defense whatever against nuclear war.

This booklet, easier to find through Public Health than it is through what is left of civil defense, is easy to understand and covers several dozen life-threatening/preserving situations that might befall the survivors of the first moments of a nuclear war. It includes advice on the care of newborns — a useful thing to have about your homestead indeed.

Anyone who has already survived American infantry or Marine training will also be familiar with the booklet, *First Aid for Soldiers,* published by the United States Army. This is a battlefield guidebook, widely available in civilian life, and it covers many of the basics, short of childbirth, while extending useful information about major wounds. Your Congressperson should be able to get you a copy, if there is no other source. Failing that, you should check with your local librarian. Librarians are wonderful people to get to know, because they have an innate fondness for useful books.

The publications mentioned above should be part of your personal library, and you should read them at least once to get the flavor of what it takes to begin planning for nuclear survival. Neither publication will allow you to help anyone over the long haul, since the object of both is simply to provide guidelines about how to keep people alive until more skilled medical care might become available. There are a host of pale imitations of these publications, many of them concentrating on various plant and herbal remedies. These may be useful, but a problem with them is that it is very difficult to teach human beings, by means of books alone, how to discriminate between one plant and another in the field.

Several other books, written some time ago, might prove useful. One is *The Ship's Medicine Chest and First Aid at Sea*, U.S. Public Health Service again, which is dated in its advice (especially if you have spoken plainly to your family doctor, as you should), but provides helpful guidelines for situations in which modern antibiotics may not be available. Another is titled *Where There Is No Doctor*, and this was written as a kind of Peace Corps manual, covering remote tropical villages, in the days when John Kennedy was President and the Cuban Missile Crisis was not yet fully understood. The latter book is, today, relatively hard to find (your librarian may help).

A number of books and publications can provide you with a useful list of medical/dental/obstetric/survival supplies. In this regard, *How to Be Your Own Doctor (Sometimes)* — still available from Grosset & Dunlap in New York — provides a list of what man thought to take along on the first voyage to the moon. *The Polar Manual* (United States Navy Medical School, Bethesda, Maryland), written for the senior Navy enlisted personnel responsible for the general health of their mates aboard American nuclear submarines, provides excellent information about dentistry-in-the-rough.

The best available lists of the medical supplies that people who wish to survive war should have are incorporated in considerable detail in the ''Packaged Disaster Hospital,'' a series of booklets put out, again, by the U.S. Public Health Service from 1965 to 1969. The books include extensive lists that may be reviewed individually by you and your family physician.

There are still other references — what does the word ''epidemiological'' mean, anyway? — that are more difficult to understand, but provide advanced information. One such tome is *Emergency War Surgery* (Superintendent of Documents, U.S. Government Printing Office, Washington D.C. 20402), which provides a perverse clinical welcome to all those cosmetologists who had the misfortune to be drafted into Alan Alda's style of M*A*S*H outfit. (There is no excuse whatever for the average layman's practicing with this book, short of nuclear war.) Two other publications deserve mention in this sort of ''advanced'' category. The first of these, a useful home-medical guide in the first place, is the *Cecil Textbook of Medicine* (W.B. Saunders Company, West Washington Square, Philadelphia, Pennsylvania 19105 and 1 Goldthorne Ave., Toronto, Ontario M8Z 5T9, Canada), which provides an encyclopedic reference to virtually all the pains the human flesh is heir to, nuclear war or not. The edition preferred, at this writing, is the 15th. The other of the advanced books that should be in your home library, however you find it, is the Physicians' Desk Reference, commonly known in the trade as the ''PDR,'' 36th edition, 1982 (Medical Economics Company, Oradell, New Jersey 07649), which provides the current standards — replete with life-size photographs — of the drugs common in American life. The latter book, highly recommended for the sophisticated family person, maintains a life of its own in our society.

There is no single book to be recommended for the subject of radiation disease.

RADIATION PROTECTION

The hazards of radioactive fallout introduce special conditions to the considerations of passive civil defense. Yet, as with most aspects of nuclear war, the extent of the peril depends greatly on where the observer lives. For most of the heavily populated East Coast, including virtually all of New England, late-arriving fallout from any Soviet assault on U.S. missile fields west of the Mississippi could prove to be a major hazard. The kind of saturation nuclear attack that would be required to degrade U.S. land-based facilities would lead to an enormous amount of fallout, all of which deposition downwind would depend upon the strength and direction of the winds that govern the weather over much of the nation.

There arc local considerations as well. Those living near the coast who might take shelter aboard a boat at sea would be faced with a risky but relatively simple expedient for reducing the danger of fallout — they could decontaminate even a tarpaulin-covered boat simply by washing the craft down periodically with buckets of water. If, after all, fallout particles are removed, they no longer constitute a danger, though, clearly, the time spent in such activities would have to be carefully calculated to reduce the danger to those doing the work.

"Decontamination" is a word that, to the general public today, conjures up visions of specially trained men dressed in space-suit-like coveralls and odd-looking helmets. In reality, decontamination is largely a matter of brushing or washing down radioactive particles. The work itself is dangerous because those doing it should be carefully monitored and protected while engaged in the activity — hence the special, disposable clothing intended to keep radioactive materials out of the body and away from the skin, hair, and natural folds of the human frame. But "decontamination" itself may be done with soap and water, so long as the rinse is disposed of properly, away from people. For the first few decades of the nuclear age, the recommended procedure for decontaminating areas made hazardous by a nuclear accident was to wash them down thoroughly with a solution of the detergent Tide and water. That brand was evidently preferred because of its ability to loosen small particles of radioactive dirt and allow them to be vacuumed or mopped away, after which the rinse water was buried. If the weather was below freezing, a small amount of Prestone-type antifreeze was added to the cleaning solution.

This is not to say that such decontamination procedures are necessarily recommended in the first hours or days after a nuclear war has salted downwind areas with fallout. In this instance, as we have seen, time is a more important factor, and it would be an urgent matter to provide people with adequate shelter until the radiation of the deposited fallout had somewhat decayed. (Again, fallout decays in its hazard by a factor of roughly ten for each seven units of time measured; the radioactive dust from a single nuclear weapon will be ten times less hazardous one full week after the contaminated dust cloud has passed.) Once the radiation rate has been reduced to the point where some outside work may be done, simple washing procedures might serve to reduce the danger still more.

In the event of nuclear war, the immediate objective should be to provide those not directly threatened by the prompt effects of blast and heat with some measure of protection against the fallout likely to arrive within a few hours or days, at most, of any detonations upwind of the location. For this purpose, it is important to understand that different types of materials provide different levels of protection, particularly against gamma radiation, which is the most penetrating type of ionizing radiation that typically results from nuclear fallout.

The Federal Defense Civil Protection Agency likes to say, "Fallout protection is dirt cheap," a statement apt to bring loud guffaws from the untutored audience. Yet there is considerable truth in this simplistic contention. Plain soil, the good earth itself, can provide considerable protection against fallout, assuming that people know what to do with it.

The object of all fallout protection is essentially to put the greatest possible amount of the densest possible material between people and the source of radioactivity. The extent of the fallout sheltering is generally stated in terms of a "protection factor," a number by which the total amount of radiation, measured in rems or roentgens, should be divided. A simple shelter with a "protection factor of 10" would be one that would reduce the amount of radiation exposure suffered by those inside to one tenth of what it would have been had they remained fully exposed throughout the same period. If, for instance, a total accumulation of 4,000 rems was measurable at a particular place in the first week after a nuclear war, anyone surviving the immediate effects of blast and heat would invariably be killed by the radioactive fallout. The 4,000 rem dosage in as short a time as one week is inevitably lethal to humans. But if everyone could be sheltered in some facility that offered a protection factor of 20, for example, the absorbed dose in the shelter would be reduced to 200 rems for the same period, an exposure that might make a small number mildly ill but would leave most largely unaware of their exposure and would not constitute an immediate danger to anyone.

Different materials reduce radiation intensity in different degrees. A protection factor of 10 may be achieved by roughly 3.7 inches of steel, 12 inches of concrete, 26 inches of plain water — which is why nuclear submarines are relatively safe from the hazards of nuclear fallout — or 50 inches of wood. The same protection factor of 10 may also be achieved by as little as 18 inches of plain dirt.

Simply taking shelter in the average basement, in areas such as New England where cellars are common, provides a protection factor of 10 against the hazards of radioactive fallout, whether the fallout comes from a nuclear blast or an accident at a nuclear plant. This is because the degree of protection rises immediately once the individuals can get below the level of the ground on which most of the fallout is being deposited. The addition of 18 inches of soil around windows, hatchways, and exposed walls would further reduce the radiation dosage absorbed by an extra protection factor of 10. Hence the idea that "fallout protection is dirt cheap." Stand outside in your back yard during a nuclear emergency of any kind, and you will be exposed to whatever total dose of radiation may befall your particular area. Seek shelter in your basement during the same period of time, and you will likely reduce the exposure to a tenth of what it would otherwise have been. If you have the time, information, and ability to sandbag 18 inches of soil around the exterior walls near the basement and the basement windows, you will reduce the dosage absorbed to a twentieth of what it would have been.

According to the best available studies, three factors would most greatly influence the overall effectiveness of any American shelter program:

1) the availability of adequate shelters in advance — or, lacking that, the extent to which people would have sufficient time, knowledge, and the materials to create expedient shelters after warning of nuclear war, but before any attack. In the past decade, government attempts to distribute plans that show how to construct expedient shelters have fallen into almost total disarray. Expedient shelters — the most famous/notorious involves shoveling dirt atop a door that covers a ditch — figure very strongly in Soviet plans for civil defense. But neither the labor required — a cubic foot of soil generally weighs 100 pounds — nor the time that would be involved are fully realized by the American public. Although most Americans do not know it, the pickaxe and shovel are among the most useful tools for the provision of extremely valuable shelter from radioactive fallout.

2) the availability of food, water, and other necessary supplies within a shelter. In a country whose population is generally overweight, most Americans have given little thought to stockpiling those minimum requirements necessary for survival in a nuclear emergency. Along the East Coast, for instance, the shelter time might vary from a minimum of a few hours or a few days to as much as a month, depending upon the intensity of the war and the vagaries of the winds.

A rendering of a typical American dwelling, showing the "protection factors" to be found against radiation at various points in the building. The safest place, clearly, is in the basement, below ground level, where direct-line radiation is attenuated by an average factor of 10. In short, if the outside radiation over a week's period were, say, 1500 rems, anyone staying inside such a basement would receive an exposure of about 150 rems.

3) the number of people who could reach and enter adequate shelter *before* peak fallout is deposited. This, too, is overlooked in most American planning and, in fact, the official government program for evacuating cities in the event of a nuclear emergency has, thus far, given virtually no consideration whatever to this factor. Once fallout begins, all those who wish to enter a shelter from outside must first be decontaminated completely, for they might otherwise track fallout dust and particles in with them. It is far better if the shelters have been created and made available in advance of fallout deposition, so that people would have adequate time to enter before the worst of the trouble arrives.

RADIATION METERS

If adequate shelters could theoretically save millions of Americans, especially on the East Coast, in the event of nuclear war, there is a further technical consideration that has been almost entirely overlooked in the past decade: how to measure the rate of fallout radiation and monitor the doses that pose a hazard to individuals and groups. The problem here is that the various kinds of radiation — alpha, beta, and gamma — are entirely beyond the ken of the five human senses. Beyond the fact that hazardous fallout can generally be seen as dust or ash, humans cannot perceive radiation or sense the extent of the danger it might present. In a nuclear emergency, you will not be able to see, smell, taste, or hear the danger from fallout. Yet reliable information concerning fallout is critical. In this instance, not knowing is dangerous, for without such knowledge there is simply no way of deciding a rational course of action in the emergency.

For all its perceptual transparency to human beings, radiation is easily monitored by several kinds of instruments. The detection and measurement of alpha particles, the fallout easiest to avoid, requires a device known as a scintillation counter. This is a specialized device that does not come specifically recommended for non-technical personnel trapped in a nuclear emergency. It is easier, instead, just to wear some form of mask to keep alpha-emitting particles out of the lungs and be sure to wash off boxes and cans of foodstuffs to preclude ingestion.

Ways to monitor and evade the hazards of alpha-particle radiation should be of special concern also to those who live near nuclear power plants or for some miles downwind of such sites. By the very nature of the fission process, nuclear power plants tend to be full of alpha-emitting radioactive elements. This type of radiation, because it can be stopped by the skin, by a piece of paper, or by a pane of window glass, presents little hazard if kept entirely external to the body. But if an alpha-emitting particle finds its way into the body, by means of ingestion or inhalation, it may take up long-term residence and its energetic form of radiation is apt to do considerable internal damage to the body in the immediate vicinity of the site where the particle is imbedded. If there is any chance whatever of a significant release of radiation from a nuclear power plant, a minimal protective first step to take is to insist that everyone in the area wear moistened towels or cloths over their noses and mouths to prevent inhalation of the dangerous alpha-emitting particles.

Gamma and beta radiation can be detected by devices generally known as "Geiger counters," but more properly entitled "Geiger-Mueller meters." Most operate by measuring the flow of electrical current produced in a gas of known conductivity by ions generated when the gas chamber of the instrument is exposed to ionizing radiation. Technically speaking, the devices measure electrical voltages produced in the so-called "Geiger plateau," an area along the theoretical curve of electrical potential where the energy measured is limited not by the magnitude of the initial energy but by the geometry of the gas-filled tube and the sensitivity of its electronics. In practice, this means that a Geiger-Mueller counter, or rate meter, cannot tell you what kind of radiation is present, but it can measure the general intensity of the overall radiation quite precisely.

A wide variety of rate meters are available in the United States today, but, unfortunately, most of them are calibrated too low for use in a nuclear fallout emergency. Most such devices are intended for use by health physicists, people responsible for radiation safety in a low-level radiation environment often found today in industry or medicine. Fallout rate meters of the civil defense type once purchased by the government have not been manufactured for the past decade, and those to be found are generally available only through commercial companies specializing in the supply of government-surplus equipment. Any equipment to measure fallout rates, however, is better than no equipment in a nuclear emergency.

For those who live in the larger cities, information about the availability of radiation rate meters is often no farther away than the nearest Yellow Pages. The listings may vary, but most of the larger directories will carry some such reference. New England Telephone, for instance, which covers five of the six New England states, lists this information under the heading "Radioactivity Instruments, Supplies and Service." The 1982 Yellow Page edition for the Boston area, for example, provides an even dozen references for this kind of equipment, most of them of companies specializing in the field or divisions of industrial giants, such as General Electric. A series of phone calls can tell you whether the equipment offered is for low-level industrial/medical use and is calibrated in "milliroentgens," or thousandths of a roentgen. This is useful, but is still on the low end of the radiation scale compared to the intensities of radiation that might be produced by a nuclear emergency. The government-approved fallout rate meters of the 1950s and 1960s, for instance, were calibrated to provide radiation rate readings in several categories, from 0 to .5 roentgens per hour (remember, for our purposes here, a "roentgen" is esentially equivalent to a "rem"), from 0 to 5, from 0 to 50, and from 0 to 500. The kind of intense radiation coming from fallout in the aftermath of a nuclear war would apt to be far off-scale, on the high side, compared to the calibration of most present-day industrial rate meters.

Several mail-order firms and suppliers of scientific instruments can also provide information about Geiger counters well suited to the civil-emergency nuclear environment. In almost all cases, the firms listed below are reputable, but the prudent consumer would be wise to seek out a catalogue first. Most rate meters calibrated from 0 to 600 rems cost anywhere from a few to more than five hundred dollars, depending upon the source and the reliability of the device. The government-surplus rate meters, are generally designated "CD V-710," and may be adjusted to take readings at various high-intensity rates. They resemble a box-shaped object small enough to be held in one hand and will generally provide several hundred hours of service life when equipped with two D-cell flashlight batteries and a single 22.5 volt extra battery. Companies that can supply useful information, in alphabetical order, include:

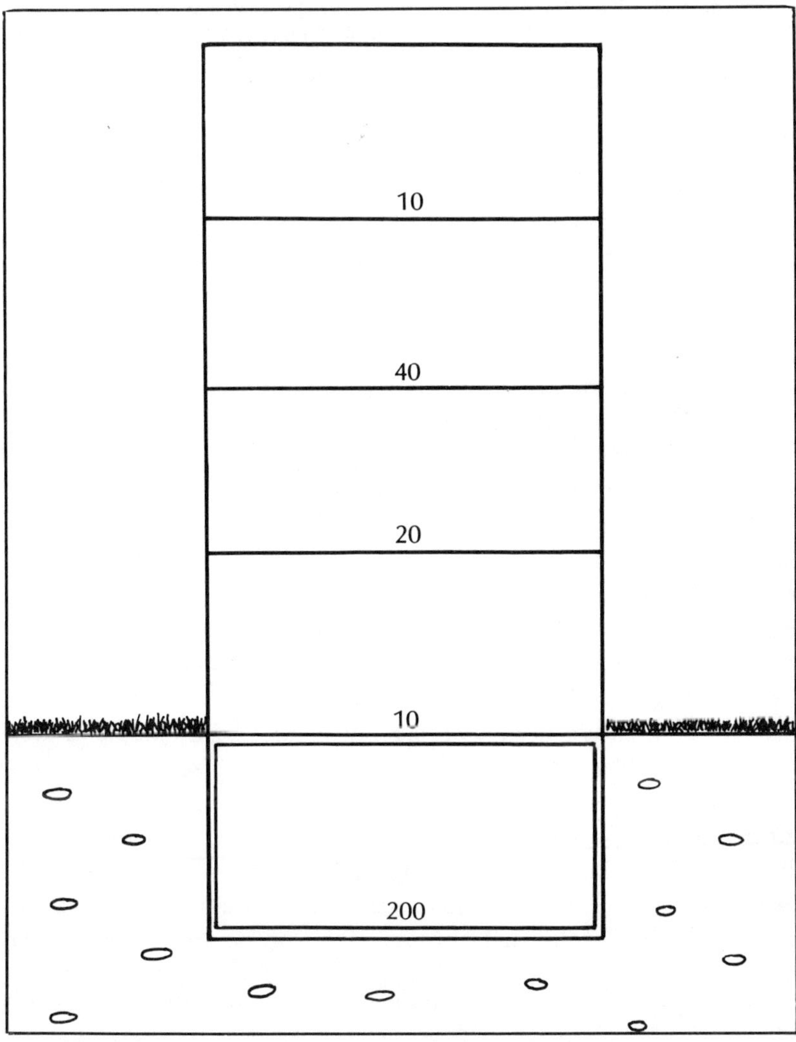

An artist's rendering of a typical small, commercial building, a few stories in height. The safest place would be in the basement, below ground level, where the building itself and the position would attenuate the fallout — provide a "protection factor" — by a factor of nearly 200. Another relatively "safer" spot during a fallout emergency is the floor just above halfway up the structure, because this is away from the fallout-emitting particles on the ground, but below those on the roof of the building.

Applied Health Physics
P.O. Box 197
Bethel Park, PA 15102

Edmund Scientific Company
1875 Edscorp Bldg.
Barrington, NJ 08007

Dosimeter Corp. of America
6106 Interstate Circle
Cincinnati, OH 45242

Nuclear Associates, Inc.
100 Voice Road
Carle Place, NY 11514

Eberline Instrument Company
P.O. Box 2018
Santa Fe, NM 87501

Survival, Inc.
16809 South Central Ave.
Carson, CA 90746

Both Edmund Scientific Company, a reputable and well-known supplier of science instruments, and Survival, Inc., a mail-order equipment supplier for dyed-in-the-wool "survivalists," have offered surplus civil defense meters in their recent catalogues.

Rate meters, of course, measure the present rate of radiation, but they can provide no measure of the total accumulated dosage received by any individual over time. For this purpose, a second kind of instrument, known as a "dosimeter," is preferred. The device looks something like a fattened fountain pen, may be hung in a pocket or on a belt, and functions in a fashion similar to the film badges used to measure cumulative dosages received by those who work in areas where low-level sources of radiation may be present. Unlike film badges, which require carefully calibrated outside analysis, pocket dosimeters can provide a measurement of the total radiation dosage absorbed by any individual wearing the device simply by a glance into the end of the tube, where a small scale will be visible. The procedure is roughly akin to looking through a telescope. Most present-day pocket dosimeters will cost $250 or less and information about them is generally available from the same firms that provide rate meters. However, dosimeters have one inherent limitation: most must be recharged once a week or more, in a special device generally supplied by the same firm that sells the dosimeter. In situations where electrical power may not be available, pocket dosimeters would have a limited application if relied upon for any prolonged period of time.

There is one other known way to provide an instrument that can read radiation rates with a high degree of accuracy, and that is to make one. The design for such a device has been worked out by scientist Cresson Kearny of the Oak Ridge National Laboratory, at Oak Ridge, Tennessee, where the enriched uranium suitable for making atomic bombs is separated from natural uranium. Realizing that government policy was apt to deprive the public of useful information about how to measure fallout, Mr. Kearny some time ago set out to invent a radiation rate meter that might be constructed by the average American from materials normally found around the typical American home. In a classic example of government boondoggling, Mr. Kearny's useful design was published by the Oak Ridge National Laboratory, but budget restrictions limited the original number of copies to about 100, most of which today are tucked into the libraries of various research laboratories. Fortunately, copies of the design are available by writing to the National Technical Information Service of the U.S. Department of Commerce (of all agencies), 5285 Port Royal Road, Springfield, Virginia 22161, at a cost less than $15. This service, incidentally, also provides a catalogue of other exceptionally useful technical documents rarely brought to the public's attention.

The homemade Kearny radiation rate meter works, and works well, and its construction requires no specialized technical knowledge. Construction of this homemade instrument requires nothing more than a large tin can with a plastic cover, some aluminum foil, a drying agent such as silica gel, and some thread and wire. The tools required include a hammer, pliers, a sharp knife and scissors, a needle, a small nail, and a ruler. This homemade device can accurately read radiation rates of more than 40 rems per hour, more than enough to provide critical information for those trapped in areas of intense fallout. Constructing the instrument requires some careful work for a few hours, and shorn of the scary implications of nuclear war that lie behind it, makes an excellent science project for parents and children working together. Once built, the device provides a family with a critical tool of exceptional value in the event of any major nuclear emergency in the vicinity of the home.

The ambient radiation level of the atmosphere can be measured with the Kearny meter by judging the separation of the two electrostatic leaves against a scale supplied with the instructions. The wider the separation, the greater the radiation intensity. The user simply pushes the device out of the shelter with some type of long probe, taking care to minimize exposures to the observers. After a short time, the instrument is fetched back into the shelter, and the scale of ambient radiation is measured against the guidelines supplied.

That so few Americans would have been informed of the mere existence of such a device is absolutely typical of the head-in-sand, oversimplified U.S. government approach to civil defense in recent years.

Sources

This chapter is the result of consultations by the author with a number of physicians, psychologists and psychiatrists in the Boston area, and other qualified personnel. The standard civil defense text sources were included in the review leading to its development, along with a series of "survivalist" manuals, few of which merit referral here. To the whole was added what the author hopes will prove to be a dollop of plain common sense.

Material on decontamination procedures was developed from interviews with personnel trained for work with hazardous nuclear wastes and contaminants. The reference to the use of "Tide" detergent may be attributed to the man who was once responsible for the radiological monitoring of the Kennedy Compound at Hyannis, Massachusetts, during the Presidency of John F. Kennedy.

The medical textbooks and similar sources of information to have on hand were the suggestions of several physicians, plus qualified personnel of the U.S. Public Health Service. Your local physician may have other suggestions to add.

The notions of how to decontaminate boats and other vessels were suggested by retired personnel once assigned to the Naval Radiological Defense Station at Hunter's Point, San Francisco, the first such facility in the United States. Suggestions concerning fallout protection factors were taken from material published by the Congressional Office of Technological Assessment and from *Fundamentals of Radiation Protection,* previously cited.

Information on private firms dealing in radiation monitoring equipment was developed by the author with the assistance of personnel at EG&G, a Boston-based company that is a special government consultant on the subject of monitoring nuclear effects.

10 National Civil Defense

*Being thus attacked by both ends of the Constitution,
the head and tail of government, what am I to do?*

Benjamin Franklin,
from "On The Price of Corn and
Management of The Poor"

According to figures published by the Federal government, between the fiscal years 1955 and 1974 the United States procured 1.4 million radiation rate meters, 3.4 million dosimeters, and their related equipment. This program ended somewhat abruptly in the mid-1970s, when the estimate was made that approximately two and one half million Americans would have had to receive formal training in radiological defense to provide any effective implementation of a national civil defense program that might provide the bulk of the American population with some protection against the hazards of fallout from a nuclear war. Little such training was ever accomplished in those years.

The enabling legislation that began this program was the Federal Civil Defense Act of 1950, a direct response to the first Soviet test of an atomic bomb in 1949. Since then, there has been constant reorganization of the government's civil defense agencies and constant re-assignment of the various responsibilities for national civil defense until, today, the history reads like a hodge-podge, alphabet-soup of Federal agencies. The most recent change came in 1978, when the U.S. Congress agreed to a change proposed by the President that called for centralizing all civil defense and peacetime disaster functions into a single Federal agency, the Federal Emergency Management Agency (FEMA). FEMA is supposed to incorporate the multitude of other government outfits that, at one time or another, have had responsibility for improvising some form of civil defense program.

Since its inception in 1978, FEMA has succeeded only in arousing the public's skepticism about its plan to evacuate American cities to countryside locations in the event of nuclear war. This program, which has justifiably contributed to the general cynicism of most Americans about civil defense, is officially termed "crisis relocation," a euphemism for the notion that the cheapest thing the government can do is to order urban populations uprooted and transferred en masse to ill-prepared host communities. By the early 1980s, the Region I office of FEMA, which is responsible for the civil defense planning for the whole of New England, consisted of fewer than half a dozen full-time personnel, whose priority rating for available government services was evidently so low that no space could be found for it in the myriad Federal buildings that dot the New England countryside. Instead, FEMA's Region I office occupied space in downtown Boston in a building owned by the State of Massachusetts. Even the telephone number for FEMA Region I was not a part of the Federal exchange in the Boston area as the 1980s began.

CRISIS RELOCATION

There are two major reasons behind the proposed Federal "crisis relocation" plan, and the two relate to each other in a way that makes the plan seem almost inevitable, given the American civil defense bureaucracy. The first is the belated recognition of the number of warheads available today to the Soviet Union. There are, in fact, so many that it is theoretically possible for the U.S.S.R. to target virtually all American military installations, yet still have enough nuclear firepower remaining to assign more than one warhead to most American centers of population. Since virtually every study ever done indicates that the immediate effects of nuclear weapons, blast and heat, are the most threatening killers, it clearly seems better to move people away from the target areas, rather than leave them to take their chances all too close to the presumed ground zero. While there is a clear contradiction when it comes to the fallout hazard posed by a Soviet attack upon American missile fields to the huge populations downwind along the East Coast, the computerized studies still seem to indicate that, if people could be gotten away from their tightly packed urban centers, more of them could presumably survive.

The second major factor is far more simple — cost. Most previous U.S. plans for civil defense called for the identification of existing structures in urban areas that might provide some protection against both blast and fallout. These are the places still marked today by the fading black-and-yellow "public shelter" signs. These marked shelters were once stocked with austere provisions, including food, canned water, and radiation monitoring equipment. The shelf life of all these survival items has long since expired, and many of the shelters never received their allotments in the first place. To repeat the attempt, at today's prices, is assumed to be far too expensive, and so crisis relocation has become the basic plan, by default. It is simply much cheaper, in theory, to move huge throngs of people than it is to plan to sustain them in place near their homes, even if the idea flies in the face of our experience of the massive American traffic jam.

In theory, the American crisis relocation plan is in its infancy in the early 1980s. Already, however, great and gaping holes in the planning are exposed daily. For one, in a great many instances, plans call for the removal of people from crowded urban areas — most of these by private transport — to "host" areas in the countryside that, regrettably, happen to be even closer to military targets than the urban population would be if it stayed put. An example of this can be seen in the planning for the highly populated Boston area. Here, nearly 2.7 million people are on some FEMA program to be moved away in the time before the onset of nuclear hostilities. But a vast number of them are to be hosted in areas of New Hampshire and Maine that themselves are under the nuclear gun from any Soviet attack on military facilities, such as Pease Air Force Base near the short coastline of New Hampshire, which are likely to be even higher on the Soviet priority list of targets.

Moreover, planning at the reception points is virtually non-existent. On paper, all such host towns and villages are to be surveyed by the U.S. Army Corps of Engineers to identify existing buildings that might serve as both housing and fallout shelter, but this end of the program is poorly funded, ill thought through, and hardly begun. According to the latest available Federal information, for instance, a total of 118,000 buildings nationwide have been marked as public shelters over the past 30 years, and another 95,000 have been identified but not yet marked. The general plan now calls for the posting of such critical sign information only after evacuation was fully under way, Who would do all this work in the short time available is left open to question, and no budget has been set aside for the purpose on a national scale, despite the public attention FEMA is now calling to its grandiose plans.

Worse still, virtually none of the countryside "shelters" have been stocked with the requisite survival items, and the controversial plan now seems to call for such stocking to be done only as the evacuation itself proceeds. How all this can conceivably be accomplished, assuming the majority of urban Americans could reach such far-flung shelters over highways jammed with vehicles — well, this gets little or no attention.

In reality, only the bare bones of the official Federal program for U.S. survival in a nuclear war is visible to the public, and much of it calls for the establishment of advance shelters for a few people, almost all of them public figures and bureaucrats. While the public will theoretically have to make do with ill-organized and badly conceived evacuations to areas far from home, where there will be little or no support, a selected minority of the population is to be protected at a string of hardened sites. The objective of these people is, on paper, to continue the functioning of the government, if only at a minimal level.

An existing DCPA program, for instance, has established eight regional centers in various sections of the nation. Each is designated an "emergency operating center," or EOC, and the majority of these sites have been hardened to provide protection against both blast and fallout. All eight regional EOCs are linked to each other by secure communications circuits that include voice, teletype, and radio. In one report to Congress by the Office of Technology Assessment, for instance, a 1980 estimate is given that, "Forty three states have EOCs, and EOCs with fallout protection are operational or under development in locales including about half the population." Which is perhaps fine for the self-selected government bureaucracy, but will little aid the vast majority of Americans.

Secure as it might be for a small minority, the American plan for civil defense shows other huge and obvious gaps when it comes to general public utility:

Item: Warning of any impending nuclear attack is supposed to come from 1,200 Federal, state, and local warning points, all of which are supposed to be manned 24 hours each day. In actuality, these "warning points" consist of local stations that control whatever outdoor air-raid sirens may still be functional in the United States today. According to this plan, "Once warning has reached local levels, it is passed on to the public by sirens and other means." Yet most of the sirens date back to the 1950s, and there is little or no public knowledge about what their signals mean. It is not necessarily a valid assumption that the U.S. government is willing, or capable, of providing warnings that would theoretically trigger mass evacuation of the cities.

Item: Information critical to the public understanding of any emergency is supposed to be broadcast over the nationwide Emergency Broadcast System, the successor to the famous "Conelrad" radio plan of the 1950s. Fallout protection is supposed to have been provided, according to official government releases, to all the radio stations participating in this national program. A check on stations in the New England area indicates, however, that few, if any, station management personnel are aware of this theoretical Federal support. Moreover, over a third of the radio stations in the Emergency Broadcast System are in areas containing very high priority targets, and very few stations have been provided with any means of protection against the electromagnetic pulse phenomenon, discussed earlier, that could easily knock them off the air. By late 1980, such protection against EMP had been planned for a total of only 180 emergency broadcast stations throughout the nation, and its implementation was so limited as to be non-existent. Even those stations which have sought such proffered assistance have sometimes been told that the aid is months or even years away.

Item: The millions of rate meters and dosimeters that would help provide some rational defense against fallout, originally purchased for use in urban shelters more than a decade ago, have been removed, plundered, or have otherwise found their way into the private market.

Virtually no radiological defense training exists in the U.S. today, with the sole exception of a tiny number of personnel trained for this work at the regional EOCs. Hence Americans who had successfully fought their way through massive traffic jams to reach their host communities would be apt to be facing an exceedingly dangerous radiation hazard, about which little was known, with no one present having the knowledge or equipment to handle the situation.

Item: Where once the Federal government made a serious attempt to provide advance information about what to do in a war emergency, the communications program for this effort has also been allowed to lapse. Today, instead, the government relies mostly on the mass media owned by private companies to provide a modicum of such essential data, even in a climate in which most of the media are extremely skeptical of the government's plans. Classroom and home-study training is now provided only for official civil defense personnel.

According to a study made by the Congressional Office of Technology Assessment,

> "On paper, civil defense looks effective. The United States has more than enough identified fallout shelter spaces for the entire population, which include underground parking, subways, tunnels, and deep basement potential blast shelters. The United States has a vast network of highways and vehicles; every holiday weekend sees a substantial urban evacuation. CB and other radios can aid communication after an attack. The United States has enormous resources (food, medical supplies, electrical-generating capability, etc.) beyond the minimum needed for survival.

> However, no one at all thinks that the United States has an effective civil defense."

SOVIET CIVIL DEFENSE

Faced with essentially the same technological advances in nuclear weaponry over the past few decades — the H-bomb, MIRVed warheads, limited warning times, fallout — the Soviet Union appears to have been embarked upon a very different program for its own civil defense. In contrast to the U.S., the Soviets have stuck to their initial ideas and evidently kept working at them, even if no one can be sure of the full efficacy of such efforts.

In the U.S.S.R., the responsibility for civil defense is vested in an agency of the Ministry of Defense. Late in 1980, the program was headed by a senior military officer, Colonel-General A. Altunin, who also bears the title Deputy Minister of Defense. The organization he heads is believed to employ more than 100,000 full-time professional personnel. Some civil defense training is required of all citizens of the U.S.S.R., and first-aid training for a nuclear environment is provided by way of classroom instruction for many as well. According to reports issued late in the 1970s by both the Central Intelligence Agency and the U.S. Defense Civil Protection Agency, there has evidently been a prolonged and quite active program in the U.S.S.R. for the advance construction of shelters.

Each Soviet citizen residing within 25 miles of the center of an urban target is assigned, in advance, to a particular farm. The farmer at that location has a list of those who would be expected to arrive for shelter at his farm in the event of evacuation. Where fallout shelters have not already been constructed, considerable emphasis is placed on the prompt construction of expedient shelters. Training in such expedient shelter construction is a formal part of the Soviet civil defense training required of all citizens in the U.S.S.R.

According to the CIA study of Soviet civil defense first released in 1978, the contrasts between the civil defense programs of the U.S. and U.S.S.R. are quite striking, and the Soviet plan is explicit to a far higher degree than American contingency planning.

Soviet shelter plans specifically call for the construction of adequate fallout shelters no closer than 25 miles from city districts, as those are defined in the U.S.S.R. The minimum requirement is for the construction to provide adequate protection from a one-megaton American warhead exploding at a distance of six to 12 miles from the shelter.

The U.S.S.R., like the United States, maintains a series of hardened and widely dispersed command posts built underground with reinforced concrete protection against all but the closest nuclear detonations. But the Soviet system appears to be much more extensive, probably providing blast-resistant and fallout-proof shelter for virtually the entire senior command structure of the nation, roughly 110,000 people.

Blast and fallout shelters already constructed near key economic centers could presumably provide protection for anywhere from 12 to 24 percent of the Soviet work force. Anywhere from one out of ten to one out of five urban residents in the Soviet Union can be accomodated in existing shelters that provide protection against blast as well as fallout. In addition, there are extensive plans long existent for urban evacuation that would resemble the newly developed U.S. crisis relocation program. The Soviet program is, however, far more detailed than that of the United States.

Other studies indicate major differences between the U.S. and U.S.S.R. programs of civil defense. One such study, conducted by Boeing Aerospace Company in 1977 (the U.S. firm that made both the B-52 bomber and the Minuteman missile), estimates that much of the Soviet plan for urban evacuation is based on the idea that urban residents of the U.S.S.R. would simply walk directly away from the center of each city for one day, since the Soviet Union is a nation with far fewer major highways and private autos. In such circumstances, a major U.S. retaliatory attack aimed at Soviet cities would be apt to kill 27 percent of this dispersed population, which is assumed to be within 30 miles of the central cities on the second day of war. If, however, the Soviet citizenry dug expedient shelters, for which training has been provided in advance, the retaliation would prove lethal to no more than four percent of the Soviet urban population.

Whether any such elaborate civil defense plans on the part of either nation would actually function effectively during a crisis, of course, cannot be known in advance. Some analysts point out the bureaucratic rigidity typical of the Soviet system and insist that this would prevent effective implementation of massive civil defense plans in the U.S.S.R. regardless of crisis circumstances. Other analysts, even more skeptical, contend that *any* evacuation attempt by either side during the course of a heated international crisis would serve only to make the other side still more nervous — precisely the wrong effect. To these analysts, any organized civil defense plan calling for evacuation upon warning in advance of hostilities is decidedly dangerous. Civil defense, these analysts suggest, is rational in the modern world of thermonuclear weapons only if it is based upon the individual decisions and training of millions of ordinary citizens. Government-ordered or sponsored mass evacuation might only lead to war in and of itself. The time for civil defense, such theorists suggest, is only after war is certain, and advanced planning should be restricted to government-supplied, voluntary training and information provided to interested individuals and their families. Anything else might prove to be pure folly.

RATIONAL CIVIL DEFENSE

If present-day U.S. government pronouncements concerning civil defense are unwise for the average American and might in fact prove harmful, then what can be done by the average American to improve his odds of survival in the event of nuclear war? Here is a kind of detailed checklist for as "rational" a program as can be presently discovered or developed. This checklist is derived in part from government documents and sources, combined with a host of private sources of similar information.

I. Well in advance of the threat, in peacetime

A.   Begin with passive civil defense, as outlined in the preceding chapter. The steps suggested there are sensible and provide extra assurance for a variety of emergency situations even more apt to occur than nuclear war. Check your family's needs in detail, including medicines, and take into consideration such factors as where you live and the weather in your area. Check the availability of emergency gear, including lights, batteries, candles, food, water supplies, and sanitation for prolonged emergencies. Establish a family emergency plan and be sure everyone knows what to do and where to go in various situations. Effort here is economical and worth the trouble, for it provides useful insurance against a host of contingencies.

B.   If nuclear war is a specific concern for you, consider learning about the hazards in detail and decide if you want to purchase equipment, such as radiation monitoring gear, that is useful only in the event of nuclear emergency. Be sure to check with your family doctor and with local libraries. Read and study.

C.   Any plan of rational action in the event of nuclear emergency, whether prompted by the threat of war or by an accident at a nuclear power facility in your area, depends largely upon where you live. The basic decision in *any* nuclear emergency will depend on your proximity to the danger. Consult the targeting lists in this book: not every urban area would necessarily be a primary target, but proximity to strategic nuclear military facilities puts you much higher on the danger list. If the target closest to you is time-sensitive and capable of producing a direct threat to the Soviet Union, then your advance planning on whether to stay or flee should be determined in terms of how far away you are from the target itself. Remember to plan for a *full, average day*, not just for times when you and your family are all gathered at home.

D.　If you are fairly near to a primary target, but far enough away to have a good chance at surviving the immediate effects of a nuclear weapon, plan in more detail to improve your shelter or how best to flee. Add to your store of medical equipment and to your knowledge of how to use it. If you conclude that escape is the best alternative available to you, give careful thought to your destination, means of travel, and what help you would require upon arrival. If you decide that it would be best to stay near hearth and home, examine the house itself and the area in its immediate vicinity. In built-up urban areas, might there be quick shelter available in the basements of nearby large buildings, in tunnels, in underground conduits? The average American home within 15 miles of a modern nuclear weapon detonation will be damaged — check the sections of this book pertaining to weapons effects again — but a bit of advance planning might serve you very well indeed. You do not necessarily need to spend a fortune uprooting your backyard garden and constructing a blast-resistant steel shelter underground. But a hard-eyed and realistic look at your basement, and at what might be done to improve its sheltering potential in the event of a nuclear emergency, might well be justified.

E.　Finally, you may wish to establish a budget for equipment that would be useful. Remember, guns and the typical equipment suggested by survivalists will likely prove far less useful than radiation monitoring gear, sandbags, shovels, food, safe water, and medical supplies. Add to your library and your storehouse of knowledge in the same degree as you make additions to the stockpile of equipment. Use common sense. Decide whether to discuss your plans with the entire family, but remember that people are far more important than things.

II.   In the event of advance warning of nuclear war

The planning you did before will now be worth the effort. First, do not panic, and keep doing things one step at a time. Your first major decision will be whether to move out or stay. Your first job will be to gather your people, re-assure them, then gather whatever is most necessary to support the chosen course of action. If there is sufficient warning time, you will be faced with two basic options.

A.   *If you decide to take shelter in or near your home* take the following steps in order of priority:

- Get everyone together. Assign one responsible person to monitor the communication line by which you would hear the news throughout the crisis period. Do not assume that such communications will be maintained, but it is still important for you to know as much as possible, in the event that some channel of official information manages to stay open.

- Alert everyone to take immediate cover if an attack is made on your area. This means NOW if the light of a weapons burst is seen or the heat from a burst is sensed. A deep basement is preferred, with everyone against the wall closest to the blast. But, if caught in the open, hit the ground immediately, feet toward the explosion, hands and arms covering the head, eyes, and ears. A ditch is better than open ground. Remember that, according to the distance you are from the explosion, the blast wave may follow the first flash after a considerable interval of time. In the early stages of the alert, stay loose and keep everyone as close as possible to shelter, consistent with the work that must be done.

- Protect all but one radio receiver from EMP by disconnecting all power cords and — hopefully — placing the instruments inside a well-grounded metal cabinet deep inside the shelter. One instrument should stay on line so that further information might be received by the person responsible for monitoring it.

- Draw all shades or venetian blinds to keep thermal effects from penetrating the house.

- Gather as much water as can be contained, in whatever will carry it. Cover the tops of the containers with clear wrapping, such as Saran Wrap, or cloth. There is no such thing as too much water in a shelter.

- Crack windows open on the bottom on the side of the home most likely to be opposite the presumed blast. This can help reduce pressure changes.

- If time permits, pile soil around the outside walls of the basement shelter, the more the better.

- Again, if there is time, add extra-strong shelter spaces within the main shelter. Prop dense objects atop, say, a desk to give more shelter to anyone tucked underneath. Books work reasonably well, as does soil poured into containers such as pillow cases or strong bags.

- Be sure that all available survival equipment, including food, radiation monitors, and fire fighting gear, is placed inside the shelter. If the basement is not feasible, pick a central point on the first floor and preferably one beneath a major archway or supporting point. Keep away from windows.

- Double-check fire-fighting equipment.

- Be sure to arrange for wet towels or masks.

- If time permits, consider bringing soil into the first floor of the home and piling it on floors and carpets. Again, the more the better.

- If there is enough time, remove several of the interior doors, take them into the basement shelter, then construct an interior sheltering space beneath the door(s) propped on several external supports. Pile soil or heavy books atop the horizontally-arranged doors, and save the space beneath them for children.

- Repeat all the above steps, double-checking that water has been secured well within the shelter.

- Take every available moment to "improve" the shelter by putting as much material as possible between you and the outside air. Seal all basement windows, and pile as much dirt as possible over any air leaks.

- Check your transportation facilities, but do *not* put extra gasoline in cans within the shelter. If your car survives, it can later be a potential supply of fuel, light, heat, some power, and perhaps communications.

- Load commercial radiation monitoring equipment, if any, with batteries.

- Stockpile food only if it is already in cans or other washable containers. Exposed food, such as vegetables and fruits, may be useful, but will have to be washed thoroughly before consumption, which will require a great deal of water.

- Conduct a final check to be sure that all electrical cords have been disconnected and all gas appliances turned off fully.

B. *If you elect to flee:*

- Check the gas available. Take with you only the most essential equipment that might promote survival. Follow the lists above.

- Keep the radio on to monitor further communications, but otherwise cut down on use of the battery as much as possible.

- BE SURE OF YOUR ESCAPE ROUTE AND KEEP IN MIND ANY ALTERNATIVES.

- The auto itself will provide useful shelter only when you have driven it atop a pre-prepared hole in the ground. If you are stuck in impossible traffic, and attack seems imminent, then get off the road onto soft ground, dig as deep a ditch as possible beneath where you will shortly move the car, then bank soil piled into blankets or sheets around the base of the car to shut off direct exposure. If time permits, consider piling soil into the open doors of the car as the vehicle sits atop your ditch. Again, the more soil, the better.

- Keep going at all costs, unless attack is certain or is apt to occur swiftly.

- IN ANY FALLOUT SITUATION WHERE YOU ARE STILL STUCK INSIDE THE CAR, close the windows and turn on the defroster or the maximum-position air conditioner, both of which treat the inside air without taking in air from outside. This will maximize the air pressure inside the car and keep the maximum amount of outside air away from the occupants.

DO NOT OPEN WINDOWS OR USE THE VENT AFTER ANY UPWIND ATTACK.

III.   In the event there is limited warning or immediate attack

A.   TAKE COVER IMMEDIATELY. If indoors, get below the level of the windows and remain flat on the floor until the blast wave has passed.

B.   Look for and extinguish any fires you can. If you cannot control the fires, prepare to evacuate immediately.

C.   Treat the injured as best you can, with whatever is on hand. The preservation of life is a primary responsibility of all those who may survive the immediate effects of nuclear weapons.

D.   If fire conditions permit and life-sustaining aid has been given to the injured, begin to construct an expedient shelter. Remember, fallout will not arrive for some minutes after a nuclear detonation, even at points within a few miles of ground zero. Farther away, it may be hours or days before the fallout hazard becomes critical. The time available may be used to construct or seek expedient shelter.

E.   Search for a safe basement, and move the injured to that location. Remember that the danger from fire is paramount. Do not plan to move far.

F.   Gather supplies in the following order or priority:

- fire-fighting equipment

- medical supplies

- water and the means to make and keep it pure

- radiation-monitoring equipment

- tools to improve the shelter

- all other equipment and supplies.

G.   Assuming that fires have been controlled and the injured cared for, use all remaining time before the arrival of fallout, if any, to improve the available shelter in the same way as outlined above. If trapped in the open, consider using the interior door approach outside, away from dangerous buildings, but place the doors atop a pre-dug ditch and cover them with as much soil or other dense material as possible. They will, in fact, sustain considerable weight. Any movable vehicle may also be used in the same general way atop a ditch.

H.   Begin monitoring fallout within ten minutes after the blast and continue this monitoring according to the following rules:

1. *Fallout radiation rate below five rems per hour but rising:*

   - Prepare fallout shelter and be ready to enter it once the fallout rate reaches five rems per hour. Until then, useful outside work may be done.
   - If fallout is at all visible in the form of ashes or falling dust particles, take shelter immediately and stay there until the rate falls below five rems per hour.
   - If you are outside when fallout is being deposited, even at comparatively low rates, it is essential to brush, wash off, or decontaminate clothing and the external surfaces of the body — especially the hair and all folds in the skin — BEFORE entering the shelter. This procedure should be followed after any visit to the outside.

2. *Fallout radiation rate between five and 50 rems per hour:* absolutely essential work might be done, but the tasks should be rotated to minimize the cumulative exposure to any one person or group. As a rule, follow the suggested list below in estimating tolerable levels of accumulated exposure:

   - oldest persons first, because they are at least risk, male or female
   - second oldest males
   - women of child-bearing age
   - teenagers
   - expectant mothers
   - younger children. IN ALL CASES, IT IS ESSENTIAL TO MINIMIZE THE TOTAL EXPOSURE OF YOUNGSTERS AND EXPECTANT MOTHERS. All others should be risked first.

3. *Fallout radiation rate of more than 50 rems per hour,* whether rising or falling:

   - TAKE IMMEDIATE SHELTER. Keep all people,

especially children and those injured, in the safest possible place, which will generally be beneath extra-sheltering interior constructions (such as the desk or door-cover type described above) or nearest one of the outside walls near its bottom.

- Do whatever can be done to increase the density of material between the fallout and the people within the shelter, BUT DO SO ONLY FROM IN-SIDE THE SHELTER.

- Prepare to decontaminate any late arrivals as well as possible.

- If a physician is available, treat radiation sickness symptomatically, according to the cumulative dosage received. Supportive therapy generally involves antibiotics if available, since radiation exposure tends to make the victim more susceptible to secondary infections.

- Remember the two precedent conditions that govern all possible cases:

  i) FIRE IS THE MOST IMMEDIATE HAZARD. IT MUST BE CONTROLLED OR ESCAPED.

  ii) YOUNG CHILDREN HAVE TOP PRIORITY, ALWAYS, FOR FALLOUT PROTECTION.

These two rules must stay in force because, even in the awful conditions of a nuclear catastrophe, there remains a chance that life may go on, with all its joys and sorrows, fears and hopes. Anything that contributes to the possibility of the survival of that spark of life cannot be overlooked. Anything that adds to the danger that this precious spark might be extinguished cannot be countenanced.

Sources

Statistics on U.S. government expenditures for civil defense and for the general history of such projects were put together with the help of personnel at the Congressional Office of Technology

Assessment, its private contractors, and consultants to the Federal Emergency Management Agency. Information on the present status of U.S. civil defense plans was supplied in part by the Office of Technology Assessment.

Information about the Soviet civil defense organization was first published, in translation, by the Oak Ridge National Laboratory, Oak Ridge, Tennessee, in 1973, but is now available from the National Technical Information Service under the American title, *Civil Defense,* at the address previously given in these Notes. Also useful is the publication "Soviet Civil Defense in the Seventies," by L. Goure (Advanced International Studies Institute, Washington D.C., 1975) and the statement on "Soviet Civil Defense" by the Director of the U.S. Central Intelligence Agency (CIA-N178-10003, July, 1978). Contrasting views on this particular subject are offered by Congressman Les Aspin in "The Mineshaft Gap Revisited," (Congressional Record for 15 January 1979) and a two part article by F.M. Kaplan, "The Soviet Civil Defense Myth" in the *Bulletin of the Atomic Scientists* for March and April, 1978.

Specific recommendations for actions to be taken in the event of nuclear war emergency are based on virtually all the relevant sources cited in these Notes, especially the ALFA NEOP guidelines and the nine-volume DCPA study previously cited, but they remain primarily the author's own composite of the many sources.

11 Long-Term Survival

But this — why, yesterday, five hours by the clock
From now, 'twas just twelve hundred, sixty and six
Years since the road was rent by earthquake shock.

Dante, *The Divine Comedy,*
the eighth Circle of Hell

It should be clear by now that even the mildest form of modern nuclear war would have immediate and disastrous consequences for many human generations still to come. People and resources destroyed in mere seconds would be an irreplaceable loss for civilization. Those killed in subsequent weeks and months by fallout would only add to the toll. The very structure of our modern social institutions would be shaken and perhaps be changed irreversibly. Most of it would be the result not of technological advance, but of the continued frailties of human wisdom and of the human spirit.

Might anyone survive at all? From a scientific standpoint, the question admits so many possible answers that any precision is virtually impossible. The whole body of knowledge of the long-term effects of modern nuclear weapons is limited to analyses of Hiroshima and Nagasaki, study of the effects produced by the nearly 600 nuclear weapons in tests in the past 35 years, and extrapolations from various laboratory experiments. In short, there has been neither enough time nor enough evidence to predict the long-term worldwide effects of a nuclear war.

LONG-TERM PROBLEMS

Cancer

In 1975, the U.S. National Academy of Sciences first attempted to summarize the issues in its report, *Long-Term Worldwide Effects of Multiple Nuclear Weapons Detonations*. Since the first publication of the report, technical knowledge of the subject has been advanced only in two basic areas — the likelihood of genetic damage to the human species, which has been shown now to occupy a somewhat narrower range of "doubling dose" (the point at which mutations can be predicted to double) between 50 and 200 rems, and the prospects of damage to the earth's protective ozone layer, where the potential hazard seems now to be somewhat increased. At the same time, the inherent limitations of human knowledge, or predictive capacity, about this subject have become even more readily apparent. We do not yet know, for instance, if very low exposures to radiation, especially those received over a comparatively long period of time, do as much damage in total, or do it in the same biological way, as somewhat higher but still sublethal doses absorbed in a shorter period of time. It seems that there is, in fact, no "threshold" dose below which radiation is safe. In this way, the basic assumptions of any formal study tend to produce very wide ranges of prediction from case to case. All the scientific uncertainties in the analysis of the effects of a single weapon upon a single place on earth are, indeed, magnified once the larger issues are approached.

The best available evidence that can be surmised in the early 1980s can be summarized as follows:

Most of those beyond the range of the immediate effects of nuclear weapons might be expected to survive over the long term, though there would be a relatively modest increase in the incidence of cancer world-side in the first 40 years after the war.

Prompt radiation, absorbed in the first month after an outbreak of nuclear war, would likely inflict sublethal doses on many who otherwise survived the effects of blast and fire. U.S. weapons, which tend to be smaller, might inflict some direct radiation on victims far enough away from the detonations to survive the blast. Ironically, Soviet weaponry, which is generally of much higher yield, can be expected to kill all those within radiation range of ground zero. On this point, there is considerable uncertainty regarding the effects on humans of fairly low levels of direct, or neutron, irradiation.

Local fallout is apt to inflict damage upon survivors who have the misfortune to take shelter on the fringes of major fallout zones. Others in comparatively high-intensity fallout areas might have attenuating shelter, but would nevertheless receive some exposure. Absorption of even sublethal doses of radiation is today assumed to have some deleterious effect on prospects of long-term survival.

Some low-level radiation hazard is apt to be present for years after a detonation, an effect demonstrated at the sites of several early weapons tests. Adverse health effects would also be influenced by the "design" of the attacks themselves. If, for instance, either side, or both, were to choose weaponry specifically designed to prolong radiation contamination, the long-term health hazards would be greatly increased for the surviving population. In almost all cases, survivors of the first month of a nuclear war would be compelled to live with substantially higher levels of background radiation than are tolerated by peacetime standards.

Fallout deposited by the detonations at the lower levels of the atmosphere would come down weeks or months later in areas far removed from the immediate danger zones. This too would add to the overall risk in the future.

Other fallout can be injected high into the stratosphere, and this fallout too will eventually descend back to the surface of earth over many years. The hazards here are posed by much longer-lived radioactive isotopes, such as strontium-90 and cesium-137, which decay so slowly as to provide some additional risk for many years to come. The radionuclides involved pose a particular risk to younger people because they tend to be mistaken by the body for elements essential to growth, such as the calcium required for the proper development of bones. The current evidence suggests that the hazards of such long-term effects would be mostly confined to the Northern Hemisphere, where the regions between latitudes 30 and 60 degrees north would be apt to receive the vast bulk of this particular form of fallout. The hazards inherent in this phenomenon were the specific motivation for the signing of the Nuclear Test Ban Treaty in the 1960s.

Cancer deaths in the millions may be predicted among all those who survive a nuclear war in the Northern Hemisphere in the first 40 years after the war. This toll, however, would actually be much less than the prompt lethalities caused by the war itself. The increased risk would simply be an extra hazard faced over the longer haul by surviving populations.

A very large nuclear exchange would also produce deaths, chiefly from fallout, "in the low millions" in areas outside the native lands of the combatants. World-wide, this would, however, represent only a relatively modest increase in the general cancer rate prevailing on the planet.

None of the above results might be as limited if any attacker possessed of a high level of nuclear technology deliberately chose to create intense levels of radiation in the course of waging war.

FOOD AND WATER

For all practical purposes, the prospect of long-term survival for anyone who has managed to endure the first month(s) of a nuclear war — assuming no subsequent attacks over a still longer period of time — would be diminished by two major factors, starvation and disease. After the first 30 days or so, these two factors, both of which would be greatly influenced by the size and scope of the nuclear exchange, would be apt to become the predominant hazards. If the war itself were confined to the exchange of a hundred or so weapons by each side, the majority of people in both the U.S. and the U.S.S.R. would likely survive the first month, only to be endangered subsequently by the disruption of economic and commercial institutions in a world often described today as possessing "no place that is more than three day's food supply away from complete panic." If the war were limited to the obliteration of purely military targets, many millions would die in the first month(s), but millions more would survive to face even more hostile conditions. If the war were all-out, prolonged over a long period of time, survival would likely become a matter of sheer luck — a village here, a small cluster of people there. Most of the luck would be bad throughout the Northern Hemisphere.

The rules of survival for those emerging from adequate fallout shelters would be harsh indeed. Very little of this has been publicized, although there is a considerable body of research available by extrapolation from the nuclear research laboratories, where years of work have been done to measure the effects of radiation on plants and on animals other than man.

Most Americans today are apt to be confused, for instance, about whether food and water would be contaminated by radioactive fallout in the aftermath of a nuclear war. The answer to the question is a qualified "yes," though much would depend on the exact circumstances, such as the season of the year in which the heaviest fallout was deposited.

Still another example of confusion is presented today by those who deem themselves "survivalists" and believe that American society could revert to hunting and fishing for food after a nuclear war. For the most part, this contention is mistaken, because most game animals and birds would suffer as much from radioactive fallout as people. And, if depletion of the ozone layer of the earth as a by-product of nuclear war proved to be as hazardous as it might, human survivors would face life in an essentially nocturnal world — the increased ultraviolet light from the sun would require it.

Yet some hazards are more controllable if appropriate knowledge is applied. Fallout-contaminated food may be safely eaten, for instance, if it is first washed thoroughly. The fallout does not make the food radioactive in itself, but the radioactive particles must be removed before the food is eaten. For this reason, food contained in cans or packages will generally be safe in the weeks after any nuclear attack, provided only that the exterior package is washed thoroughly and some care is taken to minimize contact between the contents and the packaging. Fruits and vegetables may also be eaten, assuming that they have been thoroughly decontaminated by careful washing and especially if the skin is peeled and discarded.

Safe drinking water is a similar matter, but one with its own peculiar technical characteristics. Two principal hazards are associated with drinking water exposed to a nuclear environment. The first concerns fallout particles themselves which, since they are heavier than water, tend to settle slowly toward the bottom. Care must be taken either to let them stay settled on the bottom or to filter them out before the water is taken. Passing the water first through multi-layered filters, such as layers of fine gauze, can remove some of the radioactive particles, as can distillation, which will tend to leave them behind in the residue. An important preventive step is to be sure that all open containers of potable liquids remain covered whenever possible if any potential hazard from fallout prevails. After the first week, water supplies may in fact be hazardous as sources of disease, and care should be taken to purify all drinking water with one of the kits widely available today. They are available in some pharmacies, army-surplus stores, and retailers that specialize in backpacking and wilderness camping supplies.

The other major hazard is far more technical and insidious. One of the by-products of a nuclear weapons explosion is iodine-131, a radioactive isotope of conventional iodine. This is generally released as a gas that combines all too readily with water, and its removal is very difficult, if not impossible. Taken into the body, especially by children, iodine-131 mimics regular iodine, which tends to be collected in the thyroid gland. Fortunately, radioactive iodine-131 has a relatively short half-life — which means that half its radiation decays in a fixed period — of roughly eight days. Hence potable water that can be left alone for a week or more is considerably safer than that which contains iodine-131 shortly after the blast or radiation accident. Another approach — ask your family physician about this — is to "block" the iodine by taking potassium iodide tablets or pills at the time when the danger might be greatest. The clinical evidence to date is that only so much iodine in any form can be taken up by the body; overloading the body temporarily with potassium iodide essentially reduces the uptake of the radioactive iodine-131 and thus theoretically limits the damage that might be done to the thyroid by it when the radionuclide is still at its hottest.

Asked about the safety of stockpiled food and water in the kind of dangerous world apt to exist after any nuclear exchange, several physicians suggested a wholly different approach, one reliant at the outset upon fairly new products used today in hospitals to provide sustenance for patients who cannot eat. Several such products exist in canned-liquid form, which means that they are both storable for long periods of time before use, without refrigeration, and that they could be readily decontaminated if a fallout hazard were present. Six to eight small cans of such a liquid-food product, certainly not as tasty as regular food and a touch boring if consumed exclusively over a long period, can readily provide a total intake of 2000-2500 calories per day, far more than enough to sustain life. One such product, trade-named ''Ensure,'' can provide 100 percent of all required daily amounts of vitamins and minerals while supplying needed fluids. ''Ensure'' is available at most good pharmacies without prescription.

The only drawbacks to such products as a survival stockpile option are their comparative bulk and expense. The cans, generally eight ounces, are heavy and take up valuable space. At current prices, ''Ensure'' approaches one dollar per can, and eight cans per day are required to provide 100 percent of all daily adult requirements (more than might be required on a daily basis if supplied had to be stretched). Hence, a family of four could be sustained by a liquid-food diet, such as that provided by ''Ensure,'' almost indefinitely and quite safely, provided that the family could afford $1300 or so for a month's supply and had the room to store 1280 cans of the food. Such stockpiles are also not very portable.

Those who live on farms and in rural areas are sometimes counseled, in survivalist manuals, that they are fortunate in that their local area could revert to a hunting society after a nuclear war. In fact, people living far from the madding crowds of the cities and other similar targets may have some immediate advantage — they are simply farther away from the most lethal of the direct effects of nuclear weaponry. But radiation affects virtually all animal life, as a multitude of experiments have shown, and the odds are that game animals such as deer, which would have little hope of finding effective shelter from fallout, would be more gravely injured than the men who might wish to hunt them. The effects of radiation are implacable and remorseless for all mammalian life. If there is enough radiation, everything dies, literally everything, and the greater the exposure, the swifter the effect. Grazing and browsing animals would, in fact, be more swiftly injured because they have no way to decontaminate feed grasses, twigs, and leaves. The animals of the woods, from deer to rabbit, would be similarly affected, though rabbits are thought to be among the most resistant of all mammals. Severe radiation would clearly reduce wildlife populations in any area where fallout was intense.

The same holds true for unprotected livestock and farm animals. Farmers wishing to provide the best possible protection for their stock would be advised to shelter the animals in barns, where just a roof over their heads and feed that might be less contaminated would be safer than fields and yards. (Pet owners have a similar problem, for dogs and cats are just a bit more resistant to radiation than is man.)

Most livestock, with the exception of sheep, are slightly less prone to radiation injury than is man. For example, an accumulated dose of 450 rems absorbed by an unsheltered human population in the period of a week could be expected to prove fatal to about one half the population. The figures below, derived from experiments at nuclear laboratories, indicate the average lethal dose for one half the population, species by species.

sheep	400 rems	pigs	600 rems
cattle	500 rems	chickens	850 rems

Most scientists today agree that animals grievously injured by radiation could be safely eaten by man, if they were still alive. However, the meat would have to be exceptionally well cooked because severe radiation dosages destroy the digestive tract as well as the blood-forming tissues and make the meat far more susceptible to bacterial invasion.

DISRUPTION OF AGRICULTURE

The effects of radiation on plants and crops has also been studied extensively, but simple predictions are hard to find because of the many variables involved. As a rule, plants are relatively more hardy than animals when it comes to radiation resistance. They do not, for instance, generally take up fallout from the soil very readily. Moreover, fallout particles landing directly on plants or crops may be washed away effectively by a thorough rinsing with water. As for the radiation tolerance of plants themselves, a general rule is that crops would be most susceptible to damage when they first emerged from the ground in spring. Mature crops are considerably more resistant to radiation, but the entire issue is clouded by considerations for the safety of the farmers who would have to work the fields.

A great deal of the impact of nuclear war on food supplies would likely depend on two major factors: first, the dangers of nuclear war are greatest in the Northern Hemisphere, where many of the best farmers in the world today might be killed immediately in the course of the war. The second factor is in which season the greatest fallout danger might exist after the outbreak of war. For example, a Soviet attack in February or March would do indirect damage to the American agricultural system because planting would have to be delayed while farmers sought shelter. Any major attack from April through June would likely prove disastrous to any farming country north of the Equator because it would pose a very grave danger to the young crops themselves. By late summer, crops mature to maximum tolerance to radiation. But any attack in late August, September, or October would, again, force humans out of the fields and into shelters at a critical point in the season. Attacks in the winter would have little immediate impact on food production, but would establish the conditions for the maximum take-up of fallout by the crops, if any, the following year. The most immediate human hazard from fallout-contaminated crops arises from the radioactive dust atop the plants themselves, which may be washed or rinsed off before eating. But, over time, plants may also take up a small percentage of several radioactive elements present in the soil, leading to a longer-term, if less pronounced, potential hazard.

Despite the comparative radiation resistance demonstrated by most crops, fallout might nevertheless serve to reduce the yield of some crops drastically. According to the latest available (1979) unclassified information on this subject, the following total dosages, expressed in roentgens, would be likely to reduce the overall yield of each specific crop by 50 percent:

CROP	ROENTGENS
peas	1000
rye	1000-2000
wheat, corn, cucumbers	2000-4000
cotton, most kinds of melon	6000-8000
soybeans, beets	8000-12000
rice, strawberries	12000-16000
squash	16000-24000

Compared to information on radiation effects on animals and plants, reliable data on the effects of radiation on fish and sea life is much more sparse. The general assumption is that, because water serves to attenuate the range of radiation effects, most fish would prove less susceptible to fallout than would people, plants, and animals. The Pacific tuna rendered hazardous aboard the Japanese fishing boat in 1954, for example, are presumed to have been dusted with beta-emitting particles from the U.S. H-bomb test at Bikini Atoll, 100 miles to the west. The fish were not radiactive from their internal take-up of fallout particles in the water itself.

The dust and ashes that fall downwind of a nuclear detonation, when deposited upon water, generally tend to sink to the bottom with time, theoretically minimizing the radiation threats to aquatic life. Some of the trace plutonium resulting from atmospheric weapons tests in the 1950s and early 1960s, for instance, can today be found on the sea bed. The fallout contamination has been shown to be heaviest in the belt from latitudes 30 to 60 degrees north above the equator.

For this reason, fish might be a useful source of food for humans in the aftermath of a nuclear war. Caution must still be exercised because of the paucity of reliable data available and the likelihood that the hazards might prove greater for specific species according to their life habits. Species that are habitual bottom feeders, such as the hornpout in fresh water or flounder along the coasts, might be more likely to contain a radiation hazard, while other species that seek food in the middle depths, or near the surface, such as most gamefish, might prove safer for consumption.

In all such considerations, there remain profound asymmetries in the two situations facing the United States and the Soviet Union. Both populations would be likely to suffer grievously from the effects of any major nuclear exchange, and the surviving remnants of both would face similar problems in combating disease and social disruption. It is impossible to put healthy people in cramped, crowded, damp conditions underground for long periods of time and expect them to maintain their accustomed level of health. Yet differences in production capacity and in geographic circumstance might lead to different degrees of hardship for the population of the two nations, and each might be exposed to differing extents of privation, hardship, starvation, and disease. Much of America's huge and modern agricultural capacity relies on ground that lies close to or directly in the path of the radioactive clouds that would rise from the destruction of U.S. missile silos west of the Mississippi River. A different scheme of attack, one that targets oil refining capacity, would be apt to hit Soviet agriculture much harder than it would the American counterpart because a much higher proportion of Soviet oil supplies are required for the U.S.S.R.'s much less efficient farming system.

In the last analysis, however, it is clear that any major nuclear war would kill a majority of the populations of both nations and would gravely endanger the survivors, whatever their numbers might be, by posing long-term hazards of starvation, privation, and disease.

Sources

Information about the possible long-term effects of nuclear war upon the environment is derived in large part, as described, from the 1975 study by the U.S. National Academy of Sciences, "Effects of Multiple Nuclear Explosions Worldwide." Estimates of the possible effects of nuclear war on crop production and the likelihood of starvation and disease are derived from three publications of the Stanford Research Institute, "Agricultural Vulnerability in the National Entity Survival Context" (1970); "Agricultural Vulnerability to Nuclear War" (1973); and "U.S. Agriculture Potential Vulnerabilities" (1969). Information about the resilience of various food crops to radiation can be found in "Effects of Fallout Radiation on Crop Production," by the Comparative Animal Research Laboratory (1975).

12 Two Seconds

*Man, who is the noblest part of the earth, melts so away,
as if he were a statue, not of earth, but of snow.*

John Donne, from *Devotions Upon
Emergent Occasions*

Two seconds is approximately the duration of the flash from a
nuclear weapon. The light from the weapon is unmistakable, all encompassing, like a second sunrise. It will last from two to 20 seconds,
depending on the type of weapon and other factors. The light itself is
blinding — DO NOT LOOK TOWARD IT — but the heat will be
worse. This too takes from two to as much as 30 seconds to pass. Seek
immediate shelter. Hit the ground. Immediately. Put your feet toward
the light. Cover your head and ears with your hands and arms. The
faster you move, the better your chances for the first minute of
nuclear war. If inside, get below the level of any windows. Do not
attempt to get up until the blast wave has passed. This may take mere
seconds to reach you, or it may take minutes, depending on your distance from the weapon's ground zero. If you arise too soon, the blast
may kill you if the heat has not. If you have sufficient presence of
mind, try to time the interval from the first, brilliant light to the
arrival of the blast wave. Every two seconds represents a bit more
than a mile. This may make a difference to your prospects later. So
will any advanced planning you have done.

If you can do these things in the first few moments of a nuclear
blast, your chances of survival will roughly double. You will probably
survive if you are more than five or ten miles from the detonation.
The heat will be intense and it may seem to last an eternity. The blast
will come, eventually, like a huge, sudden wind. If you survive these

two things, your first duty will then be to others. Remember, at the heart of things, people do not really live just for themselves.

In the initial stages, fight fires and do what you can to help the injured. The latter is a moral responsibility. The former is a practical matter, for fire will now become your worst enemy for many hours to come. There is little for you to fear from direct radiation at this time. The fallout may come too, later, by as much as hours or days, and it too may kill you, but not until you will have had time to contribute useful work to alleviate other conditions. The fallout will depend on the wind, and you should make careful note of this. If the wind blows away from you, toward the heart of the blast, you have more time. If you are 20 or 30 miles upwind, or a hundred or more downwind, there will be hours yet in which you should seek protective shelter. Move the children and the injured into shelter first, because they are the most susceptible to radiation. Do not panic. Do one thing at a time, then move on to the next. Always be aware of the danger of fire.

If you reach shelter, then the planning you did beforehand will prove among the most useful things you ever did in life. You will need radiation monitoring gear, or you will have to know how to make some in dire conditions. Without this, you will not know when, or if, it is safe to leave shelter. Think of the practical requirements now — water, medical help and supplies, food, sanitation. Consider the psychology of the situation, but remember that it helps greatly if you know the physics beforehand. Keep people busy with useful, practical work.

When the attack is over, or when you emerge from shelter, food, water, medicines, sanitation will be the first requirements. Even in the worst areas, fallout may decay in a few days or weeks to the point where you can risk travel outdoors. The land may be uninhabitable by peacetime standards, but the first flash has already told you that peace is no more, and the remaining radiation is not nearly as apt to kill you as are starvation and disease. Don't worry much about guns: you can't shoot a germ or an alpha particle, anyway.

Livestock and wildlife may have been badly damaged, and any animals still living should be used for food, promptly, but cooked very thoroughly. Wash what food you have. Within a few months, virtually all meat will disappear, and this condition may remain for the rest of your life, however long that may be, once people realize that it is more efficient to feed grain to people directly, rather than raising meat.

There will be privations and dangers. Money won't matter, for once, but goods and services and bartered talents — the whole sum of the human will — are going to count very much. Resourcefulness and luck will also play a part, even if most luck seems bad. Transportation will be by shank's mare, which means new thought about shoes and clothing.

No one in the United States has any experience with such disaster and disruption as would result from even the smallest of nuclear wars. It may be possible for you to survive, but it will take wisdom, far more of this commodity than our pre-war life generally requires each day. Remember that the human spirit may still prove to be unquenchable, that things take time and determination. Nothing will ever be the same again in the United States if and when a single nuclear weapon explodes on our soil. The closest historical precedent in our history is probably the agony of the South during the Civil War and for some time after. And no one yet knows whether that national experience has been fully healed in the century since it happened.

Sources

Two publications played a role: "Information Needs for Post-Attack Recovery Management," by F. Dresch, (Stanford Research Institute, 1968) and "Disaster and Recovery: A Historical Survey," (RAND Corporation report, RM-3079, 1963).

Afterword

As this book has approached completion in the first half of 1983, news and commentary about nuclear war has grown increasingly frequent. Among the headline items has been the seemingly endless debate about the MX missile. In Congress, this debate comes as a choking bone in the throat, because the nation consciously chose, in the early 1970s, *not* to field weapons of first-strike capability, such as the MX. To more than one observer, the MX debate has been made necessary by Soviet intransigence and their decision, late in the 1970s, to deploy gigantic new rockets with first-strike capability.

To cool the fiery politics of the MX issue, President Reagan turned to a special commission for recommendations about how to deploy the MX. The commission's report was, no doubt, both more and less than MX supporters might have hoped. Build a small number of the giant MX rockets, the commission said, and house them in existing Minuteman missile silos (where they would be as vulnerable to Soviet attack as are the Minuteman missiles today). In addition, however, the commission noted that missiles of the MX type might tend to make Soviet fingers even more itchy on the nuclear trigger. On balance, then, such giant new rocketry should be looked upon as diplomatic bargaining chips. But perhaps the national interest would be better served if we construct a host of much smaller new missiles, each with a single warhead incapable of wiping out a hard target, such as a Soviet missile silo, and widely disperse them.

A second newsworthy event was the election of Chancellor Kohl's party in West Germany. The Kohl election is widely viewed as a rejection of Soviet attempts to influence a free election in the West. That Soviet sabre-rattling and economic threats were overlooked by a majority of the West Germans is seen as clear evidence that most Europeans may support the deployment of new American missiles to offset Soviet forces. The loudest, longest, and most visible by-product of this election is apt to be violent street demonstrations throughout Europe late in 1983, as the first American Pershing II missiles and Tomahawk cruise missiles are deployed in Europe. The Soviets have made a particular issue of the new Pershing missiles, which are rockets of relatively short range but capable of bringing Moscow under nuclear fire from bases in West Germany within eight minutes of a decision to launch. Soviet objections to the cruise missiles have not been as strident, although this particular technology carries with it a high risk of completely unverifiable deployment of the weapons in huge numbers. Perhaps, in fact, the Soviets believe they have the ability to shoot down the slower and lower flying cruise missiles, given their extensive air defense system. But the question remains why the Soviets have taken so strong a stance against the Pershing II when, in fact, missiles fired from U.S. submarines in the Baltic could reach Moscow in ten to 12 minutes, and the subs to fire them have been on station for years.

The third major announcement of 1983 was the speech by President Reagan on March 23. In it, Mr. Reagan signalled what could be the largest single shift in American strategic thought since the dawn of the nuclear age, away from offense and toward defense. Little understood as yet by the general public, and though it remains uncertain how much of the Reagan plan will ever be implemented, this speech has spawned a broad review of nuclear war doctrine.

What would change, under the Reagan plan, would be reliance on the notion of "Assured Survival" rather than on the traditional all-out-offense doctrine of "Mutually Assured Destruction" that has been the linchpin of U.S. nuclear strategy for nuearly four decades.

To analysts familiar with the science and technology involved, the Reagan proposal is intriguing because, historically, nuclear weaponry has given virtually all advantage to the offensive side, from cost factors to ease of deployment and likelihood of successful operation. That technology has advanced to the point that the nation could rely upon it for *survival* in times of international nuclear emergency is, in fact, stunning.

To the public, the debate seems to be about exotic new weaponry, lasers in space and beam-shooting space fighters, with the basic question being whether all the equipment would function. Actually, however, Mr. Reagan's startling proposals seem to be based on the proposals in the "High Frontier," a privately-organized study of what America might do to maintain its security in the face the Soviet build-up of recent years. Various elements of "High Frontier" are themselves both more and less exotic than the reader might suspect.

For instance, the High Frontier proposals openly acknowledge the likelihood that lasers, particle-beam generators, and solar-heat weapons are not yet ready and that such ideas are hardly much beyond the theoretical stage. According to High Frontier, reliance upon such weaponry would not be possible until the deployment of second-generation defensive weaponry in the 1990s.

What then constitutes a bolstering of U.S. nuclear defenses today? One thing, High Frontier says, is weaponry based on technology already in existence. For example, in one of its proposals, High Frontier envisions the deployment of four or five 30-millimeter automatic cannons in hardened turrets around each Minuteman missile silo. Such silos today represent almost two-thirds of the U.S. deterrent force that could be fired in the first half hour of any nuclear conflict, and these installations have grown increasingly vulnerable to a Soviet first strike. The automatic cannons, made by General Electric, were designed to be mounted in the A-10 tank-fighting aircraft deployed by NATO. The weapon is well-proved, potentially useful for a measure of final, close-in, defensive support. In gatling-gun fashion, the weapon fires a stream of explosive 30-millimeter shells at a rate of fire so high that it can literally form a wall of exploding shells around an installation. According to High Frontier, this kind of weapon could be used at Minuteman sites to fire on incoming Soviet warheads, hoping to damage or set them off prematurely, well above the silo. High Frontier analysts give this weapon a 90 percent chance of disabling or setting off an incoming Soviet warhead between 8,000 and 1,000 feet above the silo, far enough away, barely, to keep the warhead from obliterating it.

A more significant defensive layer would be the next to be constructed under the High Frontier proposals. This involves a near-space network of more than 400 new earth satellites, each launched with an inclination of 65 degrees away from the earth's Equator. Each such "defensive" satellite would be armed with several dozen Phoenix-like missiles (the Phoenix is a U.S. Navy air-to-air interception rocket of great range), intended to shoot down outgoing Soviet missiles as they first emerged from the atmosphere. The attacking Soviet missiles would be traveling comparatively slowly, still in their full-stage assembly thus presenting fairly large targets. The same network would theoretically have a second, smaller chance to degrade the intensity of the attack when the surviving Soviet warheads had separated from their booster rockets and were arcing down to their targets. Some High Frontier proponents argue today that such a system, theoretically could reduce the impact of an all-out Soviet first strike on the United States by 40 to 90 percent. To them, the persuasive arguments are that the system would not have to rely on nuclear weapons and much of the work could be done with proven techniques and equipment, for deployment in just a few years.

Should such proposals seem relatively mundane, High Frontier has a few corker ideas as well, such as the building of a one-man space fighter-plane that could be launched from a carrier jet and then travel anywhere in near-space from the earth to the moon.

Yet, in a larger sense, the High Frontier proposals espoused by President Reagan bring up once again the question about what represents the most stable condition for the world and its armaments. Might, for instance, the mere likelihood of success for such a defensive system not lead the Soviets to be even more nervous, to fear that their retaliatory stance was being made less credible? In these perilous nuclear times, a comparative break-through in defense might produce grave tension, as the two nations try to estimate who is stronger and by how much.

Moreover, the extension of advanced technology into space bears implications for past treaties, such as the original pact not to establish anti-ballistic missile defenses and to prevent the stationing of assault weaponry in near-space. It should be noted, for instance, that the High Frontier anti-ICBM satellites could conceivably carry other missiles to attack ground targets.

Lost in the dispute about such subjects is the ever-increasing manned use of near-space by such devices as the American space shuttle and the Soviet manned orbiting laboratory. The Soviet system, much larger, is irrevocably fixed in one relative orbit above the earth. The Shuttle, in theory, is sufficiently maneuverable to serve as a kind of space fighter in its own right. Both sides are now clearly engaged in a race, whatever its philosophical underpinnings, to extend their direct influence to the space that surrounds the immediate vicininty of our planet. What may come out of this race is almost beyond ken, for the neat distinctions between offense and defense, between threat and assurance of survival, are apt to be made still more complex than they are today. Place a host of nuclear weapons of various kinds aboard several hundred satellites hovering near earth, provide some degree of intelligent control of the weaponry directly aboard the spacecraft, and you will have created a situation fraught with potential hazard.

It was once thought that the nation that controls the oceans controls the earth. Today, the ''ocean'' is the space around us. If the race between the two superpowers is allowed to proceed there, the planet will invariably face greater danger. Offense or defense, assured survival or certain destruction, nothing could be more clear than the fact that man has never yet stopped his desire to expand his empires, to settle his causes by force of arms.

That the answers to the human quandaries reside not so much in advanced technology as they might in a re-examination of the human heart has never been so transparently obvious as it is today, as the world prepares to extend its conflicts into the universe that surrounds us all.

Needham, Massachusetts
July, 1983